We Are Aztlán!

We Are Aztlán!

Chicanx Histories
on the Northern Borderlands

Edited by Jerry García

WSU
PRESS

Washington State University Press
Pullman, Washington

WSU PRESS

Washington State University Press
PO Box 645910
Pullman, Washington 99164-5910
Phone: 800-354-7360
Fax: 509-335-8568
Email: wsupress@wsu.edu
Website: wsupress.wsu.edu

Library of Congress Cataloging-in-Publication Data

Names: García, Jerry, 1963- editor of compilation.
Title: We are Aztlán : Chicana/o histories in the northern borderlands /
    edited by Jerry Garcia.
Other titles: Chicana/o histories in the northern borderlands
Description: Pullman, Washington : Washington State University Press, [2017]
    | Includes bibliographical references and index.
Identifiers: LCCN 2016047758 | ISBN 9780874223477 (alk. paper)
Subjects: LCSH: Mexican Americans--Northwest, Pacific. | Mexican
    Americans--Middle West. | Aztlán. | Chicano movement--Northwest, Pacific.
    | Chicano movement--Middle West.
Classification: LCC E184.M5 W39 2017 | DDC 979.5/0046872--dc23
LC record available at https://lccn.loc.gov/2016047758

On the cover: Farmworker children at a meeting at La Escuelita (The Little School) in Yakima, ca. 1970. From the Irwin Nash Collection of Photographs of Yakima Valley Migrant Labor, 1967-1976. *Courtesy of Manuscripts, Archives, and Special Collections, Washington State University Libraries, PC8901f3.*

In Memory

Carlos S. Maldonado
(1953-2008)
and
John E. Kicza
(1953-2016)

Friends and Mentors

Contents

Acknowledgments

There are many individuals who helped bring this book to its conclusion who I wish to acknowledge. The genesis for this book came while I was at Michigan State University and worked with Dionicio Valdés, who at the time was the interim director of the Julian Samora Research Institute. Under his leadership we held a conference that brought in a variety of scholars who examined the Chicanx/Latinx experience beyond the Southwest. The seeds for this book were planted as we listened to scholars who presented on these experiences from Washington, Oregon, Michigan, North Carolina, Pennsylvania, and Illinois.

I also wish to thank my current institution, Northern Arizona University and the NAU Ethnic Studies Program for providing the space to complete this project. The Ethnic Studies Program welcomed and supported me with open arms. I also found committed intellectuals within the program vital in not only sustaining friendships, but also in engaging, stimulating conversations. I wish to acknowledge them here: Angelina Castagno, Mark Beeman, Frederick Gooding Jr., Mark Montoya, L. Greg McAllister, Sara Aleman, Ricardo Guthrie, Eva Barraza, José G. Moreno, Jessi Quizar, Rose Soza War Soldier, Christine Lemley, Daisy Purdy, Gerald K. Wood, An Nguyen, Michelle Tellez, and Nicole Selinger.

A special acknowledgement goes out to the staff of WSU Press, including the editor-in-chief, Robert Clark, who was the first to see an early draft of this project and saw its merits and significance. Another special thanks to Beth DeWeese, our manuscript editor who worked collaboratively with me and the other contributors throughout the book and made *We Are Aztlán!* a better manuscript. We also want to thank the anonymous reviewers who provided insightful critiques and suggestions throughout the manuscript. Finally, thanks to Marc S. Rodriguez for looking over the manuscript and making important suggestions.

Lastly, I want to thank the contributors to this book for their hard work and patience. *Mil Gracias!*

INTRODUCTION

We Are Aztlán!

Jerry García, Editor

> …This land was Mexican once, was Indian always.
> And will be again.—*Gloria Anzaldúa*[1]

Historians, sociologists, demographers, and scholars in other fields are taking greater notice of the rapidly increasing presence of Chicanxs[2] throughout the United States. Chicanxs form a majority of the overall Latinx population, which has become the largest underrepresented group in the nation. Indeed, there are significant Chicanx communities in all fifty states. This book has assembled scholars to address specifically the historical and current conditions of Chicanxs beyond the well-studied U.S. Southwest. Ten Chicanx scholars present some of their latest research, offering academic and non-academic perspectives on the Pacific Northwest and the Midwest.[3] The papers have a multi-disciplinary and interdisciplinary focus, addressing colonialism, gender, history, immigration, labor, literature, sociology, education, and religion.

This volume builds on the historiography of the Chicanx presence in the Pacific Northwest and Midwest by examining various forms of resistance, community mobilization, culture, and how people negotiated their precarious position in regions that lacked a critical mass of Chicanxs. Here *El Movimiento* (the Chicanx movement) and the Chicanx experience are set beyond the boundaries of the Southwest, offering readers insight into distinct strategies developed in mobilizing communities in the northern borderlands. In this manner we gain a better understand-

1

ing of the contested terrain of race, race relations, political mobilization, and community. More important, this volume illuminates how Chicanxs overcame racialization, marginalization, and isolation by using their sense of identity and the search for social justice.

Another aim is to situate the Chicanx experience in the Pacific Northwest and the Midwest within the national narrative and *El Movimiento*. The articles provide critical scholarship from an academic perspective, but also discuss the personal lived experience far removed from the U.S.-Mexican borderlands. The presence and history of Chicanxs in the Northwest and Midwest have commonalities with the Southwest and California, especially regarding their treatment and marginalization. However, because the field of Chicanx studies has established a monolithic approach to its master narrative—that the Chicanx experience is predicated on the Southwest experience—the important contributions made by regions outside of that zone are marginalized or not seen as central to the experience or the Chicanx movement. We argue that there are a multiplicity of lived experiences and identities within the field of Chicanx studies and the community. Thus, a goal of this book is to insert and weave together the regional histories of the Northwest and Midwest into the national Chicanx experience.

We Are Aztlán! Chicanx Histories in the Northern Borderlands remains a study of borderlands history and its experience, but shifts geographically to the northern borderlands, an area not only neglected by the field of Chicanx studies, but by borderlands history as well. More specifically, *We Are Aztlán!* examines Chicanxs along the U.S.-Canada border in the states of Oregon, Washington, and Michigan. Chicanx studies scholars in the Pacific Northwest and Great Lakes[4] region have advocated for a broader approach to the field and the collection of essays in this volume represent that continued effort. Once it is understood that scholarship on the Mexican experience in the Midwest and the Pacific Northwest has been continuous for over one hundred years, any notion that these regions are new to the field dissipates.

These articles also challenge the accepted narrative of the origins of *El Movimiento*, which embodied "not only patriarchal practices, but also a nationalist ideology," that confined the overall movement to a narrow geographical space.[5] Michael Soldatenko, in his study on the genesis of the field of Chicanx studies, argues that the standard narrative begins with a "creation myth," which homogenized the Chicanx student movement and *El Movimiento*. Soldatenko suggests that the field move away from this homogenization by placing greater emphasis and importance on the multiplicity and particularity among student protests. Although Soldatenko primarily used California universities and colleges as examples of student protests, *We Are Aztlán* extends the movement to the Pacific Northwest and Midwest, in particular Seattle and Yakima, Washington, Mt. Angel and Woodburn, Oregon, and [Azt]lansing (East Lansing), Michigan.[6]

Rodolfo F. Acuña, in *The Making of Chicano Studies: In the Trenches of Academe*, provides a brief examination of the Chicanx student movement at the University of Washington and Washington State University and by doing so expands, albeit in limited fashion, the national narrative of the Chicanx movement beyond California and Texas.[7] When we include regions outside California and the southern borderlands it becomes apparent the Chicanx Movement, and in this specific case, the student movement, resonated nationally. Thus, Michigan, Washington, Minnesota, Oregon, Idaho, and other areas of the United States embody the essence of *El Movimiento* and Aztlán. The collection of articles in this book is one attempt to nudge the field into a broader trajectory and understanding of the overall Chicanx experience, but also to remind the field that the presence of Mexicans in these regions is not new.

WE ARE AZTLÁN!

Aztlán, the legendary and mythical homeland of the Mexica, who founded the Aztec Empire, became perhaps the strongest unifying symbol of the Chicanx movement of the late 1960s and early 1970s. For Chicanxs, dispossessed and marginalized since their incorporation into the United States, Aztlán symbolized a homeland, a connection to a land long indigenous, but stolen by conquest and later usurped by the encroachment of the expansionist empire of the United States. According to Luis Leal, Aztlán emerged as a symbol in the 1960s with two distinguishing characteristics: one, a geographic region that encompassed the conquered territories of Northern Mexico after the 1848 Mexican-American War, which gave Chicanxs a sense of belonging—a homeland;

two, and more important to this collection, Aztlán signaled the spiritual union of Chicanxs within the heart, no matter where they may live or where they find themselves.[8] "In this respect, the saga of Aztlán functions to provide identity, location, and meaning for a people who were previously directionless in their collective existential pilgrimage through earth," wrote Michael Pina, or as art historian Dylan Miner articulates, "Aztlán…became the metaphor used to refer to the collective 'national' identity and consciousness of Chicanxs."[9]

As the Chicanx experience moved beyond the 1970s, the meaning of Aztlán has taken twists, turns, and criticisms. Aztlán is no longer confined to a rigid unmovable location; rather, this symbol of unity has transformed into the metaphorical and shifted with the movement of people who carry within them the liberatory essence of Aztlán. For example, the 2004 publication by Chon A. Noriega and Wendy Belcher, *I AM AZTLÁN: The Personal Essay in Chicano Studies*, quotes Rudolfo A. Anaya's novel *Heart of Aztlán* (1976), specifically the protagonists' search for the Chicanx homeland and the realization that its location is not in the past or defined by space; instead he discovers that Aztlán exists spiritually within him:

Time stood still, and in that enduring moment he felt the rhythm of the heart of Aztlán beat to the measure of his own heart. Dreams and visions became reality, and reality was but the thin substance of myth and legend. A joyful power coursed from the dark womb-heart of the earth into his soul and he cried out I AM AZTLÁN![10]

With this proclamation, *I AM AZTLÁN* jettisoned the monolithic approach to the concept of a homeland for Chicanxs and instead positions it within the lived experience of those yearning for liberation in its many manifestations. As the editors articulated, "We focus on the process of self-naming—the ubiquitous 'I am…'—because it is found not just in early Chicano literary, performing, and visual arts, but in Chicano scholarship as well."[11] Further, the editors argued that incorporating the personal challenged conventional scholarship from non-Chicanx scholars, who rarely used the "I" or the personal. Several contributors to our collection position their research from this perspective. Along with rigorous inquiry, intertwined throughout the articles is the personal experience of individuals, which conveys a level of intimacy often missing from scholarly studies.[12]

Because the Pacific Northwest and Midwest are significant regions of the United States, what follows is demographic information in order to provide the reader with a brief historical overview of the growth of the Mexican population in those areas over the past one hundred years. We also provide information on the scholarship produced on Mexican communities in the Northwest and Midwest during the same period.

A BRIEF DEMOGRAPHIC AND HISTORICAL OVERVIEW

Consisting of twelve states, the region known as the Midwest is a massive geographical zone with a population of nearly 68 million (see note 3 for list of states). Based on U.S. Census data the total Hispanic population in this region is approximately 5 million, with people of Mexican origin representing 3.5 million of that total.[13] In this volume Michigan is examined as part of the Great Lakes region. The state of Michigan has a population of 9.9 million people, with Hispanics numbering 476,283 or 4.8 percent of the total population. The most populated state in the Midwest is Illinois, which currently has a population of 12.8 million people with over 2 million individuals of Hispanic origin or 16.7 percent of the state's total population.[14]

Although Oregon and Washington are the primary Pacific Northwest states examined in the anthology, as a comparison we include demographics on Idaho. These three states have a total population of 12.6 million people with an overall Hispanic population of more than 1.5 million individuals.[15] Broken down individually, Oregon has a total population of 4 million people with Hispanics numbering approximately 500,000 or 12.5 percent of the total population of the state. Washington State has a total population of 7.1 million individuals with people of Hispanic ancestry numbering 874,782 or 12.2 percent of the total state population. The state of Idaho consists of 1.6 million individuals with Hispanics numbering 198,860 people or 12 percent of the total population. Hispanics in the three Pacific Northwest states make up a significant portion of each state's overall population. As in the Midwest, the origins of this population are deep-rooted.

The Mexican presence in the Pacific Northwest can be traced to the late eighteenth century with the arrival of Spanish explorers to the region, and later during the mid- to late-nineteenth century, Mexican mule packers hired by companies and early settlers of the Northwest. However, scholarship on these historical moments did not emerge until the twentieth century, including Chicanx research that provided insight to the significant contributions of Mexicans. In the Pacific Northwest, early twentieth-century Mexican communities remained largely invisible because of the small and transient nature of the population. Scholarship on Mexican communities in the Pacific Northwest during this period is also limited because there simply were no studies conducted on Mexicans in this region similar to the studies commissioned by the University of Chicago or by individuals such as Paul S. Taylor or George T. Edson. Nevertheless, the first four decades of the twentieth century saw a steady increase in the number of Mexicans in the Northwest. The need for food production during World War I, immigration restrictions on Europeans and Asians, and the Mexican Revolution all contributed to the movement of Mexicans away from the U.S.-Mexico borderlands and into areas such as the Pacific Northwest and Midwest. The 1930 census (see below) provides an indication of the small Mexican population in the Pacific Northwest. However, the transitory nature of the Mexican population during this era as Mexican migrants traveled from region to region seeking employment, especially in agriculture, made it easy for them to be overlooked by census enumerators.

Another important contrast to the Midwest is that the Mexican community developed at a slower pace in Washington, Oregon, and Idaho, which can be attributed to the gradual development of permanent labor-intensive agriculture in the Northwest. The expansion of reclamation projects during the early- to mid-twentieth century—especially in North Central Washington's Columbia Basin, the Puyallup and Skagit Valleys in Western Washington, the Willamette and Hood River Valleys in Oregon, and Snake River Valley in Idaho—brought water to these semi-desert regions. The result of these efforts not only meant increased acreage for agriculture, but a need for laborers. For example, the Mexican population in Washington in 1930 was approximately 562 individuals, in

Oregon, 1,568, and in Idaho, 1,278.[16] This population would not grow in any significant manner until after World War II, coinciding with the completion of major government-funded projects that siphoned water from the Columbia and Snake Rivers.

In contrast, and during the same period, Michigan had a Mexican population of 13,336, Iowa, 4,295, Kansas, 19,150, and Minnesota, 13,336.[17] These selected Midwest states provided greater economic opportunities where agriculture was better established, as in Minnesota and Iowa, which attracted thousands of Mexican laborers to the sugar beet industry. In the Midwest, Mexicans were not only recruited for agriculture, but also to the railroad industry in Iowa and Kansas, and the factory floors of the automobile industry in Michigan, which provided long-term permanent employment.[18] The post-World War II era brought employment opportunities in the Pacific Northwest, which in turn stimulated population growth in the region.

The 1940s introduced a shift in the presence of Mexicans throughout the United States. The outbreak of World War II, the internment of Japanese Americans, and the need for the United States to control the flow of labor from Mexico led to the creation of the Mexican farm and railroad labor programs popularly known as the Bracero Program. This was an emergency labor mechanism utilized by the U.S. government, in agreement with the Mexican government, that brought tens of thousands of Mexican laborers to the area. In fact, from 1943 to 1947 nearly fifty thousand braceros entered the Pacific Northwest as emergency labor, second only to California during the same period.[19] Like braceros in other areas, many of these workers broke their contracts and did not return to Mexico. Others went to Mexico, then re-entered the United States and returned to their places of employment without contracts, before gaining employment visas and becoming permanent residents.[20] Historian Erasmo Gamboa wrote that "the Chicano community in the Pacific Northwest had its genesis in the Bracero program…and the program was a watershed moment for Chicano communities in the Northwest."[21] Gamboa, in one early exposé on the Chicanx community in the Northwest, made a critical observation:

Chicano Culture in the Pacific Northwest is truly distinct because of certain historical and regional factors. Principal among these factors are the migration patterns of Chicanos and Mexicans...Moreover, [in the 1940s] most of the migrants to Washington came from Texas... As people migrated to Washington state they brought this culture relatively unchanged...Once in the Northwest both the geographical distance and isolation from the Southwest and the alienation from the local Anglo culture guaranteed that the cultural matrix of the communities would remain in a near state of encapsulation and consequently unvaried.[22]

For Midwest Mexican communities the decades leading up to World War II provided opportunities, but also economic hardships. When Mexicans became exempt from the provisions of the 1917 Immigration Act, the formal recruitment of Mexican workers for the sugar beet fields of the Midwest commenced and by the end of the decade thousands had been recruited.[23] Indeed, according to historian Dennis (Dionicio) Valdés, the recruitment for Mexican labor increased through the 1920s and by 1927 over 15,000 Mexicans were working in the beet fields in the Midwest.[24] These migrants were vulnerable to economic contraction in the sugar beet industry, and the automobile industry, the other major employer of Mexicans in the Midwest, which faced a crisis as the Great Depression intensified in the early 1930s and continued throughout the decade.

Mexicans in the Midwest experienced two different periods of economic hardship. The first began in the early 1920s when a national depression impacted the agriculture and automobile industries. The late 1920s depression slowed further movement of Mexicans into the Midwest and many became scapegoats for the economic ills of this period.[25] With the onset of the Great Depression during the 1930s the Mexican population working in the automobile industry were the first to be fired in favor of "American" citizens, and the thousands who had migrated north for the agriculture season found themselves without employment or struggling to survive on depressed wages. As the bottom fell out of the economy Mexicans previously employed in such places as Detroit found it difficult to find relief from the city or U.S. government because of rampant discrimination.[26] As the depression became entrenched and prolonged many cities throughout the United States began to implement repatriation or the mass deportation of people of Mexican ancestry. Formal efforts to deport Mexicans commenced in states such as Indiana, Illinois, and Minnesota.[27] The city of Detroit implemented a program for the removal of Mexican and Mexican Americans with the help of the U.S. and Mexican governments.

In the Pacific Northwest, Mexicans also faced deportation as a result of the economic depression. At McNeil Island Federal Penitentiary, located in Steilacoom, Washington, ninety Mexican inmates in 1932 were deported to Mexico to save costs for the institution.[28] Scholars Francisco E. Balderrama and Raymond Rodríguez also report in their path-breaking study, *Decade of Betrayal: Mexican Repatriation in the 1930s*, that Mexicans repatriated to the U.S.-Mexican border included families from Washington, Idaho, and Montana who complained of maltreatment and hardship encountered during repatriation.[29]

With U.S. involvement in World War II, the Great Depression began to subside in the late 1930s and in the 1940s the Midwest again began to import bracero labor. A total of 28,156 braceros were utilized in the Midwest during the war period, whereas over 50,000 were used in the Pacific Northwest. The smaller number of braceros in the Midwest is attributed to a larger domestic Chicanx labor force. The use of braceros in the Midwest increased after the war period until the program's demise in the 1960s, which is in contrast to the Pacific Northwest, where the Bracero Program, by and large, ended in the late 1940s.[30]

The post-World War II period brought significant change to the Mexican population in the Midwest and Pacific Northwest. In the late 1960s Michigan had one of the largest migrant labor populations in the country, and the Midwest overall employed over 200,000 migrants in agriculture. Table 1 shows the significant increase of the Mexican population in selected Midwestern states from the 1930s to the second half of the twentieth century. And, although agriculture played an important role bringing Mexicans to the region, the majority of the Mexican population lived in urban zones such as Detroit, Minneapolis, Kansas City, and Chicago.[31] Nevertheless, the increase in the Hispanic population in the United States commenced with the economic restructuring that began in the 1970s.

Table 1
Mexican Population in the Midwest

State	Mexican Foreign Stock				
	1970	1960	1950	1940	1930
Ohio	13,349	9,960	5,959	2,792	3,099
Indiana	18,325	14,041	8,677	4,530	7,589
Illinois	117,268	63,063	34,538	23,545	20,963
Michigan	31,067	24,298	16,540	9,474	9,921
Wisconsin	9,160	6,705	3,272	1,716	1,853
Minnesota	4,575	3,436	3,305	2,976	2,448
Iowa	4,546	3,374	3,973	3,959	2,760
Missouri	8,353	8,159	5,862	4,783	3,482
Nebraska	5,552	5,858	6,023	5,333	4,178
Kansas	13,728	12,972	13,429	13,742	12,900
Total	225,923	151,866	101,578	72,476	69,193

Source: U.S. Bureau of Census, Census of Population, 1850-1970, U.S. Government
Printing Office, Washington, DC. See Gilbert Cárdenas, "Los Desarraigados: Chicanos in
the Midwestern Region of the United States," *Aztlan: International Journal of Chicano Studies
Research* 7 (Thematic Issue—Chicanos in the Midwest, Gilbert Cárdenas, Special Issue
Editor) no. 2 (Summer 1976): 153-186.

Although the origins of the Chicanx community in the Pacific Northwest are found prior to World War II, the region witnessed a significant increase in its Mexican population during and following the war period. In 1947 the U.S. government ended its subsidy for transporting bracero workers from Mexico to their U.S. destinations. For Northwest growers, transporting Mexican labor from the U.S.-Mexico border to the Pacific Northwest became cost prohibitive. Subsequently, growers and labor contractors began to heavily recruit domestic labor from the state of Texas (resulting in the Tejano diaspora). Although Mexican Americans resided in the Northwest long before the 1940s, the population remained relatively stagnant for reasons already discussed. The post-World II movement of Tejano labor began a decades-long migration to the Northwest that became the foundation for many communities throughout the region.

In general, the permanent movement and settlement of Mexican labor to the Pacific Northwest can be divided into four periods. From 1900 through the 1930s the initial movement of ethnic Mexicans to the region consisted of small numbers of permanent and itinerant residents who worked in the sugar beet and fishing industries. The 1940s witnessed the recruitment of Braceros and Mexican American labor to the Northwest, with many becoming permanent fixtures in region. During the 1950s through the1980s, hundreds of thousands of migrants moved to the Northwest from the state of Texas in what became known as the Tejano diaspora. In fact, one study indicates that in 1957, Oregon was the recipient of the sixth largest movement of Tejanos in the country.[32] From 1970 to 1980 the Spanish-speaking populations of Oregon and Idaho doubled, with Washington not far behind.[33] The decades of the 1980s through the 2000s represent a shift from domestic migration to international immigration, primarily from Mexico, but also significant numbers from Central America.

In 1970 there were 760,000 Mexican-born residents in the United States and by the year 2000 that number had increased to 8.8 million.[34] Countless studies have examined the dramatic increase of the U.S. Mexican population since the 1970s. Most of these studies point to economic restructuring, which saw the U.S. economy shift from heavy industry and manufacturing to service, manual labor, and labor-intensive manufacturing industries that drew heavily on immigrant labor.[35] The economic crises that shook Mexico in the 1980s and 1990s also contributed to this immigration. It should also be noted the transnational nature of the movement of Mexicans to the United States became more pronounced when coupled with the embeddedness of immigrant labor into the country's economic structure. By the beginning of the twenty-first century the migration of Mexicans beyond the U.S.-Mexico border region included the movement both to rural agricultural zones and to urban centers. For example, Seattle, between 1990 and 2000, saw a 105 percent increase in its Mexican population and Portland, Oregon, witnessed a 175 percent surge during the same period.[36] The movement of Mexicans to the United States during the twentieth and twenty-first centuries represents one of the longest sustained movements of human

Table 2
Hispanic Population in the Pacific Northwest

State	2015	2010	2000	1990	1980	1970
Washington	879,410	790,000	441,509	214,570	121,570	70,734
Oregon	511,168	450,062	275,214	112,707	84,835	44,000
Idaho	201,901	182,000	101,690	52,927	42,377	27,932
Total	1,592,479	1,422,062	818,413	380,204	248,782	142,666

Source: U.S. Census Bureau, Quick Facts, Oregon; Washington State, Office of Financial Management: Data Center; U.S. Census Bureau, Quick Facts, Idaho; Campbell Gibson and Kay Jung, U.S. Census Bureau, Population Division, Historical Census Statistics on Population Totals by Race, 1790 to 1990, and by Hispanic Origin, 1970 to 1990, for the United States Regions, Divisions, and States; U.S. Census, Table 99 1980; U.S. Census, Table 135 1990.

migration in history. Table 2 is a representation of that movement to the Pacific Northwest.

SCHOLARSHIP ON THE REGIONS

To better understand the history of the Chicanx presence in the Pacific Northwest and Midwest, we provide a brief overview of some of the studies from these regions. Grounding our book within the well-established scholarship of these two areas highlights and better situates this collection. We also believe it is important to illuminate the research and scholarship advanced by pioneering scholars of twentieth and early twenty-first century that reinforce the Chicanx presence in these regions and the scholarship produced on these communities.

Forty years ago Gilberto Cárdenas echoed similar sentiments in a special thematic issue of *Aztlán: International Journal of Chicano Studies Research*:

> The Southwest regional approach has also failed to incorporate an adequate perspective toward the Chicano experience outside (north) of its boundaries. Thus, apart from the numerous problems associated with the study of the Chicano and Chicano Studies in the Southwest, the regional approach as a conceptual category has become a major limitation. The historical presence of Chicanos outside the South-

west suggests that the scope of Chicano Studies must be expanded to include a national perspective.[37]

In his article in the same issue of *Aztlán*, "Los Desarraigados: Chicanos in the Midwestern Region of the United States," Cárdenas provided a scathing critique of the early approach of Chicano studies and its lack of inclusion. Cárdenas was especially concerned with research and policy position papers on the Mexican origin community in the United States that only provided figures for California and the Southwest, rendering other regions with substantial Mexican enclaves invisible.[38]

In the decades since Gilberto Cárdenas wrote those words, scholarship on the Midwest and Pacific Northwest has expanded dramatically, but an inclusive national perspective of Chicanx studies remains elusive. Research on both communities has grown since "el grito de Cárdenas" in *Aztlán*'s special issues on the Midwest, and we believe it is imperative to demonstrate the early twentieth century scholarship and its continuity into the twenty-first century. Scholars such as Dionicio N. Valdés, Zaragosa Vargas, Louise Año Nuevo-Kerr, and others initiated the pioneering work, along with the earlier studies by the University of Chicago organized in the 1920s that provided our first understanding of the Mexican presence in the Midwest.[39]

For example, the groundbreaking work, *The Mexicans in Chicago* (1931), by Robert C. Jones and Louise R. Wilson, gave one of the first detailed accounts of the Mexican experience in the Midwest.[40] Others such as Paul S. Taylor, George T. Edson, and Manuel Gamio originated research on Mexicans in the Midwest during this period as well. Taylor also provided field notes and research on the recruitment of Mexican railroad section gangs to the Pacific Northwest and the movement of California's Mexican migrant workers to Idaho, Oregon, and Washington.[41] In fact, scholars doing historical research on Mexicans in the Midwest and Pacific Northwest often refer to these early pioneering scholars.

Paul S. Taylor's papers are located at the University of California, Berkeley, Bancroft Library and primarily consist of research in the field of agriculture including studies on Mexicans in the United States, migrant workers, and the farm worker strikes of the 1930s and 1960s. Also in this collection are field reports conducted by George T. Edson on sugar beet workers in the north and north central states of Iowa, Illinois, Minnesota, Michigan, and Wisconsin from 1926 to 1927.[42] Taylor and Edson's extensive research and vast field reports on the Mexican presence in the Midwest and beyond remain as relevant today as they were nearly a century ago.[43]

Anthropologist and sociologist Dr. Manuel Gamio did widespread research on Mexican immigration and labor in both Mexico and the United States. Important to our understanding of the Mexican experience in the Midwest are Gamio's publications *Mexican Immigration to the United States: A Study of Human Migration and Adjustment* (1930), *The Life Story of the Mexican Immigrant* (1931), and *El inmigrante mexicano: La historia de su vida* (1969). Each of these publications contains interviews with Mexican immigrants who came to the United States in the early years of the twentieth century.[44] A significant number of immigrants interviewed indicated they were recruited in Mexico and contracted to work in the railroad and automobile industries in such places as Nebraska, Kansas, Montana, and Michigan.[45]

Norman D. Humphrey and John Thaden conducted research on Mexican communities in Michigan during the 1930s and 1940s.[46] The second half of the twentieth century saw the emergence of sociologist Julian Samora conducting research on Chicanxs in Chicago.[47] Samora eventually trained a cadre of Chicanx scholars who continued research on Mexicans in the Midwest. Although not a complete list of early scholarship on the Midwest, the above-mentioned individuals and their work provide a solid indication of the presence of the Mexican communities in the Midwest during the early twentieth century.

The second half of the twentieth century witnessed the continuation of scholarship on the Mexican diaspora throughout the Great Lakes region and the appearance of research on Chicanxs in the Pacific Northwest. Mentioned earlier is Gilbert Cárdenas' seminal work in the journal *Aztlán*, aptly titled "Chicanos in the Midwest."[48] This significant thematic issue provides important scholarship on the Chicanx experience throughout the Midwest ranging from demographics, to comparative study on the Midwest and Southwest, to Chicanx teatro. More important are Cárdenas' introduction, "Who Are the Midwestern Chicanos: Implications for Chicano Studies," and his article, "Los Desarraigados: Chicanos in the

Midwestern Region of the United States." Through these articles Cárdenas made the call to expand the master narrative of Chicanx studies beyond California and the Southwest, a sentiment that remains as valid today as it was forty years ago.[49]

The expansion of Chicanx scholarship on the Midwest is seen through important publications during the 1990s, such as Chicano and labor historian Dionicio Nodín Valdés' two important books: *Al Norte: Agricultural Workers in the Great Lakes Region, 1917–1970* (1991), and *Barrios Norteños: St. Paul and Midwestern Mexican Communities in the Twentieth Century* (2000). *Al Norte*, a meticulously researched book, examines the important role of agriculture in the recruitment and movement of Mexican labor into the upper Midwest from the early to late twentieth century. More important, the book focuses on the class struggle between capitalist employers and seasonal farmworkers, providing a strong class analysis of the lived experience of Chicanx in the region.

With the publication of *Barrios Norteños*, Valdés shifted from the rural to the urban setting, but remained focused on the Chicanx community. Valdés argued that *Barrios* was a sequel to *Al Norte* and continued the social history he began with the former book. Up until the publication of *Barrios Norteños* the urban history of Chicanxs in the Midwest had remained an untold story. Valdés argued that the field of Chicanx studies had failed to examine and recognize *El Movimiento* from a national perspective. To broaden this perspective, *Barrios Norteños* provides an analysis of the movement as it developed in the 1960s and 1970s in St. Paul, Minnesota. Dionicio Valdés' contributions to the historiography of Chicanx studies are important as he provided some of the first sweeping scholarship on the Midwestern Chicanx experience.

Another important piece of scholarship for our understanding of the midwestern Mexican experience is Zaragosa Vargas' *Proletarians of the North: A History of Mexican Industrial Workers in Detroit and the Midwest, 1917–1933* (1993). Here Vargas provides one of the first historical analysis of the Mexican industrial worker in the automobile industry between the end of World War I and 1933, especially in the Ford Motor Company in Detroit. Vargas maps the contours of Mexican migration to the Midwest from such places as Texas and Mexico. By focusing on Detroit we are able to see the development of Mexican colonias, residential patterns, founding of Mexican businesses, and the situation of Mexican women.

Our understanding of the Mexican experience in the Midwest was further developed with the publication of Gabriela Arredondo's *Mexican Chicago: Race, Identity, and Nation, 1916-1939* (2008). Arredondo's study is a stark reminder that Mexicans in the Midwest, and Chicago in particular, developed distinct communities that challenge the Southwest-centric perspective approach to the Mexican experience in the United States. This book expands our knowledge of the Mexican experience in the United States, providing additional insight into urban experiences outside the Southwest; illuminating gender differences in response to life in Chicago; and broadening our understanding of the racialization of Mexicans in the United States.

Shifting to another state of the Midwest, Marc S. Rodriguez's book, *The Tejano Diaspora: Mexican Americanism and Ethnic Politics in Texas and Wisconsin* (2011), provides important insight into the history, experiences, and organizing in Chicanx communities in Texas and Wisconsin. A more recent publication by Theresa Delgadillo, *Latina Lives in Milwaukee* (2015), uses oral histories to illuminate the experiences and lives of Latinas—Chicanas, Mexican Americans, Puerto Ricans, and Salvadoran Americans—in this Midwestern city.[50] Delgadillo submits that her approach, in moving beyond just the Mexican experiences, provides a richer understanding of the experience of Latinas/os in regards to how Latinas organized socially, culturally, and politically.

The Midwest has a significant number of universities with established departments and programs specializing in the Chicano/Latino experience; over twenty-seven schools offer some type of degree in the field of Chicanx/Latinx studies.[51] Michigan, a focus of this volume, is home to some well-established programs. One of the oldest is located at Wayne State University. The Center for Chicano-Boricua Studies (CBS) originated as the Latino en Marcha Leadership Training Program in 1971 created by Wayne State, Latin Americans for Social and Economic Development (LA SED), and New Detroit, Inc. In 1972 it became an academic center.

Before creating its Chicanx/Latinx studies program, Michigan State University (MSU) developed the Julian Samora Research Institute in 1989, considered one of the leading research institutes on Latinxs in the

Midwest. Since 1999 MSU has offered an undergraduate specialization in Chicanx/Latinx studies. Like some others throughout the country, the creation of this program was student driven, prolonged, and met with resistance by university administrators. Nevertheless, students at MSU overcame this struggle through persistence and perseverance (see Ernesto Todd Mireles' chapter in this volume for detailed analysis). This crucial victory set the stage for another vital development, the establishment of the second PhD program in the country in Chicano/Latino studies in 2007. Three individuals who worked tirelessly on this creation were Ernesto Todd Mireles, Theresa Meléndez, and Dionicio Valdés, all contributors to this volume.

In the Pacific Northwest, research and scholarship on the Chicanx experience gradually emerged in the early 1970s as graduate programs were expanded.[52] Some of the rationalizations for the slow development of Chicanx scholarship in this region, especially in comparison to the Midwest, were that the region simply was not producing individuals who studied this experience, or the examination of the Mexican experience was not deemed a legitimate area of study by mainstream academics who controlled graduate studies. Nevertheless, in the early 1970s a handful of master's and doctoral studies from the region's universities examined Chicanxs from the historical, educational, migrant, and political perspectives. In 1971 Anne Marjorie Brunton produced "The Decision to Settle: A Study of Mexican-American Migrants" as her doctoral dissertation from Washington State University.[53] In 1973 Erasmo Gamboa wrote two important pieces: "A History of the Chicano People and the Development of Agriculture in the Yakima Valley, Washington," his master's thesis from the University of Washington, and, what is believed to be one of the earliest publications on Chicanxs in the Northwest, "Chicanos in the Northwest: An Historical Perspective," in *El Grito*.[54]

José Manuel Romero produced "The Political Evolution of the Farm Workers," as his master's thesis at the University of Oregon in 1973.[55] In 1974 Jesus Lemos Jr. wrote "A History of the Chicano Political Involvement and the Organizational Efforts of the United Farm Workers Union in the Yakima Valley, Washington" as his master's thesis at the University of Washington.[56] Also in 1974 Senon Monreal Valadez produced "An

Exploratory Study of Chicano Parents' Perceptions of School and the Education of Their Children in Two Oregon Community Settings," as a PhD dissertation from the University of Oregon.[57] In 1974 Richard W. Slatta produced "Chicanos in Oregon: An Historical Overview," as his master's thesis from Portland State University.[58] Slatta's thesis evolved into the second published article on Chicanxs in the Pacific Northwest, "Chicanos in the Pacific Northwest: An Historical Overview of Oregon's Chicanos," which appeared in *Aztlán* in 1975.[59] Overall, these theses and dissertations indicate that the Chicanx population in the Northwest had become more visible and warranted scholarly attention. However, it would not be until the 1980s that additional scholarship appeared in academic journals and university presses. For example, in 1980 Patricia K. Ourada published what was considered the most thorough documentation of the Hispanic community in Idaho, *Migrant Workers in Idaho.*[60]

Perhaps the first published material on the Chicanx experience in the Pacific Northwest is a little-known, out-of-print booklet written by Erasmo Gamboa in 1971. This publication, simply titled *The Chicano Experience in the Northwest: An Historical Overview* began a more than forty-year publishing career that revolved around the Chicanx experience in the Northwest.[61] Gamboa's book *Mexican Labor and World War II: Braceros in the Pacific Northwest, 1942-1947* (1990), based on his PhD dissertation from the University of Washington, was the first major publication to begin the process of inserting the Northwest Chicanx experience into the national narrative of Chicanx studies, as well as bringing that history to the general population. At the time of this writing the University of Washington Press is set to release Professor Gamboa's next publication *Mexican Railroaders: The Forgotten World War II Story of Mexican Workers in the U.S. West* (2016), which examines Mexican railroad workers in the Pacific Northwest and beyond.[62] Gamboa's voluminous production of historical and cultural literature is responsible for inspiring and encouraging students throughout the region to engage and study the Chicanx experience in the Northwest.

The 1990s and early 2000s brought additional research and scholarship on the Chicanx experience in the Pacific Northwest. Isabelle Valle, an investigative reporter, published *Fields of Toil: A Migrant Family's Journey* (1994), which explored the migratory patterns of a Mexican family from South Texas to the Pacific Northwest, specifically the southeastern Washington community of Walla Walla.[63] Another example, and one of the few book length studies on Chicanx in Idaho was the 1995 book *Los Dos Mundos*, a unique ethnographic study of a small Idaho community with a large Mexican population examines many dimensions of the impact race relations have on everyday life for rural Mexican Americans. The late Robert C. Dash from Willamette University published in 1996 "Mexican Labor and Oregon Agriculture: The Changing Terrain of Conflict," which provided an understanding of the efforts by the Pineros y Campesinos Unidos del Noroeste (PCUN) (Northwest Treeplanters and Farmworkers United) union to organize Mexican migrant farmworkers in the Willamette Valley, Oregon.[64]

The arrival of Carlos S. Maldonado in 1987 as the new director of the Chicano Education Program at Eastern Washington University (EWU) ushered in further development of Chicanx studies in the state of Washington and the region. Maldonado, a product of the Tejano diaspora in Oregon, and a graduate of the University of Oregon, wrote a PhD dissertation "The Longest Running Death in History: A History of Colegio César Chávez, 1973-1983 (1986), that eventually was published by Routledge Press as *Colegio Cesar Chavez, 1973-1983: A Chicano Struggle for Educational Self-Determination* (2000). Colegio César Chávez was located at Mt. Angel, Oregon, and was the first accredited, four-year independent college for Chicanx students in the United States, and during the 1970s became a bastion of radicalism and activism for the Pacific Northwest.

Since the advent of the Chicanx movement in the Pacific Northwest, the region has struggled to establish stand-alone Chicanx Studies programs. University of Washington's program was eventually merged into American Ethnic Studies, and Washington State's disappeared altogether. Oregon State University and the University of Oregon each have a derivative of an ethnic studies program with a Chicanx-Latinx track. In Idaho, Boise State University currently offers a minor in Latin American and Latinx studies. However, it should be noted that a Chicanx studies curriculum was developed at numerous institutions of higher education throughout the Northwest. One of earliest institutions to do so was Yakima Valley Community College, which began offering courses in

1971.[65] Currently, there are three institutions with stand-alone Chicano studies programs in the Northwest: Eastern Washington University (The Chicano Education Program); Yakima Valley Community College (Chicano Studies); and Portland State University (The Chicano/Latino Studies Program).

Eastern Washington University established its Chicano Education Program in 1977 and will celebrate its fortieth year in 2017. For nearly a decade after its inception its primary focus was on student support services, recruitment, and the teaching of Chicano studies courses. With Maldonado's hire in 1987 the program began to concentrate on the importance of Chicanx scholarship in the Pacific Northwest. Pushing this agenda, Maldonado founded the Pacific Northwest National Association for Chicano Studies Foco and was the National Coordinator of the National Association for Chicano Studies (NACS) from 1991 to 1992.[66] Maldonado brought the NACS national office to EWU where it was housed from 1992 to 2000. During that period the Pacific Northwest hosted the national NACS conference in Spokane, Washington (1995), where NACS was re-named National Association for Chicana and Chicano Studies (NACCS). It also hosted the 2000 national conference in Portland, Oregon. Furthermore, Maldonado was co-editor of *The Chicano Experience in the Northwest* (1995), the first comprehensive examination of the Chicanx experience in the region.[67]

In 2001, Antonia I. Castañeda published "Que Se Pudieran Defender (So You Could Defend Yourselves): Chicanas, Regional History, and National Discourse." This important article "centered on gendered, sexualized, racialized, and historicized lives of working-class Chicana bodies and the transregional migration of farm workers from Texas to Washington state during the mid-twentieth century."[68] Professor Castañeda examined the lives of Chicanas in such places as Idaho and Washington providing crucial and missing research on Chicanas in the Northwest.

In 2005 and following in the vein of *The Chicano Experience in the Northwest*, the book *Memory, Community, and Activism: Mexican Migration and Labor in the Pacific Northwest* was published, providing another comprehensive examination of the Chicanx experience.[69] University of Oregon anthropologist Lynn Stephen has published several books on the Mexican Indigenous experience in Oregon as well as the farmworker movement in the state. Stephen's *Transborder Lives: Indigenous Oaxacans in Mexico, California, and Oregon* (2007) provides an insightful account of Mexican Mixtec and Zapotec indigenous communities as they traversed the multiple borders on their way to the U.S. and eventually Oregon. Stephens also explores the involvement of these groups in labor organizing with such groups as Pineros y Campesinos Unidos del Noroeste (PCUN).[70] Individuals seeking a solid understanding of the farmworker movement in Oregon will find it in Stephens' *The Story of PCUN and the Farmworker Movement in Oregon* (2012).[71] Mario Jimenez Sifuentes' recent publication, *Of Forest and Fields: Mexican Labor in the Pacific Northwest* (2016) is a concise examination of the evolution of the movement of Mexican labor to the region. At the heart of this study is the genesis and evolution of the Willamette Valley Immigration Project (WVIP), which morphed into PCUN.[72]

In 2008 Yolanda Alaniz and Megan Cornish wrote *Viva La Raza: A History of Chicano Identity and Resistance*.[73] Their book describes heroic battles, surveys the Raza youth movement, focuses attention on the role of women, and examines issues such as police brutality, the emergence of Chicana feminism, Chicanx lesbians and gays, and the role of radical organizations. Alaniz provides broad examination of the Chicanx Movement, but important to this study are the sections that examine the Pacific Northwest. The authors provide some insight to the movement in the state of Washington in Appendix 1: "Farmworker Organizing in the Yakima Valley" and Appendix 2: "Uproar at the University of Washington."[74] The publication in 2010 of *Mexicans in Oregon: Their Stories, Their Lives* by Erlinda Gonzales-Berry and Marcela Mendoza is one of the first books on Mexicans in Oregon. This important volume sheds new light on the stories and lives of Mexicanos in Oregon, including why migrants come to Oregon fields, an overview of various occupations, their experiences when settling, and how they adapt to life in the United States.[75]

Lastly, providing additional insight to the Chicanx movement in the Northwest is Glenn Anthony May's publication *Sonny Montes and Mexican American Activism in Oregon* (2011).[76] May's book both examines the role of Montes as Chicanxs in Oregon began to demand their full rights as citizens and equal treatment, and serves as broader examination of the Chicanx movement in Oregon.

Overall, the late twentieth and early twenty-first century ushered in important research on the Midwest and Pacific Northwest. The Hispanic populations in both regions underwent considerable change from the early to mid-twentieth century, with the Mexican population representing the largest segment of the overall Hispanic diaspora. The Mexican population in the Midwest garnered early attention from social scientists and later historians and sociologists. The Midwest and its twelve states have enjoyed a longer duration of research for the reasons discussed. Research on the Chicanx experience in the Pacific Northwest came late in the twentieth century, but during the last twenty-five years research on the region has been continuous.

Like other states in the region, Idaho has seen considerable growth in its Hispanic population during the last twenty years, and Mexicans have been present in the state since the late nineteenth century. Today, Hispanics represent over 12 percent of Idaho's population at nearly 200,000 individuals, with 85 percent of Mexican origin.[77] Although a handful of studies in article and book form have been published, there has not been the intense examination of the community that we have seen in Oregon and Washington. The exception to this is the research conducted by Erasmo Gamboa, Errol Jones, Kathleen R. Hodges, Richard Baker, and Laurie Mercier.[78] The overwhelming majority of information on Idaho's Mexican community is in the form of newspaper articles, government reports, and ephemera.[79] Reasons for this disparity are similar to what the region as a whole experienced earlier in the twentieth century, specifically, Idaho's universities are not producing individuals with the academic training to conduct the rigorous research needed to explore the rich Chicanx experience. However, Erasmo Gamboa and others have laid the foundation for continued research with the Idaho Hispanic Oral History Project, the Mexican American Oral History Project, and the Latino Experience in Idaho. In all, these oral history projects contain over sixty oral histories that have been under-utilized by scholars.[80]

The Book

We Are Aztlán! is divided into three parts: Empire, Aztlán, and Sovereignty; *El Movimiento* in the Northern Borderlands; and Community, Labor, and Immigration.

Part I—Empire, Aztlán, and Sovereignty provides a broad, theoretical overview of the Chicanx experience as it relates to labor and capitalism. Both articles in this section critique colonialism and settler-colonialism, and capitalism. This section also provides personal insight into the lived experience and the role of settler-colonialism on the northern borderlands of Michigan-Canada. The chapters provide a foundation for the remainder of the book by illustrating the importance of the northern borderlands and its link to the overall Chicanx experience.

Part Two—*El Movimiento* in the Northern Borderlands, features articles that provide path-breaking case studies that examine community mobilization and the Chicanx Movement in the state of Washington; a critical assessment of the Chicano movement and the establishment of Xicano studies at Michigan State University; and an examination of the often-neglected role of Chicanas in Oregon during the Chicano movement.

Recognizing that the movement of Mexicans to the United States is one of the longest sustained labor movements in history, the articles in Part Three—Migration, Race, and Community attest to the fact that Mexican communities have been long established in regions beyond the Southwest. The three articles in this section explore the movement of Mexican origin people to Oregon, Michigan, and Washington. This exploration provides insight to community development, identity, and race relations.

CONCLUSION

Resounding the declaration issued by *I AM AZTLÁN: The Personal Essay in Chicano Studies*, the authors of this collection cry out *We Are Aztlan!* The articles affirm their place in Chicanx studies and claim the Pacific Northwest and Midwest as embodiments of Aztlán. All the articles in this collection are based on meticulous research using primary and secondary sources, as well as oral history and the personal experience. Nearly all of the contributors are original inhabitants of the Pacific Northwest, the Great Lakes region, or represent the Tejano diaspora. Their roots in the regions run deep, with many born and raised to migrant farmworker parents born in Mexico or Texas, who became part of the migratory stream to these regions as early as the 1920s and 1930s.

With this anthology we are reminded that Aztlán emerged as part of the male-centered Chicano nationalism of the 1960s and 1970s. Nevertheless, Aztlán as a concept and part of the "decolonizing imaginary to signify a homeland" provides an important place for Chicanxs, while simultaneously it represents a form of resistance to their unequal position within the U.S.[81] In this manner, the collection of articles in *We Are Aztlán!* summons the foundational document, "El Plan Espiritual de Aztlán," to promote and illustrate that Aztlán is a collective symbol of memory, lived experience, liberation, and spirituality regardless of geographical dispersion:

With our hearts in our hands and our hands in the soil, we declare the independence of our mestizo nation. We are a bronze people with a bronze culture. Before the world, before all of North America, before all of our brothers in the bronze continent, we are a nation, we are a union of free pueblos, **We Are Aztlán.**[82]

Notes

1. Gloria Anzaldúa, "The Homeland, Aztlán/El Otro México," in *Aztlán: Essays on the Chicano Homeland*, eds. Rudolfo A. Anaya and Francisco A. Lomeli (Albuquerque: Academia/El Norte Publications, 1989), 193.
2. Since at least 2014, student organizations, academics, and institutions of higher education have shifted toward the identifiers "Chicanx" and "Latinx," born out of a collective aim to move beyond the masculine-centric "Chicano" and "Latino" and the gender inclusive but binary embedded Latin@. (This definition is taken from the María R. Scharrón and Alan A. Aja discussion on Latinx at www.latinorebels.com.) In this introduction I prefer Chicanx(s) and Latinx(s) in an attempt at inclusiveness and to move beyond the binary model of Chicana/o and Latina/o; however, like other contributors to this collection, I have chosen to use a variety of these terms, as well as Mexican American, Xicano, and Tejano.
3. According to the U.S. Census Bureau the Midwest consists of twelve states: Illinois, Indiana, Iowa, Kansas, Michigan, Minnesota, Missouri, Nebraska, North Dakota, Ohio, South Dakota, and Wisconsin. In this volume the two Midwestern states discussed are Michigan and Iowa.
4. The Great Lakes region of North America is generally considered to be the U.S. states of Illinois, Indiana, Michigan, Minnesota, New York, Ohio, Pennsylvania, and Wisconsin, and the Canadian province of Ontario. Although not traditionally included, within our collection Iowa is integrated as part of the region.

5. Michel Soldatenko, *Chicano Studies: A Genesis of a Discipline* (Tucson: University of Arizona Press, 2009), 10.
6. Ibid., 14–15.
7. Rodolfo F. Acuña, *The Making of Chicanx Studies: In The Trenches of Academe* (New Brunswick: Rutgers University Press, 2011), 56–57.
8. Luis Leal, "In Search of Aztlán," in *Aztlán: Essays on the Chicano Homeland*, Rudolfo A. Anaya and Francisco A. Lomeli, eds. (Albuquerque: Academia/El Norte Publications, 1989), 8.
9. Michael Pina, "The Archaic, Historical and Mythicized Dimensions of Aztlán," in *Aztlán: Essays on the Chicano Homeland*, 37. Dylan A.T. Miner, *Creating Aztlán: Chicano Art, Indigenous Sovereignty, and Lowriding Across Turtle Island.* (Tucson: University of Arizona Press, 2014), 13.
10. Chon A. Noriega and Wendy Belcher, eds., *I AM AZTLÁN: The Personal Essay in Chicano Studies* (Los Angeles: UCLA Chicano Studies Research Center Press, Regents of the University of California, 2004).
11. Ibid., v.
12. Jerry García, "The Measure of a Cock: Mexican Cockfighting, Culture, and Masculinity," in Noriega and Belcher, eds., *I AM AZTLÁN*, 109–38. One of my first publications is located within this collection. *I AM AZTLÁN* allowed me to share the personal experience of my childhood, which resembled many of the experiences in the collection, but with one major difference. My adolescent years were not spent along the U.S.-Mexican border or in some major Chicano or Latino enclave such as Chicago or Los Angles, but rather along the U.S.-Canadian borderlands, the state of Washington.
13. United States Census Bureau, Quick Facts, Hispanic or Latino Percent, July 2014 and 2015. See also Demographics: Profile of General Population and Housing Characteristics for each Midwestern and Pacific Northwest state.
14. Ibid.
15. Ibid.
16. Jerry García and Gilberto García, *Memory, Community, and Activism: Mexican Migration and Labor in the Pacific Northwest* (East Lansing: Michigan State University and Julian Samora Research Institute, 2005), 2. See also U.S. Census of the Population, 1930.
17. Ibid.
18. For a full discussion on the recruitment of Mexican labor to the Midwest see the following: Dennis Nodín Valdés, *Al Norte: Agriculture Workers in the Great Lakes Region, 1917-1970* (Austin: University of Texas Press, 1991); Zaragosa Vargas, *Proletarians of the North: A History of Mexican Industrial Workers in Detroit and the Midwest, 1917-1933* (Berkeley: University of California Press, 1993); Dionicio Nodín Valdés, *Barrios Norteños: St. Paul and Midwestern Mexican Communities in the Twentieth Century* (Austin: University of Texas Press, 2000).

19. Erasmo Gamboa, *Mexican Labor and World War II: Braceros in the Pacific Northwest, 1942-1947* (Austin: University of Texas Press, 1990), 58. The number of braceros who came to the Pacific Northwest is 46,934.
20. The best-known study on the bracero program in the Pacific Northwest remains Erasmo Gamboa's *Mexican Labor and World War II.*
21. Ibid., 131.
22. Erasmo Gamboa, "Raíces," *Metamorfosis* 2 (Teatro En El Noroeste), no. 1&2 (1979): 3.
23. Valdés, *Al Norte,* 8-9. According to Valdés the 1917 Immigration Act exempted Mexican workers from the literacy test and eight-dollar head tax. Furthermore, sugar beet companies introduced the use of *Enganchistas* (recruiters) and sent them to the U.S.-Mexico border and into Mexico, and by 1920 the Michigan, Holland-Saint Louis, Columbia, and Continental sugar companies had recruited more than five thousand Mexican workers for the Michigan and Ohio beet fields.
24. Ibid., 10–11.
25. Vargas, *Proletarians of the North,* 78–79.
26. Ibid., 170–71.
27. Valdés, *Al Norte,* 30–31.
28. Francisco E. Balderrama and Raymond Rodriguez, *Decade of Betrayal: Mexican Repatriation in the 1930s,* 2nd ed. (Albuquerque: University of New Mexico Press, 2006), 65.
29. Ibid., 142.
30. Gilbert Cárdenas, "Los Desarraigados: Chicanos in the Midwestern Region of the United States," in "Chicanos in the Midwest," ed. Gilbert Cardenas, special issue, *Aztlan: International Journal of Chicano Studies Research* 7, 153–86. Hereafter cited as Cárdenas, "Los Desarraigados."
31. Cárdenas, "Los Desarraigados," 155.
32. Mario Jimenez Sifuentes, *Of Forests and Fields: Mexican Labor in the Pacific Northwest* (New Brunswick: Rutgers University Press, 2016), 36–37.
33. Erasmo Gamboa, "A Social Portrait: Chicano and Latino People of the Pacific Northwest," in Lauro Flores, et al., *Chicano and Latino Artists in the Pacific Northwest.* (Olympia, WA: Evergreen State College, 1984), 8–11.
34. David G. Gutiérrez, ed., *The Columbia History of Latinos in the United States Since 1960* (New York: Columbia University Press, 2004), 62.
35. Ibid.
36. Ibid., 67–68.
37. Gilbert Cárdenas, "Introduction—Who Are the Midwestern Chicanos: Implications for Chicano Studies," in "Chicanos in the Midwest," ed. Gilbert Cárdenas, special issue, *Aztlan: International Journal of Chicano Studies Research* 7, no. 2 (1976): 141–52.
38. Cárdenas, "Los Desarraigados," 156–57.

39. Louise Año Nuevo Kerr, "The Chicano Experience in Chicago: 1920–1970" (Ph.D. diss. University of Illinois at Chicago Circle, 1976); Valdés, *Al Norte*; Vargas, *Proletarians of the North*.

40. See Robert Redfield, "Mexicans in Chicago, 1924–1925," Robert Redfield Papers, Special Collections, University of Chicago; Robert C. Jones and Louise R. Wilson, *The Mexicans in Chicago* (Chicago: Comity Commission of the Chicago Federation, 1931); Edith Abbott, *The Tenements of Chicago 1908–1935* (Chicago: University of Chicago Press, 1936).

41. Gamboa, *Mexican Labor and World War II*, 9, 13.

42. For Paul S. Taylor, see: Paul Schuster Taylor Papers, Bancroft Library, University of California, Berkeley; *Mexican Labor in the United States: Chicago and the Calumet Region*, University of California Publications in Economics, vol. 7, no. 2. (Berkeley and Los Angeles: University of California Press, 1932); "Migratory Farm Labor in the United States," *Monthly Labor Review* 44 (March 1937), 537–49; "Mexicans in Detroit, Michigan," 1928, Paul S. Taylor Collection Bancroft Library, University of California, Berkeley. See also George T. Edson, "Mexicans in Our Northcentral States," 1927, Paul S. Taylor Collection, Bancroft Library, University of California, Berkeley, 24.

43. Vargas, *Proletarians of the North*. Includes an extensive bibliography on the studies examining the Mexican and Chicano experience in the Midwest.

44. Manuel Gamio, *Mexican Immigration to the United States: A Study of Human Migration and Adjustment* (Chicago: University of Chicago Press, 1930); *The Life Story of the Mexican Immigrant* (New York: Dover Publications, Inc., 1931).

45. Ibid., *The Life Story of the Mexican Immigrant*, 226–27.

46. Norman D. Humphrey, "Mexican Repatriation from Michigan: Public Assistance in Historical Perspective," *Social Service Review* 15 (September 1941), 497–513; "The Migration and Settlement of Detroit Mexicans," *Economic Geography* 19 (October 1943), 358–61; "The Detroit Mexican Immigrant and Naturalization," *Social Forces* 22 (March 1944), 332–35; "Employment Patterns of Mexicans in Detroit," *Monthly Labor Review* 61 (November 1945), 913–23.

47. Julian Samora and Richard A. Lamanna, "Mexican-Americans in a Midwest Metropolis: A Study of East Chicago," *Mexican-American Study Project*, University of California, Los Angeles, July 1967.

48. Cárdenas, "Chicanos in the Midwest," special issue, *Aztlán: International Journal of Chicano Studies Research*.

49. Cárdenas, "Who Are the Midwestern Chicanos," in "Chicanos in the Midwest," special issue, *Aztlan*, 141–52; "Los Desarraigados."

50. Theresa Delgadillo, *Latina Lives in Milwaukee* (Urbana: University of Illinois Press, 2015).

51. Acuña, *The Making of Chicanx Studies*. See Appendix: Academic Programs in Chicanx Studies and Related Areas, 273.

52. Two studies emerged in 1967: Nadine Frances Nelson, "Health Resources Utilized for Various Health Conditions as Reported by Twenty-Five Mexican-American Mothers in the Yakima Valley, Washington" (master's thesis, University of Washington, 1967); and Joan Soderstrom, "An Investigation of Mexican-American Migrant Children Population in Idaho and the Educational Opportunities Provided by Select School Districts" (master's thesis, Idaho State University, 1967).

53. Anne Marjorie Brunton, "The Decision to Settle: A Study of Mexican-American Migrant" (PhD diss., Washington State University, 1971).

54. Erasmo Gamboa, "A History of the Chicano People and the Development of Agriculture in the Yakima Valley, Washington" (master's thesis, University of Washington, 1973); Erasmo Gamboa, "Chicanos in the Northwest: An Historical Perspective," *El Grito* 6, no. 4 (Summer 1973): 57–70.

55. José Manuel Romero, "The Political Evolution of the Farm Workers" (master's thesis, University of Oregon, 1973).

56. Jesus Lemos Jr., "A History of the Chicano Political Involvement and the Organizational Efforts of the United Farm Workers Union in the Yakima Valley, Washington" (master's thesis, University of Washington, 1974).

57. Senon Monreal Valadez, "An Exploratory Study of Chicano Parents' Perceptions of School and the Education of Their Children in Two Oregon Community Settings" (PhD diss., University of Oregon, 1974).

58. Richard Wayne Slatta, "Chicanos in Oregon: An Historical Overview" (master's thesis, Portland State University, 1974).

59. Richard W. Slatta, "Chicanos in the Pacific Northwest: An Historical Overview of Oregon's Chicanos," *Aztlán* 6, no. 3 (Fall 1975): 327–40. See also Richard W. Slatta, "Chicanos in Oregon: An Historical Overview" (master's thesis, Portland State University, 1974); Richard W. Slatta and Maxine P. Atkinson, "The 'Spanish Origin Population' of Oregon and Washington: A Demographic Profile, 1980," *Pacific Northwest Quarterly* 75, no. 3 (July 1984): 108–16.

60. Patricia K. Ourada, *Migrant Workers in Idaho*, (Boise: Boise State University, 1980).

61. Erasmo Gamboa, *Chicanos in the Northwest: A Historical Perspective* (Sacramento: Montal Education Associates, 1971).

62. Erasmo Gamboa, *Mexican Railroaders: The Forgotten World War II Story of Mexican Workers in the U.S. West* (Seattle: University of Washington Press, 2016). The following is a partial list of Gamboa's publications not included elsewhere in these notes: "Mexican Migration into Washington State: A History, 1940–1950," *Pacific Northwest Quarterly* 72, no. 3 (July 1981): 121–31; "Mexican Labor in the Pacific Northwest, 1943–1947: A Photographic Essay," *Pacific Northwest Quarterly* 73, no. 4 (October 1982): 175–81; "Braceros in the Pacific Northwest: Laborers on the Domestic Front, 1942–1947," *Pacific*

Historical Review 56 (August 1987); "Washington's Mexican Heritage: A View into the Spanish Explorations, 1774–1792," *Columbia* 3 (Fall 1989); "Mexican Mule Packers and Oregon's Second Regiment Mounted Volunteers, 1855–1856," *Oregon Historical Quarterly* 92 (Spring 1991); and *Nosotros—The Hispanic People of Oregon: Essays and Recollections*, Erasmo Gamboa and Carolyn M. Buan, eds. (Portland: Oregon Council for the Humanities, 1995).

63. Isabel Valle, *Fields of Toil: A Migrant Family's Journey* (Pullman: Washington State University Press, 1994).

64. Richard Mabbutt, "Hispanics in Idaho: Concerns and Challenges," Boise: Idaho Human Rights Commission, 1990; Padilla, Fernando, "The Mexicanization of the Lower Yakima Valley," *Revista Apple* 2, no. 1-2 (Spring 1991): 59–63; Richard Baker, *Los Dos Mundos* (Logan: Utah State University Press, 1995); Robert C. Dash, "Mexican Labor and Oregon Agriculture: The Changing Terrain of Conflict," in *Agriculture and Human Values* 13, no. 1 (Fall 1996): 10–20; Jerry García, "A Chicana in Northern Aztlán: An Oral History of Dora Sánchez Treviño," in "Varieties of Women's Oral History," special issue, *Frontiers: A Journal of Women Studies* 18, no. 2, (1998): 16–52.

65. Gilberto García, "Organizational Activity and Political Empowerment: Chicano Politics in the Pacific Northwest," in *The Chicano Experience in the Northwest*, Carlos S. Maldonado and Gilberto García, eds., 2nd ed. (Dubuque: Kendall/ Hunt Publishing Company, 2001), 76.

66. The National Association for Chicano Studies (NACS) adopted the new name of the National Association for Chicana and Chicano Studies (NACCS) at the 1995 national conference in Spokane, Washington, in recognition of the contributions Chicanas have made to the association and the experience of Chicanxs.

67. Maldonado and García, eds., *The Chicano Experience in the Northwest* (Dubuque: Kendall/Hunt Publishing Company, 1995, 1998, 2001).

68. Antonia I. Castañeda, "Que Se Pudieran Defender (So You Could Defend Yourselves): Chicanas, Regional History, and National Discourse," in "Women's West," special issue, *Frontiers: A Journal of Women Studies*, 22, no. 3 (2001): 116–42.

69. García and García, eds. *Memory, Community, and Activism.* Another excellent example of emerging scholarship during this period is E. Mark Moreno, "Mexican American Street Gangs, Migration, and Violence in the Yakima Valley," *Pacific Northwest Quarterly* 97, no. 3 (Summer 2006): 131–38.

70. Lynn Stephen, *Transborder Lives: Indigenous Oaxacans in Mexico, California, and Oregon.* (Durham, NC: Duke University Press, 2007).

71. Lynn Stephen, *The Story of PCUN and the Farmworker Movement in Oregon* (Eugene: University of Oregon, Center for Latino/a and Latin American Studies, 2012).

72. Mario Jimenez Sifuentes, *Of Forests and Fields: Mexican Labor in the Pacific Northwest* (New Brunswick: Rutgers University Press, 2016).
73. Yolanda Alaniz, *Viva La Raza: A History of Chicano Identity and Resistance* (Seattle: Red Letters Press, 2008).
74. Ibid., Appendix 1 and 2, 287–326.
75. Erlinda Gonzales-Berry and Marcela Mendoza, *Mexicans in Oregon: Their Stories, Their Lives* (Corvallis: Oregon State University, 2010).
76. Glenn Anthony May, *Sonny Montes and Mexican American Activism in Oregon* (Corvallis: Oregon State University, 2011).
77. Cyndi MacFarland, "Growing Hispanic Population Part of Idaho's History," *Idaho State Journal*, August 15, 2015. Accessed April 15, 2016 at www.idahostate-journal.com/members/growing-hispanic-population-part-of-idaho-s-history/article_f65db386-4315-11e5-b41e-e731d99a9f78.html
78. Errol Jones and Kathleen R. Hodges, "A Long Struggle: Mexican Farm Workers in Idaho, 1918–1935," in García and García, *Memory, Community, and Activism*, 41–84. This article provides an excellent analysis of the Mexican experience between post World War I and the Great Depression. See also Erasmo Gamboa, *Voces Hispanas: Hispanic Voices of Idaho: Excerpts from the Idaho Hispanic Oral Project*, Boise: Idaho Humanities Council, 1992; Laurie Mercier, "Idaho's Latin Americans," in Laurie Mercier et al., *Idaho's Ethnic Heritage Guide* (Boise: Idaho's Ethnic Heritage Project, 1990); Laurie Mercier, "Creating a New Community in the North: Mexican Americans of the Yellowstone Valley," in *Stories From an Open Country*, ed. William L. Lang (Billings, MT: Western Heritage Center, 1995).
79. The following are examples: "Profile of the Hispanic Population of Idaho," Boise: Idaho Department of Commerce, 1990; Richard Mabbutt, "Hispanics in Idaho: Concerns and Challenges," Idaho Human Rights Commission, Research Report, Spring 1990; Hispanic Youth—Dropout Prevention, Report of the Task Force On the Participation of Hispanic Students in Vocational Education Programs, Boise: State Division of Vocation Education, 1990; "Report of the Task Force on Hispanic Education," State of Idaho Board of Education, January 18, 1991.
80. Gamboa, *Voces Hispanas*; "Oral History Projects," *Idaho State Historical Society*, accessed on April 15, 2016, at history.idaho.gov/oral-history-projects. The Idaho State Historical Society houses the various oral history transcripts on the Hispanic communities mentioned. Very few have been digitized.
81. Maylei Blackwell, *Chicana Power! Contested Histories of Feminism in the Chicano Movement*, (Austin: University of Texas Press, 2011), 102–103.
82. Anaya and Lomelí, eds., "El Plan Espiritual de Aztlán," 1–5.

PART ONE

EMPIRE AND BORDERS

CHAPTER 1

Empire, Colonialism, and Mexican Labor in Greater Aztlán

Dionicio Valdés

A notable feature of the third wave of Chicana/o studies theory in the twenty-first century is the resuscitation of internal colonial theory, which focuses on the descendants of the conquered and enslaved people of the United States, particularly Native Americans, Mexicans, and African Americans.[1] Popularized in the 1970s, it came under attack by a second generation of scholars in the 1980s and 1990s, some demonstrating flaws and adding to an already rich criticism in Chicano studies and other disciplines, others openly rejecting it as outmoded, inapplicable, and not even worthy of discussion.[2] The latter were influenced in particular by current trends in post-colonialism, post-structuralism, and especially post-modernism, arguing that internal colonialism and other efforts to generalize about society and broad characteristics of the population were totalizing, inconsistent with their own experiences, and therefore invalid.

Unfortunately, those who rejected systemic analysis in effect deterred theoretical discussion and engagement, which left a vacuum in efforts to understand the broader forces that explain inequality and other aspects of the Mexican experience. Despite our internal divisions and individual successes, the Mexican population as a group continues to enjoy far fewer fruits of our labor than the majority population, and it is necessary to examine inequality systematically to deal with it more effectively. It is necessary to approach theory and generalization on different levels, and this essay is a modest effort in this direction.

I want to return to colonial theories and demonstrate how they can enhance our understanding of Mexicans in the United States. Rather than try to create an immutable definition of colonialism or its variants such as internal colonialism, neocolonialism, or post-colonialism, I agree with authors who emphasize its link to imperialism, and I concur with Pablo González Casanova, who argues that it involves "above all the domination of some people by others," and has a "violent connotation."[3] In fact, imperialism is not simply a phenomenon of the past, but has intensified markedly since the early years of Chicana/o studies scholarship, and it is therefore incumbent on us to examine it as a dynamic phenomenon.

My present concern is the history of the United States as an imperialist nation and its impact on Mexico and Mexicans during the past two centuries. In order to place this conversation firmly in the context of the discipline, I will briefly discuss the historiography of internal colonialism, the earliest popular colonial model in Chicana/o studies literature, its importance in advancing knowledge, as well as the value and limitations of subsequent criticism. Then I will offer an historical framework for examining the United States empire and its relations with Mexico, with particular attention on how that relationship has influenced the lives of Mexican workers in both countries during the past two centuries.

THE BARRIO AS INTERNAL COLONY: EARLY CHICANA/O STUDIES

While internal colonial theories have deep roots, early Chicana/o studies literature on the topic was influenced by scholars from Mexico, particularly Pablo González Casanova and Rodolfo Stavenhagen, and from the Black Power movement, sociologist Robert Blauner.[4] Mario Barrera, Carlos Muñoz, and Charles Ornelas, in "The Barrio as Internal Colony," introduced the concept of the internal colony to the youthful discipline of Chicano studies in 1972.[5] Many scholars influenced by the concept were later characterized by remarkable diversity of thought, including Rodolfo Acuña, *Occupied America* (1972); F. Chris Garcia and Rodolfo O. de la Garza, *The Chicano Political Experience* (1977); Ruben Martínez, "Internal Colonialism" (1982/83); and Ramón Gutiérrez, "Mexican Migration to the United States: The Chicano and Internal Colonialism" (1976).[6] Meanwhile other authors spoke to colonialism while not specifically addressing its internal variety.[7]

The popularity of internal colonialism stemmed from several factors particular to the era. This included the Chicano movement, in which Chicanos could identify as distinct from other groups in the United States as well as from Mexico, and as a political strategy that emphasized commonality of the group within the diverse Chicana/o experience. It was harmonious with Chicano nationalism as articulated at the time, in which the Southwest was unique space, and popularized in the notion of Aztlán, linked to but distinct from Mexico. It also emphasized the violent nature of conquest as the defining moment in the birth of the Chicano people.

In Chicana/o studies literature of the 1970s, internal colonialism emphasized race, but it simultaneously addressed political, economic, cultural, and ideological dimensions. It explicitly challenged several current approaches to inequality among Mexicans in the United States, particularly those that focused on the individual or family as the source of inequality, the so-called "blame the victim" varieties. It also criticized a range of structural accounts, particularly Marxism, for its ostensibly exclusive focus on "economic" class, although Marx referred to himself as a political economist, and he and many early adherents spoke to ideology and culture, and further offered profound gender analyses.[8]

Meanwhile internal colonialism as applied to Chicana/o studies scholarship demonstrated serious weaknesses evident from the start. The geography it depicted (the barrio) was indeed vague. It was locked in time and not dynamic. It did not adequately incorporate class or gender. Furthermore, its adherents did not address the simultaneous impact of the U.S. imperial project on the people of the "internal colonies," including African Americans, Native Americans, Chicanos, or the conquered people of other countries like Mexico, and the formal colonies in Latin America and the Pacific.

Yet Chicana/o studies scholarship quickly transcended the early work on internal colonialism, evident in Barrera's 1979 classic, *Race and Class in the Southwest*. Barrera explicitly asserted that colonial theory (not specifically internal colonialism), a structural explanation of inequality focusing on race, must be modified by including class. He expanded the geography of the barrio to include a more specific and larger entity—the United States Southwest. The choice made it possible for him to consider the United States invasion and conquest of Mexico in 1846 and 1847 as a critical factor accounting for Chicano inequality in the former Mexican territories. A final important addition was his emphasis on the necessity of offering an historical framework using interdisciplinary methods.[9]

THE SECOND GENERATION CRITIQUE

Much of the new scholarship appearing in the 1980s and 1990s turned to issues distinct from the collective concerns of the Chicana/o movement, focusing heavily on the autobiographical. Its adherents were often adamant in eschewing broad generalization, while focusing on the personal, stressing a world filled with complexity, ambiguity, and difference, and the infinite divisions among individuals of Mexican origin.[10] It was influenced by but also contributed to leading tropes in the literature of post-modernism and cultural studies. Perhaps its most notable contribution was the concept of the border and the "borderlands," articulated in boldest fashion by Gloria Anzaldúa in her classic *Borderlands*.[11] The concept of borderlands proliferated beyond Chicana/o studies circles as authors from hegemonic sectors of academia peered into the subaltern.

The internal colony did not strike a positive chord with postmodern scholars, for whom "micro-theory" was more appropriate to their concerns of multiple identities, ambiguity, confusion, and individualism than macro-theory concerned with broader historical relations. Their works made a number of important contributions to the field, particularly the inclusion of gender-based accounts and the independent power of language. The postmodern fear of systemic generalization, however, turned up short when its leading adherents directly confronted Marx and macro-theoretical approaches.[12] As Samir Amin argued, postmodernism is impotent against capitalist globalization, "which in fact they readily accept by claiming that the real problems lie elsewhere."[13] Another major weakness was that its relativism and ambiguity played effectively into the hands of the newly-ascendant language of neoliberalism and globalization, whose ultraconservative and counterfactual ideology emphasized the individual as the unit of analysis. The neoliberal focus on the individual resuscitated the individualistic blame-the-victim accounts for inequality whose premises earlier Chicana/o studies scholarship had effectively shredded.

The broad trends affecting the Mexican population as a whole merit continued attention. Since the Chicana/o movement peaked in the 1970s, educational attainment for Mexicans has lagged, residential segregation has increased, health services to the poor have not improved, and income and wealth gaps between the Euro-American and Mexican populations in the United States have skyrocketed. Not surprisingly, in the past generation, attacks on Mexicans by politicians, academics, and sectors of the media in particular, have intensified sharply.

Our research and writing must go beyond the barrio, beyond the borderlands, and beyond the individual. In retrospect, the colonial/class approach of the late 1970s was fruitful in its day, but did not go far enough. In his subsequent work, *Beyond Aztlán*, Barrera offered one of several productive avenues of investigation that some Chicana/o studies scholars have pursued, namely comparison with peoples in other parts of the world.[14] Further understanding can be gained by examining how micro-level and macro-level theories interact, and how they change over time.

In the sketch below, I offer a historical framework to analyze the interplay of United States imperialism and colonialism with Mexico and Mexicanos in both countries. Scholarly discussions about internal colonialism in the United States during the 1970s did not emphasize sufficiently the dynamic but unequal relationship between the United States and Mexico. That relationship continues into the present, and is neither an ambiguous empire nor a phenomenon of the past.[15]

The United States has had imperial ambitions since its own political independence, and even earlier, and Mexico and Mexicans have been impacted in a variety of ways. The imperial agenda evolved over time and initially was not focused directly on Mexico. My examination of the impact of empire on Mexican populations in both Mexico and the United States is influenced by the one of the earliest published works in English to use the term "internal colonialism"—Pablo González Casanova's "Internal Colonialism and National Development." González Casanova observed that "colonialism functions as a phenomenon which is not only international but intranational," having an impact simultaneously between and within nations. While his own analysis addressed Mexico, the framework he adopted and the following observation he made apply also to the United States: "The notion of 'internal colonialism' has its roots in the great independence movement of the old colonies."[16]

CONQUEST, RACE, AND THE EARLY REPUBLICAN EMPIRE (1776–1848)

The United States' imperial pretensions were already developed during its own struggle for political independence. As Roxanne Dunbar Ortiz argues, the United States' struggle for independence aimed at founding "a settler-colonialist and imperialist-aggressor state."[17] The Declaration of Independence sought not only to establish a republic of white males, but more importantly to remove protections against what it referred to as "merciless Indian savages," which had been agreed upon at the end of the French and Indian War to prevent illegal encroachment by white squatters on Native American lands west of the Allegheny/Appalachian boundary.

The era the nation's historians refer to as the Early Republican period represented an early phase of its empire. It was in part a continuation of colonial English policies, although the United States remained an economic periphery of Great Britain. The expanding British empire was already engaged in its headlong rush as the first nation to enjoy the fruits of the Industrial Revolution, and the United States was an important provider of raw materials and agricultural goods, whose trade depended upon the work of its subjugated and conquered peoples of color. While maintaining close economic links, the United States itself engaged in imperial challenges against Great Britain, particularly during the War of 1812, when it attempted to conquer Canada, and with its declaration of the Monroe Doctrine in 1823, which asserted that European imperial activities in the Americas were not acceptable. Adopting an imperial posture, the United States claimed exclusive status and power over all its neighbors to the south.

As an imperial republic, the United States' treatment of the ancestors of the reservation and the ghetto influenced its treatment of the people of Mexico, its most significant military conquest of the era. Slaves of African origin were racialized in the Constitution, where they counted as only three-fifths of a "citizen" (an attribute allowed only white people), and as chattel had few rights. Native Americans were treated as impediments to be removed, in order to permit the advance of "civilization," as only whites merited the designation of being "civilized." Even the treaties they were forced to sign did not allow them citizenship status, unlike the "civilized" white people of French Louisiana, who were readily incorporated into the body politic and retained their land.

In the United States, Native Americans were members of nations, but interpreters of law consistently violated their treaty rights, withholding the respect granted citizens. Andrew Jackson, U.S. president from 1829-1837, emphasized that they must be removed beyond the boundaries of "civilized" people onto reservations. As early as the 1790s, his strategy was "Indian removal." He invaded peaceful Indian nations during the War of 1812, and later attacked Native Americans in Florida and elsewhere in the Southeast. He achieved great success in 1837 with outright removal in the Trail of Tears of even those who met the white man's legal criteria of "civilized": living in settled communities, having written languages and established governments.[18] Ultimately, formal United States policy and laws that justified the removal of Native Americans and the enslavement of Africans contradicted the democratic pretensions of the era, and could only be resolved by an imperial ideology of inequality that justified conquest and subjugation based on race.

Mexico's period as a formal colony of Spain ended in 1821, when it achieved its independence and was soon recognized as a civilized nation in international law. Imperialism had shaped its colonial racial order, with Europeans dominating a huge indigenous population and imposing African slavery, yet by the early nineteenth century, slavery in Mexico was moribund. Colonial structures of domination remained largely intact, although the Mexican nation was not yet subordinated by foreign economic or military interests. But as Aníbal Quijano notes, "from the point of view of the dominators, their social interests were much closer to the interests of their European peers, and consequently they were always inclined to follow the interests of the European bourgeoisie. They were, then, dependent."[19] Their dependence on a Eurocentric ideology ensured that they viewed their own interests in opposition to indigenous and African peoples. Despite the efforts of some among the Mexican elite to eliminate the language of race, the repression and enslavement of indigenous people continued, along with their resistance.[20] However, the relative isolation of Mexico from foreign military and economic interference and domination was short-lived, as the United States quickly asserted its imperial designs on the Mexican north.

The Conquest of Mexico and the U.S. Empire (1846–1876)

The Early Republican era of the United States culminated with an obvious act of imperialism, an unprovoked invasion and conquest of a nation in what would become known in early twenty-first century parlance as "preemptive war." The United States justified its actions by claiming that Mexico had committed aggression against the lives of United States citizens in the disputed territory of Texas, although its primary aim was to wrest the territories of far northwestern Mexico, particularly Alta California, to which it lacked any legal or historical claim.

At the beginning of the nineteenth century Mexicans were barely within the conscious scope of the United States imperial agenda. Racial norms differed in the two nations, as Euro-Americans recognized few Mexicans as white.[21] Still another point of contention was that in the immediate aftermath of its struggle for independence from Spain, Mexico abolished slavery, an institution Mexican popular opinion vehemently opposed. Its elites preferred less direct forms of coercion, including debt labor.

During the invasion, as the United States military pushed into the heart of the nation, sentiments to acquire all of Mexico intensified. At that time, the U.S. coveted Mexico for its natural resources and not for its labor or its people, as the *Democratic Review* made clear in August 1847:"The annexation of the country to the United States would be a calamity. 5,000,000 ignorant and indolent half-civilized Indians, with 1,500,000 free Negroes and mulattoes, the remnants of the British slave trade, would scarcely be a desirable incumbrance, even with the great natural wealth of Mexico."[22]

But there were strong sentiments in both major parties and among Southern slaveholders that acquiring all of Mexico would upset the nation's institutions, including slavery and the racial order in the United States. Thus the movement to acquire all of Mexico floundered and collapsed. In the Treaty of Guadalupe Hidalgo of 1848, Mexican citizens from the conquered territories were incorporated as U.S. citizens and recognized as white. The critical years of racial formation were in the immediate aftermath of the treaty, when leading citizens of the United States devised a hypocritical and complicated framework to deny Mexicans that "whiteness" and dispossess them of their lands. Even people from the former Mexican elite were affected, like Manuel Domínguez, a signatory of the California constitution of 1850, who was barred from testifying in court by the end of the decade because of his "Indian blood." Indigenous Mexicans, who had been granted Mexican citizenship and whose collective landholdings were recognized in Mexican law, lost those citizenship rights and were treated as wards of the state. Both political rights and economic power, particularly in the form of lands held individually and in common, were largely wrested away from the former citizens of Mexico within a generation. As Kenneth Stewart and Arnoldo DeLeón demonstrate, in Texas the total per capita wealth of Mexicans was higher than Anglos in 1850, but fell to only one-fifth that of European Americans by 1870.[23] The conquerors had taken most of the Mexicans' lands and made a mockery of the treaty.

Industrial Capitalism and Imperialism during the Porfiriato (1876–1910)

Visions of empire and racial ideology became intertwined in the minds and actions of European nations and the United States as industrial capitalism advanced in the late-nineteenth and early-twentieth centuries, an era in Mexico referred to as the Porfiriato, dominated by the dictator Porfirio Díaz, 1877-1911. It was also the era to which Vladimir Lenin referred in his classic *Imperialism as the Highest Stage of Capitalism.* Once it had conquered and subjugated the indigenous peoples of its own West, in the 1890s the United States joined the scramble to acquire foreign territories it had long coveted, as demonstrated by its unprovoked conquest and annexation of Hawaii and its provocation of war with Spain to acquire its former territories, particularly Puerto Rico, the Philippines, and the "protectorate" of Cuba. Meanwhile the United States engaged in a form of "soft" imperialism by subordinating Mexico through a combination of loans, commerce, exchange, and investment, thus establishing a neo-colonial relationship with its southern neighbor.

The primary goals of imperialists were to acquire land and raw materials, as well as cheap labor, to enhance industrial production and consumption at home. France, England, and the United States all had Mexico in their sights, but in the 1850s and 1860s Mexico successfully fended off their imperial attempts, including a French military invasion and occupation. Representatives of the United States government and leading industrialists realized they could accomplish their ends without direct military conquest or settler colonialism, depending instead on an ideology of racism and a strategy of collaboration with the Mexican government and its elite, who they accepted as leaders of an already "civilized" nation who considered themselves white.

The Mexican elite adapted European ideologies to justify actions that paralleled measures being taken simultaneously in the United States, namely the reduction of native peoples and the forcible wresting of their lands through legislation, and when that failed, through military force. In Mexico it involved altering established Spanish colonial laws that protected native lands and communities, and adopting a labor regime that included extreme forms of labor, even outright slavery, to produce on behalf of international capitalist investors for the markets in the United States and Western Europe. The foreign industrial capitalists and mine owners shared the strategies of land grabbing and labor repression with collaborationist Mexican elites. They justified their actions in Mexico, as in the United States, through scientific, race-based popular ideologies of the era. Belief in Social Darwinism was widespread among English-speaking peoples, and positivism among the French, who had a greater impact on the Mexican *científicos* (scientists) who popularized the ideology in Mexico. A particular racist notion used to justify colonialism was the idea of the White Man's Burden—the presumed paternalistic duty of the white race to care for nonwhite inhabitants of their colonies.

Science and Mexican labor made possible the opening of railroads north to El Paso by the 1880s and allowed Mexican workers from the more densely populated sections of the country to move to the sparsely populated mines and work on the railroads on both sides of the international border. The neocolonial relationship between the two countries was evident in their social relations, as owners and bosses commonly were European Americans from the United States, along with skilled railroad and mine workers, who received superior wages and treatment. Meanwhile, Mexican workers were excluded from the political process, relegated to menial and contingent labor, and isolated culturally. In effect, the scientific ideologies of the era that racialized Mexicans and other colonized peoples further contributed to the shift in popular thought from defining Mexicans as white at the time of the Treaty of Guadalupe Hidalgo to nonwhite by the turn of the twentieth century. The racialization was reinforced by the United States conquest and subjugation of peoples deemed nonwhite in the Caribbean and Pacific, sustained by economic, political and cultural mechanisms, as well as military intervention.

THE MEXICAN REVOLUTION, WORLD WAR I, AND THE CLOSING OF EUROPE (1910–1940)

The United States and European nations, particularly England and France, in their quest for raw materials, agricultural products, and labor during the Porfiriato upset the economic and political order of the nation and set the stage for revolution in Mexico. As they set up railroads and factories and established an industrial form of migrant agricultural labor that sent products to the borders of the nation, the investors created an industrial working class. The migrant workers in the Laguna region of Durango and Chihuahua, as well as miners and railroad workers and the urbanizing industrial workers of the nation, participated as soldiers in different factions during the Mexican Revolution.

Meanwhile European imperialists struggled over the wealth of colonies in Africa and Asia and set the stage for World War I, which disrupted labor migration from Europe to the industrializing United States. As a result, industrialists from the United States were induced to recruit workers from Mexico to replace Europeans who had been cut off. While many Southwest-focused histories suggest that Mexican migration to the United States in the early twentieth century was primarily a consequence of economic development in the Southwest, more importantly it stemmed from the disruptions in Mexico that led to revolution, and from the European imperial struggles that led to World War I. Industrial employers lured Mexican workers far beyond the Southwest, and Mexicans formed colonias in Kansas City, Chicago, Detroit, Philadelphia, New York, and other northern cities.

The migration of this era was influenced by ideology stemming from the Mexican Revolution. Mexican Revolutionary Nationalism compelled the government and its ruling classes to remain sensitive to popular nationalist sentiments. It protected natural resources and infrastructure projects from direct foreign control, and it did not support a formal program of labor migration. Capitalists from the United States encountered a more independent and contentious Mexican government, and operated mostly independent endeavors including labor recruitment, initially seeking short term workers, particularly young and unattached males, while families remained in Mexico to reproduce themselves in a classic form of colonial labor relations. Agricultural capitalists were even more effective in blocking legislation that applied to the mostly white working class, while they were soon able to attract women and children for their operations.

At the end of the 1920s an early theoretical contribution to understanding empire, colonialism and Mexican labor appeared: *Los latino-americanos en los Estados Unidos,* by Communist Party members Leon Slavín Ruiz and Alberto Moreau. They offered a globalized and "totalizing" account, linking United States imperialism to the migration and exploitation of workers from Latin America, particularly Mexico and Puerto Rico, and the role of ideology in making them racialized minorities.[24]

GOOD EMPIRE, GOOD NEIGHBORS (1940-1980)

The onset of the Great Depression marked the beginning of an era of sharply reduced international migration, and in the United States conversations about the nation and its workers turned inward. Worker struggles contributed to this shift as the working classes of the United States, Mexico, and the European empires, "gained a legitimacy and status that they had never heretofore possessed," and established welfare states based on national Keynesian policies that resulted in collective bargaining, social insurance, and wage increases proportionate to increases in productivity.[25] A sector of the Mexican working class participated in this upward movement by identifying with the United States and considering themselves American and white, a strategy of upward mobility and incorporation into civic life.

At the same time, the U.S. policy of open military intervention in Latin America dating from the 1890s was reversed when Franklin D. Roosevelt articulated the Good Neighbor Policy. Meanwhile, the war forced many European nations to accept formal decolonization in exchange for support from the people of their colonies to join the struggle on their side, and in response to demands for independence. Similarly, the United States supported less-heavy handed tactics toward its neighbors to the immediate south. The Roosevelt administration refused to intervene when the Mexican government nationalized its oil in 1938, or when Guatemala elected a progressive democratic government in 1944. If the United States was a Good Neighbor, at the time it represented a Good Empire. Once World War II ended, it became engaged in a war against a new evil empire, the Cold War against its former ally, the Soviet Union.

As the ideology of the struggle between the good and evil empires took a sharper nationalist turn by the early 1950s, politicians turned against foreign workers, particularly Mexicans who they dubbed "wetbacks." The interplay of reduced international migration and the turn to the individual in academia and popular culture influenced many Mexican Americans to adopt insular and provincial theories to separate themselves from Mexico and its citizens, which influenced the first generation of self-identified Chicano scholarship, including the early accounts of internal colonialism.

Meanwhile European empires were weakening as Third World liberation movements spread throughout Asia and Africa. In the Americas, liberation movements were inspired by Cuba, which had retained a neo-colonial relationship with the United States. Its revolution encouraged people to see commonality and community in their struggles against colonialism and racism. These movements, along with the accompanying anti-colonial writings of Frantz Fanon, Albert Memmi, and other authors, directly inspired rebellions in the United States among its own Third World peoples.[26] The anti-colonial thought of the Black Power, American Indian, and Chicano movements included its own literature on internal colonialism.

THE NEW WORLD ORDER: GLOBALIZATION AND ILLEGALS

The United States responded to challenges against its imperial domination from Latin America and from Third World peoples within its own borders by means of wide-ranging and concerted attacks. In Latin America, through national elites, and particularly the military, which it trained, it sought to systematically destroy national liberation movements, often using the pretext that they were linked to the Soviet Union. It supported the installation of military dictatorships throughout the continent. Its military and ideological attacks on the Latin American movements did not cease with the collapse of the Soviet Union in 1990. As Samir Amin observed, United States "imperialism is once again on the offensive." The current wave of imperialism functions both militarily and through the ideology of global neoliberalism, which claims that unregulated individual competition and free trade are the normal and necessary course of affairs in the world. The rhetoric obfuscates its defense of monopolistic and corrupt practices by corporate elites, supported by governments and by organizations including the World Bank, the International Monetary Fund (IMF), and the World Trade Organization. The ideology of globalization, Amin observes, is "nothing but a new way in which the inherently imperialist nature of the system asserts itself."[27]

Lacking the counterweight of the Soviet Union, the United States intensified its efforts to increase domination, particularly over nations formerly under the sway of Great Britain, France, and the Soviet Union, in Eastern Europe, the Middle East, Asia, and Africa. The most visible consequence has been an expanded U.S. military presence accompanied by "pre-emptive" invasions and provocations, often in alliance with the North Atlantic Treaty Organization (NATO) in Eastern Europe, Asia, the Middle East and Africa. Targets include Iraq, Afghanistan, Syria, Ukraine, and Libya—nations that challenged the empire's desire to control the world's oil supply. The imperialist military ventures, having caused massive destruction and disruption in those nations, provoked unprecedented waves of refugee migration to many parts of the world. In countries that have received the refugees, there has been an intensifying level of hostility, articulated as Islamophobia, and the formation of another distinct non-European racial group. The link between imperialist military intervention and subsequent racial formation in this case has been clear and direct. By invading and conquering people of a vaguely Islamic and Muslim appearance and identifying them as "terrorists," imperialism has created another colonized people who, not surprisingly look quite a bit like Mexicans.

The United States also intensified its political, economic, and military presence in Latin America in an effort to reassert domination in Central and South America to upend the "Pink Tide" of progressive governments that came to power in the late 1990s and first decade of the twenty-first century. The governments it targeted were all democratically elected and more profoundly responsive to the demands of their citizens than any predecessors, but in their quest for autonomy, regional economic and cultural integration, and freedom from foreign interference, they encountered sharp reactions from the United States.

In Mexico, the "Pink Tide" made little headway, as the United States' presence was more deeply entrenched and it had more ways to influence politics and block the accession to power of progressive governments. The imperialist efforts included supporting openly fraudulent elections, including those for President in 1988 and 2006, and imposing debt on Mexico that led to repeated economic crises as part of a neoliberal agenda that included austerity and privatization through closed agreements including the North American Free Trade Agreement (NAFTA) and the Mérida Initiative, all part of "the soft imperialism of free trade."[28] In conjunction with the dealings of the IMF and World Bank, the agreements revoked many of the achievements of the Mexican Revolution as they privatized natural resources and public utilities, displaced the owner-occupants of rural and communal lands, and imposed austerity on the working class. It was a direct assault on small farmers and workers, who in the face of the loss of their lands and their means of livelihood, along with plummeting living standards, were forced in massive numbers to seek other means of survival. The disruption had a parallel to the impact of United States assault on the oil-rich lands of the Middle East and Africa in forcing migration, as it drove millions of Mexicans into the United States, where it provoked a new wave of nativism and racial antipathy toward the newcomers that led to new laws further restricting the legal rights of immigrants and other working people. The results further demonstrate that the neoliberal claim that it promotes democracy is empty rhetoric.[29]

Formal agreements between the two countries have permitted elites in control to intensify the neocolonial relationship and intensify class

warfare on workers from both countries. Extending beyond classic imperialism which focused primarily on acquiring raw materials, land, and
other natural resources, it also involves shifting industrial production for
the United States market to Mexico, while accelerating the migration of
workers from Mexico. This wave of neocolonial imperialism involves a
more pervasive effort to spread United States culture and its ideology of
globalization by luring the elites to the United States for training. Many
top executives in Mexico, as well as presidents elected in 1982, 1988,
1994, and 2006, attended graduate or law school in the United States,
while another, Vicente Fox, elected in 2000, was a former executive of
Coca Cola, the most pervasive symbol of U.S. capitalist culture in Latin
America. The effort included an intensified War on Drugs, highlighted
by the Mérida Initiative started under President Felipe Calderón, which
involves the United States training Mexican military for counterinsur-
gency operations in Mexico, resulting in the wanton deaths of tens of
thousands of Mexicans. While exporting its popular culture and its
weapons, the United States imports and trains Mexico's political leaders,
business executives, and military officers.

Neoliberal globalization, NAFTA, the Mérida Initiative and similar
agreements sustained by the World Bank and the IMF, while ostensibly
aimed primarily at trade, have in fact shifted a great deal of industrial
production from the United States to Mexico, and to even poorer Third
World countries. While migration from Mexico hollowed out many small
towns in the northern part of the country, in the United States it caused
deindustrialization that devasted thriving cities and the industrial working
class, along with the unions that advocated for workers. The bulk of the
new working class in the United States does not make things, but rather
serves other people, with growth sectors in health care and sales. The
new jobs are largely low-wage and increasingly contingent, in contrast
to earlier factory jobs, with conditions that are more akin to those of
migrant agricultural workers of the twentieth century. With the collapse
of union protection, it has become much more difficult for workers to
defend themselves from assaults by employers who found it easier to enact
hostile labor legislation and to engage in outright robbery. Wage theft by
employers in the United States, literally the failure to pay wages due, in
the early twenty-first century exceeds all other reported classes of theft

and robbery combined.[30] These same forces have destabilized the lives of millions of Mexicans, forced their migration northward, and sharply increased inequality within and between Mexico and the United States.

In the United States hostility against Mexicans and negative stereotypes have been increasing. The most popular dominant stereotype of Mexicans in Greater Aztlán from the 1940s to 1970s was the migrant worker, a United States citizen who lacked residency status, the right to vote, and experienced other political and economic drawbacks. It then shifted to the "illegal alien," an individual who lacked even the possibility of establishing residence to obtain such rights, because of the lack of citizenship. But since inauguration of the so-called "War on Terror," dominant popular parlance has been shortened to "illegal," a curious sleight of hand involving a complication of colonial racial ideology.[31]

Meanwhile, the brown person became a suspect in terrorism, resulting in increasing arrests of Mexicans and other misdemeanants; justification of the intensifying militarization of the U.S. Border Patrol; and an expanded use of state and local police forces to prosecute immigration offenders, performing tasks that constitutionally reside in the federal government.[32] The designation as illegal was linked to new prison initiatives and skyrocketing levels of incarceration. With the formation of Immigration and Customs Enforcement (ICE), a division of the Department of Homeland Security, the longstanding misdemeanor of crossing or re-crossing the border gained increasing attention, and the Immigrant Detention Center, an entirely new category of prison, was created primarily for thousands of newly-illegal Mexicans.[33] As U.S. Attorney Mike Shelby acknowledged, "in 2002, we changed our policy to move as many cases as we could from the administrative side of the house to the criminal side of the house, even if that meant that we just filed misdemeansor cases on those people and they just got time served and were deported."[34] Finally, the term "illegal," not explicitly "illegal alien," could be applied more randomly to the individual of foreign and swarthy appearance. It acquired particular importance in locations where the Mexican population surged, including Atlanta, or in New Orleans following Hurricane Katrina, when the federal government encouraged hiring Mexican misdemeanants by suspending employer sanctions on hiring them, and by not obligating employers to pay prevailing wages.[35] The term "illegal," could also be more readily applied to Guatemalan and Honduran immigrants, Mexican-born residents, and United States-born Chicanos and other people of vaguely similar appearance. This justified to many a heightened degree of exploitation and mistreatment of the "illegal," an individual not entitled to the rights and protections of citizens, or even basic human rights.

The War on Terror was accompanied by a wave of discriminatory legislation, voter suppression laws and other efforts to discourage people of Mexican origin from participating in governance.[36] This included unconstitutional legislation aimed at denying them the human rights to which they are entitled regardless of residence. The ideologies supporting globalization and so-called free trade agreements aimed at easing exchanges between the two countries were accompanied by rising clamor to block human movement between the two countries, as the construction, reinforcement and expansion of the great wall at the border proceeds apace.

It further gives lie to expectations that democracy and equality apply to Mexicans, and glosses over the massive and increasing material gap between European Americans and Mexicans in the U.S. Since the early 1980s, rising indexes of inequality have been evident in residential segregation, formal schooling, incomes, wealth, and other material indicators.[37] By the year 2013, per capita Euro-American wealth was more than fourteen times greater than that of the average person of Mexican origin in the United States.[38] In addition, recent surveys have indicated record numbers of Mexican immigrants are dying and facing mistreatment simply trying to cross into the United States, and that staying in the U.S. is bad for one's health.[39] While authors including Samir Amin suggest that with increasing mechanization, there should be less need to work, in fact working hours in the United States have increased sharply since 1980.[40] This may suggest that the attractiveness of Mexicans to employers is not primarily to increase production in order to obtain meager profits amidst growing competition, but rather to intensify exploitation to heighten inequality and keep the workers of the world divided.

CONCLUSION

Adopting colonial theories in Chicana/o studies focusing on imperialism enables us to examine much more profoundly how the agenda of the United States empire, like other empires, has shifted markedly over time, and how it has impacted the nations and peoples it encountered. In its early years the United States treated Mexico, while recognized among the European family of nations, only modestly differently than other indigenous nations. The U.S. empire was still an economic periphery of England and provided raw materials including lumber and agricultural products, which motivated it to expand its land base at the expense of its neighbors. Its agression in 1846, the imperial conquest of Mexico, accomplished its goal of expanding its land base to acquire natural resources to extend commercial agriculture. The war also broke its dependency on England by enabling it to fuel its own industrial revolution.

As competition over empire intensified in the late nineteenth century and the United States was becoming a major world industrial power, its aggression increased, accompanied by investments in neighboring countries. It elaborated on Eurocentric race-based ideologies to justify its conquests and its domination over Mexico and its neighbors, as well as its treatment of the new subject people, not all deemed black, indigenous, or white but nevertheless deemed inferior, and toward whom the threat of invasion and conquest loomed over the not-too-distant horizon.

The conquest of lands in the Caribbean and Pacific represented its most visible imperial action as a nation. In the aftermath of 1898, the Caribbean was often referred to as an "American Lake," and the United States military repeatedly invaded nations that it bordered, including Mexico twice during its Revolution. In 1914 it occupied the port of Veracruz and in 1915 it invaded Chihuahua to thwart Pancho Villa.

Soon the United States was distracted by World War I, a scramble over the spoils of empire. The war cut off the flow of workers to the United States from Europe, while many European nations took stronger steps to protect their own citizens from poor treatment they perceived was being dealt them by capitalists in the United States by curtailing immigration. Meanwhile European living standards were catching up with those of the United States, and many European workers realized that the American Dream had little to offer them. The cessation of large-scale European labor migration induced capitalists from the United States to look elsewhere, and many turned to the much cheaper and by now readily accessible workers of Mexico. But many representatives of the Mexican government and its elites, swept up by the nationalism stemming from the Revolution, adopted more guarded behavior toward the United States, and were not eager to assist the northern capitalists to gain easy access to Mexican labor. They recognized that Mexican workers in United States were treated poorly, a later example being the humiliating repatriation programs of the Great Depression.

When World War II broke out, the declining European empires had to make promises to their colonies for greater independence in exchange for support during the war. The United States did the same with Mexico, and it gained an inter-governmental agreement that afforded legal protection for its citizen workers who came to the United States under contract. But after the war ended, the United States empire faced few challengers in the Americas and Mexico's leverage was reduced. The Mexican government readily collaborated with employers and the government of the United States to send a much greater number of contingent workers with fewer protections.

The rebellions that erupted throughout Latin America in the 1960s and 1970s, inspired in large part by Cuba, were also a reaction against United States' imperial arrogance. They were brutally supressed by the United States, the military allies it had trained, and the dictators it had helped to put in power. Social movements in the United States faced similar, if less extreme opposition, which was accompanied by an ideological assault in academia aimed at taming the scholars who challenged the imperial project, while a new generation adopted theories that failed to challenge the neoliberal ascendancy.

Soon another insurgency erupted in Latin America, the "Pink Tide," a nationalist, leftist reaction against the imperial ambitions of neoliberalism. But the United States faced fewer obstacles to intensifying foreign investment, privatization, and austerity on Mexico, sending its own industries to the south while devastating and destabilizing the lives of workers and promoting a regime of violence and imprisonment on both sides of the border. Despite the attacks on livelihoods and the campaigns of violence and criminalization, Mexican workers have been joining allies on both sides of the border, including academics, to assert their political, economic and cultural rights, and challenging the regime of rising violence, austerity, and privatization.

Notes

1. John R. Chávez, "Aliens in Their Native Lands: The Persistence of Internal Colonial Theory," *Journal of World History*, 22 (December 2011): 785–809; Ramón Gutiérrez, "Internal Colonialism: An American Theory of Race," *DuBois Review* 1 (September 2004): 281–95; Adrian Groglopo, "Dependency Theories and Internal Colonialism," in Richard Dankell, Anna Larsson, and Per Wisselgren, eds., *Social Science in Context: Historical, Sociological, and Global Perspectives* (Lund, Sweden: Nordic Academic Press, 2013): 205–19; Charles Pinderhughes, "Toward a New Theory of Internal Colonialism," *Socialism and Democracy*, 25 (June 2011): 235–56; Rosaura Sánchez and Beatrice Pita, "Rethinking Settler Colonialism," *American Quarterly* 66 (December 2014): 1039–55.

2. See e.g., John Walton, "Internal Colonialism: Problems of Definition and Measurement," Northwestern Univerversity Center for Urban Affairs, November 6, 1974; María Montoya, "Beyond Internal Colonialism: Class, Gender and Culture as Challenges to Chicano Identity," *Voices of a New Chicana/Chicano History*, Refugio Rochín and Dionicio Valdés, eds. (East Lansing: Michigan State University Press, 2000): 183–95; Michael Soldatenko, *Chicano Studies: The Genesis of a Discipline* (Tucson: University of Arizona Press): 51ff.

3. Pablo González Casanova, "Internal Colonialism and National Development," *Studies in Comparative International Development* 1: 4 (St. Louis: Washington University Social Science Institute, 1965): 29.

4. Pablo González Casanova, "Sociedad Plural, Colonialismo Interno y Desarrollo," *América Latina*, 6 (1963); Rodolfo Stavenhagen, "Classes, Colonialism and Acculturation," *Studies in Comparative International Development*, 1: 6 (St. Louis: Washington University Social Science Institute, 1965); Robert Blauner, "Internal Colonialism and the Ghetto Revolt," *Social Problems* 16 (Spring 1969): 393–408.

5. Mario Barrera, Carlos Muñoz, and Charles Ornelas, "The Barrio as an Internal Colony," *Urban Affairs Annual Reviews* 6 (1972): 465–98.

6. Rodolfo Acuña, *Occupied America: The Chicano's Struggle Toward Liberation* (San Francisco: Canfield Press, 1972); F. Chris García and Rodolfo O. de la Garza, *The Chicano Political Experience: Three Perspectives* (North Scituate, MA: Duxbury Press, 1977); Rubén O. Martínez, "Internal Colonialism: A Reconceptualization of Race Relations in the United States," Humboldt Journal of Social Relations 10 (Fall/Winter 1982/1983): 163–76; Ramón Arturo Gutiérrez, "Mexican Migration to the United States: the Chicano and Internal Colonialism," (master's thesis, University of Wisconsin-Madison, 1976).

7. Tomás Almaguer, "Toward the Study of Chicano Colonialism," *Aztlán* 2 (Spring 1971): 7–21.

8. The most notable case of cultural applications of Marx, of course, was Antonio Gramsci, in *The Prison Notebooks*. The most influential early Marxist gender

analysis was Fredrick Engels, *The Origin of the Family, Private Property and the State* (New York: Pathfinder, 1972).

9. Mario Barrera, *Race and Class in the Southwest: A Theory of Racial Inequality* (Notre Dame: University of Notre Dame Press, 1979), 2–3.

10. Tey Diana Rebolledo and Eliana S. Rivero, comp., *Infinite Divisions: An Anthology of Chicana Literature* (Tucson: University of Arizona Press, 1993).

11. Gloria Anzaldúa, *Borderlands = La Frontera: The New Mestiza* (San Francisco: Spinsters/Aunt Lute, 1987).

12. Jacques Derrida, *Specters of Marx: The State of the Debt, the Work of Mourning, and the New International* (New York: Routledge, 1994), offers a very disappointing and shallow analysis of Marx, in particular when read in juxtaposition of the structural analysis *Spectres of Capitalism*, by Amin, below.

13. Samir Amin, *Spectres of Capitalism: A Critique of Current Intellectual Fashions* (New York: Monthly Review Press, 1998), 66.

14. Mario Barrera, *Beyond Aztlán: Ethnic Autonomy in Comparative Perspective* (New York: Praeger, 1988).

15. Michael Hardt and Antonio Negri, *Empire* (Cambridge and London: Harvard University Press, 2000).

16. Casanova, "Internal Colonialism and National Development," 27.

17. Roxanne Dunbar-Ortiz, "The Grid of History: Cowboys and Indians," *Monthly Review* 55:3 (July–August 2003), www.monthlyreview.org/2003/07/01/the-grid-of-history-cowboys-and-indians.

18. Robert V. Remini, *Andrew Jackson and His Indian Wars* (New York: Penguin Books, 2001).

19. Aníbal Quijano, "Coloniality of Power, Eurocentrism, and Latin America," *Nepantla* 1 (2000), 566; Sánchez and Pita, "Rethinking," 1046–48.

20. John R. Chávez, "Beyond Domestic Empire: Internal- and Post-Colonial New Mexico," *History Faculty Publications* (Paper 3, 2015), 9–10. http://digitalrepository.smu.edu/hum_sci_history_research/3.

21. Joel Roberts Poinsett, *Notes on Mexico Made in the Autumn of 1822* (New York: Frederick A. Praeger, 1969), 120.

22. *Democratic Review*, XXI, 101, quoted in John Douglas Pitts Fuller, *The Movement for the Acquisition of all of Mexico 1846–1848*, The Johns Hopkins University Studies in Historical and Political Science, 54: 1 (Baltimore: The Johns Hopkins Press, 1936): 63.

23. Kenneth L. Stewart and Arnoldo de León, *Not Room Enough: Mexicans, Anglos, and Socioeconomic Change in Texas, 1850–1900* (Albuquerque: University of New Mexico Press, 1993), 34–35.

24. Leon Slavín Ruiz and Alberto Moreau, *Los Latino-Americanos en los Estados Unidos: La Situación de los Trabajadores en Norte America* (New York: Vida Obrera, 1929).

25. Amin, *Spectres*, 40.

26. Frantz Fanon, *The Wretched of the Earth* (New York: Grove Press, 1963); Albert Memmi, *The Colonizer and the Colonized* (Boston: Beacon Press, 1965).

27. Amin, *Spectres,* 45.

28. Alex Callinicos, *Imperialism and Global Political Economy* (Cambridge: Polity 2009), 190–191; Brianna Lee, "Mexico's Drug War," CFR Backgrounder, March 5, 2014, www.cfr.org/mexico/mexicos-drug-war/p13689.

29. Amin, *Spectres,* p. 24, observes that the key labor factor is that the law of value required markets to become integrated in all their dimensions (for capital, commodities and labor power), but in fact it has not for labor power, because the world market is truncated, as the law of value in globalized form is subservient to polarization between central and peripheral economies. On contradictions in NAFTA preventing integration of labor market that hurts workers and middle classes while allowing relatively free flow of capital, goods, services, and information, see Douglas S. Massey, "Thinking Out Loud: Immigration—A 'Free Market' Includes Labor," *Los Angeles Times,* July 31, 2005; Stuart Laidlaw, "One Country, Two Economies," *Toronto Star,* October 10, 2005, C1; Bill Lambrecht, "Low Prices Force Mexicans from Fields," *St. Louis Post Dispatch,* October 30, 2005.

30. Ross Eisenbrey, "Wage Theft is a Bigger Problem Than Other Theft—But Not Enough is Done to Protect Workers," *Economic Policy Institute Economic Snapshot,* April 2, 2014, www.epi.org/publication/wage-theft-bigger-problem-theft-protect/.

31. See e.g., "Facing the Crisis of Illegal Immigration," *New York Daily News,* August 17, 2005, 28.

32. On militarization of the border and politics, see e.g.: Jean O. Pasco, "O. C. Race Shapes Up as a Duel—Gilchrist's Strong Finish Tuesday Makes Him Chief Rival to the GOP's Campbell," *Los Angeles Times,* October 6, 2005, B1; Tillie Fong, "Protesters Slam Border Trip," *Rocky Mountain News,* October 6, 2005, A31. On local enforcement of immigration laws, see Edward Allen, "A Border War," *Financial Times,* August 29, 2005, 11. On federal mandate to increase prosecutions, see Gina Barton, "Millions spent to jail the deported," *Milwaukee Journal Sentinel,* August 28, 2005, 1.

33. U.S. Government Accountability Office, *Criminal Alien Statistics: Information on Incarcerations, Arrests, and Costs,* GAO-11-187, March 2011; Peter Wagner and Bernadette Rabuy, "Mass Incarceration: The Whole Pie 2016," *Prison Policy Initiative,* March 14, 2016, www.prisonpolicy.org/reports/pie2016.html.

34. James Pinkerton, "Routine immigration violators prosecuted," *Houston Chronicle,* September 19, 2005, B1.

35. Monica Campbell, "Post-Katrina Easing of Labor Laws Stirs Debate," *Christian Science Monitor,* October 4, 2005, O1.

36. "Voter Suppression and Victories in 2016." *El Hispanic News,* March 3, 2016, www.elhispanicnews.com/2016/03/03/voter-suppression-and-victories-in-2016;

Advancement Project Voter Registration Program, "Segregating American Citizenship: Latino Voter Disenfranchisement in 2012," September 21, 2012, www.advancementproject.org/resources/entry/segregating-american-citizenship-latino-voter-disenfranchisement-in-2012.

37. On school resegregation, see e.g., Gary Orfield and Jack Boger, eds., *School Resegregation: Must the South Turn Back?* (University of North Carolina Press, 2005); "Has it Worked?," *Washington Post,* May 13, 2004, p C14; "Brown's Forsaken Dreams; Flawed Rulings of 1954 Color Today's Schools," *Boston Herald,* May 16, 2004, p. O27; Ellis Cose, "Beyond Brown v. Board: The Final Battle for Excellence in American Education," *Rockefeller Foundation Report,* ca. May 13, 2004; Gary Orfield and Chungmei Lee, *Harvard Civil Rights Project,* 2004. On graduation rates, see Gary Orfield, Daniel Losen, Johanna Wild and Christopher B. Swanson, *Losing Our Future: How Minority Youth Are Being Left Behind by the Graduation Rate Crisis,* Cambridge, MA: The Civil Rights Project at Harvard University, 2004; Contributors: Urban Institute, Advocates for Children of New York, and The Civil Society Institute, www.civilrightsproject.harvard.edu. On incomes and wealth, see Pew Hispanic Center, "Wealth Gap Widens Between Whites and Hispanics," October 18, 2004, pewhispanic.org/newsroom/releases/print.php?ReleaseID=15. On impact of difficulty of obtaining health services because of fear see "Borderline Healthcare," *Los Angeles Times,* October 18, 2005, B10.

38. U. S. Census Bureau, *Average Number of People Per Household, by Race, Hispanic Origin, Marital Status, Age and Education of Householder: 2011,* www.census.gov/population/...tabAVG1.xls.; Chuck Collins, "Accelerating Racial Wealth Inequality," *Inequality.org,* December 13, 2014. inequality.org/racialwealthinequality-pew/.

39. Richard Marosi, "Crossing Deaths Set a 12-Month Record," *Los Angeles Times,* October 1, 2005, A1; Leslie Berestein, "460 Border Crossers Died in Past Year; Posters on Fence Tell of 3,600 Found Dead in 11 Years," *San Diego Union-Tribune,* October 1, 2005. On deteriorating health over time, Silvia Helena Barcellos, Dana P. Goldman, and James P. Smith, "Undiagnosed Disease, Especially Diabetes, Casts Doubt on Some Reported Health 'Advantage' of Recent Mexican Immigrants," *Health Affairs* 31 (2727–2737); Osea Giuntella, "Why Does the Health of Immigrants Deteriorate? Evidence from Birth Records." August 21, 2014. www.oseagiuntella.com/giuntella_mx_health_aug2014.pdf.

40. Amin, *Spectres.*

CHAPTER 2

Gaagegoo Dabakaanan miiniwaa Debenjigejig: No Borders, Indigenous Sovereignty

Dylan Miner

"NO FENCES, NO BORDERS. FREE MOVEMENT FOR ALL."

During the mid-1990s, I frequently crossed the Canada-USA border—as was common for youth living in the borderlands—to go to clubs and restaurants and, more importantly, for punk and hardcore music shows. I was an art student (and later, art school dropout) living in Detroit, on the U.S. side of the Detroit River, just across the Medicine Line from Windsor, Ontario. Before the arrival of Europeans in the late seventeenth and early eighteenth centuries, this place was called Waawiyaataanong, "at the curved shores." Historically, Waawiyaataanong was—and remains—an intertribal space, where Kiwikapawa (Kickapoo), Meskwaki (Fox), Sauk (Sac), Wendat (Wyandot or Huron), Anishinaabeg (Odawa, Potawatomi, and Ojibwe), Miami, Mascouten, Métis, and other peoples gathered or settled at various times.[1] Today, Detroit remains a vibrant urban Indigenous center.

In 1996, following the release of Propagandhi's second album, *Less Talk, More Rock*, I decided to cross the Ambassador Bridge and see the Winnipeg-based punk band play a show somewhere in southern Ontario (maybe London or Guelph or Hamilton, I don't recall). Traveling with an Arab-American friend, we were stopped and questioned for potential gang involvement. This border stoppage delayed us enough so that we barely made the show—that was what seemed important to us at the time, as teenage punks. Although I am an Indigenous person, my white privilege (or what might be better called "light-skin privilege"—a topic that light-skinned Indigenous and Latinxs should talk more about) and class privilege allow me to cross the border with less violence than brown-skinned Indigenous peoples, Latinxs, Arabs, Black folks, and other people of color. Although borders are inherently violent, settler-colonial nation-states enact border violence in ways that are not distributed equally.

Poster advocating Indigenous-Migrant Solidarity. *Dylan Miner*

Historian Jürgen Osterhammel defines colonialism as "a relationship of domination between an indigenous (or forcibly imported) majority and minority foreign invaders."[2] He continues: "Rejecting cultural compromises with the colonized population, the colonizers are convinced of their own superiority and of their ordained mandate to rule."[3] The systemization of colonialism enables racist, classist, and heteropatriarchal structures to infiltrate nearly everything, while the interconnectedness of these machinations may, at times, be hidden by the system itself. The xenophobic language of Donald Trump's 2016 presidential campaign is only the most recent articulation to lay this bare.

Here on Makanak-minis, what we may call Turtle Island or the Américas, we are all very much still contained within colonial structures and their hegemonic reproduction. While independence movements of the twentieth century offered self-determination for many former colonies in Africa and the Caribbean, the United States and Canada—as nation-states—remain colonial powers in which Indigenous nations are legally constructed as dependent entities within the settler-colonial nation-state.

Historian Patrick Wolfe distinguishes between the systematized workings of colonialism, on the one hand, and those of settler colonialism, on the other. Wolfe writes that "the primary object of settler-colonization is the land itself rather than the surplus value to be derived from mixing native labor with it. Though, in practice, Indigenous labor was indispensable to Europeans, settler-colonization is at base a winner-takes-all project whose dominant feature is not exploitation but, replacement."[4] Settler-colonialism is, at its core, a project of land appropriation, destruction of societies, and the repopulating of Indigenous territories.

In the so-called "New World," we could argue that French and Spanish colonial projects expanded through more classical examples of colonialism, while British "colonialism" more actively employed strategies of direct land and resource appropriation that accelerated after the "colonies" gained political "independence." Of course, as Wolfe argues, these colonialisms often used both strategies, one of exploitation and one of replacement. It is important to recognize that the "American Revolution" was "won" by settlers, not Indigenous or colonized peoples, and that Anglo-Americans then pursued an aggressive project of Euro-American expansionism, land appropriation, and replacement. Manifest Destiny required the creation of legal and economic systems that permitted European colonists and their descendants to become legal title-holders of the land. Manifest Destiny is, quite simply, settler colonialism. However, both projects—colonialism and settler colonialism—are also integrated with the racializing logics and the employment of colorism, the practice of discriminating against darker skinned individuals. And both colonialisms—as systems and as structures—employed racialization, blood quantum laws, and colorism within their own regimes. We can see the violent ramifications of these practices in some Indigenous and Latinx communities. On the one hand, many tribal communities continue to use blood quantum policies in determining who is eligible for enrollment; on the other, light skin (as a marker of being less Indian and less African) is commonly viewed as a positive. How do we undermine these racist and colonial logics that impede so much of what we do?

Remembering my own border-crossing experiences, and thinking about my current work as an artist-activist-intellectual, brings to mind one particular eighty-eight-second Propagandhi song, "Fuck the Border." As these Winnipeggers proclaimed in their searing song: "No fences, no borders. Free movement for all. Fuck the border." There is no ambiguity here. The anarchist orientation of certain sub-genres of 1990s hardcore helped me, as a youth, understand the implications of global capitalism and the intersectionality of colonialism, capitalism, and heteropatriarchy, among other structural oppressions. Bands like Propagandhi, Los Crudos, Limp Wrist, Chokehold, and Bikini Kill were particularly relevant to me at one time or another. Punk was simultaneously an epistemology and an ontology. However, what does punk have to do with Indigenous sovereignty, migration, and to the Canada-USA border? This is a question that I have asked myself for over two decades and one that I hope in this chapter to begin to think through.

While my own political commitments are quite similar to those articulated in Propagandhi's "Fuck the Border" song, as an adult with daughters attending university and secondary school I have struggled to find ways to talk about radical political positions that may complicate the simplicity of North American sound bites. Academics love to complicate what are often, in reality, not overly complicated issues; inversely, the news media frequently oversimplifies what may, in fact, be complicated. My own activism has likewise emerged from a place of direct opposition, an epistemology that does not always facilitate a way of being that understands my own hegemonic complicity. So the question becomes: how can we think about the intersectionality of our own lives—our various privileges and oppressions—without reducing the potential for everything to be linked in a network of ambiguities?

What is crucial to my thinking here is how, as a teenager and young adult, I was unable to fully comprehend the manner that colonial and capitalist ways of being in the world restrained my own ability to think (and act) outside them. The border—as a manifestation of the settler-colonial and capitalist nation-state—constrained my own being and, in turn, constrained my capacity to think beyond the limits of its own borders. Although I may ask this question frequently, I earnestly inquire if we can truly think outside or beyond the limits of colonialism? In his articulation of the "coloniality of power," Peruvian sociologist Aníbal Quijano would tell us, in fact, that we cannot.[5]

In the 1990s, I screamed "Fuck the Border" because it had very real implications on the lives of my ancestors and those of my partner, Estrella Torrez. My paternal ancestors crisscrossed the Canada-USA border and literally fought against its creation, while Estrella is the child of migrant farmworkers and was herself a seasonal laborer and student (and then teacher) in schools for migrant children. Her family has been in what is now the United States since time immemorial, but as is commonly said: "they didn't cross the border, the border crossed them."

Saying "Fuck the Border" was a cathartic and medicinal act that, although I did not name it such at the time, moved me towards decolonization. But, are decolonization and healing the same for those who can easily cross borders with little or no trouble (or, more likely, do not need/want to cross borders to leave the USA or Canada)? What about the individuals and communities who are violently affected by these same borders? I cannot help but think about those Mexican and Central American migrants who die—some might say structurally murdered—while migrating north in response to the contemporary ramifications of centuries of colonialism and capitalist globalization.

By saying "Fuck the Border," or voicing similar political provocations, are we actually moving toward a decolonized border and immigration practice? Are we individually and collectively seeking to create a world where Indigenous sovereignty exists beyond the limits of the settler-colonial nation-state? While I would not hesitate to say no, I do believe that in hearing this song—and the radical political ontologies associated with it—many middle-class and suburban settler-youth began to challenge their own privilege, even if they did not seek to fully dismantle a system that gave them this privilege in the first place.

As Jean-Paul Sartre reminds us, "colonialism is a system" and, as such, we are all implicated in its vicious systemization.[6] Colonialism is violent to both colonizer and colonized, as Frantz Fanon and others have long noted. Sartre writes that, "when we talk of the 'colonial system,' we must be clear about what we mean. It is not an abstract mechanism. The system exists, it functions; the infernal cycle of colonialism is a reality. But this reality is embodied in a million colonists, children and grandchildren of colonists, who have been shaped by colonialism and who think, speak and act according to the very principles of the colonial system."[7] To some extent, colonialism has shaped and informed every single one of us and our ancestors whether Indigenous, settler, or arrivant.[8] As Caribbean intellectual Aimé Césaire acknowledged in the early 1950s, colonization "dehumanizes even the most civilized man; that colonial activity, colonial enterprise, colonial conquest, which is based on contempt for the native and justified by that contempt, inevitably tends to change him who undertakes it."[9]

On Mikinaak-minis (Turtle Island), and I am not certain that Sartre or Fanon—or their peers—fully understood how colonialism functioned in this hemisphere, we are all implicated in *settler colonialism as a structure*. Recent work by Audra Simpson and Glen Coulthard, among other Indigenous scholars—often in the pages of *Decolonization: Indigeneity, Education & Society*—have brought earlier anti-colonial theorists into conversation with the uniquely North American variant of settler-colonialism. Coulthard argues, with credit to anticolonial theorist and psychiatrist Frantz Fanon "that the reproduction of a colonial structure of dominance like Canada's rests on its ability to entice Indigenous peoples to come to identify, either implicitly or explicitly, with the profoundly asymmetrical and non-reciprocal forms of recognition either imposed on or granted to them by the colonial-state and society."[10] Coulthard and Simpson both advocate the refusal of colonial forms of recognition and governmentality.

Since we—Indigenous, settlers, and arrivants alike—are physically located on Indigenous lands and yet still situated within settler colonial nation-states, we must fully understand what it means to say "Fuck the Border" and the implications that this statement has on both Indigenous, settler, arrivant, and mixed communities. While, I may no longer walk around yelling "Fuck the Border," the political ontology embedded in Propagandhi's song nevertheless assists me in understanding how settler-colonial and capitalist structures seek to disaggregate various parts of an otherwise intersectional structure. Moreover, this song may help us think about how these colonial systems (and settler-colonial structures) should not be intellectually unlinked. Rather, understanding them as an integrated unit shows how they must be simultaneously and reciprocally dismantled, not attacked on the isolated or individual level. If intersectionality helps us understand various oppressions and privileges, it will also help us understand the inseparability of structural and systematic inequalities.

Immigration policy—in the USA, Canada, and even Mexico—cannot be understood outside a history of longer and deeper systemic and systematic appropriation of Indigenous lands, seizure of resources, and denial of sovereignty. As Coulthard argues, we must also acknowledge the establishment of violent assimilative systems to convince Indigenous people that they were/are Canadians, Americans, or Mexicans. To identify with the nation-state is to undermine the capacity for authentic Indigenous governmentality. At the beginning of the 2016 presidential election season, Republican presidential hopeful Rand Paul said that, "I think assimilation is an amazing thing. A good example of how even in our country assimilation didn't happen and it's been a disaster for the people has been the Native American population on the reservations. If they were assimilated, within a decade they'd probably be doing as well as the rest of us."[11] Contextualization is not even needed to understand how Rand understands the workings of hegemonic systems and what this means.

In North America, settler colonialism is, in fact, *the* system. The question becomes, I think, how do we dismantle the many-headed hydra of settler colonialism, capitalism, and heteropatriarchy? How do we work to revitalize Indigenous sovereignties—including aesthetics and artistic articulations of sovereignty—in ways that acknowledge how capitalist-globalization precipitates migrations across settler-colonial borders by Indigenous, detribalized, and other oppressed peoples? What does it mean when Indigenous people migrate onto the traditional homelands of other Indigenous people? Moreover, can we ever escape the systematization of colonialism, as Sartre convincingly writes, or the coloniality of power, as Quijano has it?

ENACTING SOVEREIGNTY, OR IMAGINING AWAY THE COLONIAL NATION-STATE

I have been accused of imagining or wishing away the settler nation-state. At first I did not fully know what this critique even meant, but have grown to embrace this criticism coming from a very limited way of being in the world. As I have heard this response to my work a few times now, I think it means that my line of thought imagines that we can somehow live as if the settler-colonial nation-state is not always in control. While I understand the limits of settler-colonial and capitalist hegemony, I wonder why we cannot live in ways that are not fully contained by it. While this criticism was, at some point, a hurtful one (I am not certain why I felt inadequate for this challenge), I now wear this critique as an honor and intentionally work in ways that creatively seek to dismantle the nation-state, while also imagining a world without it.

Is it a contradiction to understand that colonialism, capitalism, heteropatriarchy, and associated structures are always encapsulating us, but simultaneously try to locate and exacerbate fissures in their structure? Or better yet, can we imagine a world without limitations and commence building new worlds – based in the teachings of the ancestors – that are not overdetermined or delimited by settler-colonial and capitalist constraints? Can I acknowledge the presence of existing systems, but live as if they are not in control? I am not a political scientist or a politician, and do not arrive at this proposition as one committed to "politics" as we know them. Instead, I ask if we should not all be imagining a world where nation-states and corporations do not control things. What is the meaning of our collective existence if we cannot imagine something beyond colonial ontology?

As an artist, my task is not to simply work inside the contours of this existing world and its political and ontological structures. Artists must fundamentally express ambiguity, while creating tangible works that exist both inside and outside structural limitations. It is for this very reason that I have been thinking through and writing about "Indigenous Aesthetic Sovereignty," a concept similar to that printed on a T-shirt in celebration of the tenth anniversary of the Aboriginal Curatorial Collective (ACC). On this shirt, the ACC advocates "Activating Indigenous Creative Sovereignty."

What aesthetic or creative sovereignty means, exactly, is unclear. The opacity of Indigenous sovereignty is part of what makes it, as a concept, so powerful. Just as the Idle No More movement was not entirely fixed, so too is Indigenous sovereignty somewhat indeterminate.[12] Sovereignty, in this context, is shorthand for self-determination or self-governance or autonomy and should not be understood in its purely Westphalian interpretation. Westphalian sovereignty is a principle of international law which holds that nation states maintain sovereign power over their own territories and domestic affairs. This principle came to prominence in Western Europe following the Peace of Westphalia (1648). Through colonial and imperial interventions, Westphalian sovereignty emerged as the dominant practice.

Indigenous sovereignties existed long before—and will long after—the nation-state became the dominant global polity. As a political manifestation that emerges from within Indigenous ontologies, Indigenous sovereignty is not limited by the nation-state, even if the settler-nation-state can still exert authority over it. While I am committed to reclaiming "aesthetics" (can we talk about aesthetic self-determination?) from its colonization by Kantian thinkers, both the ACC (a multiplicity of voices, of which I am a member) and I understand that there is an undeniable relationship between Indigenous sovereignty and the maintenance or revitalization of Indigenous aesthetics. All of this exists within colonialism and capitalism and heteropatriarchy, but is not contained by it. I guess that is what I am trying to get at here: the nation-state can, in fact, be imagined away, if only we envisage living without it.

Being utopian and desiring a place for true Indigenous liberation does not come from a place of naïvety. To not imagine a way of being that is simultaneously *beyond* and *before* (and *after)* colonialism, is much more naïve. I have read Fanon and understand the "pitfalls of national consciousness." Even so, imagining that "*otro mundo es posible*" (to borrow from Marcos and the Zapatistas) is what we must all be struggling for. Didn't the Zapatistas imagine away the nation-state, while also working within it? If you read the EZLN communiqués, you will certainly see how the Zapatistas imagined away the nation-state and, at the same time, created alternative governance models (*caracoles*).[13]

As I write this chapter, Indigenous communities are continuously forced to assert themselves against capitalist and colonial encroachment. In the unceded territory commonly known as British Columbia, Canada, the Unist´ot´en Camp is protecting the interests of Shkaakaamikwe (Mother Earth) by exercising their own sovereignty to stop the encroachment of big oil in their traditional territory. In Anishinaabewaki, the Indigenous lands that we know by the Dakota name Mne Sota (Minnesota), Anishinaabe harvesters are confronting the Minnesota state government as it interferes in their harvesting of *manoomin* (wild rice) and *giigoonyag* (fish).

Would imagining away the nation-state mean that you or I, or folks harvesting *manoomin* in Minnesota, or that the Unist´ot´en resistance to oil pipelines, would not face state confrontation or enforcement by the nation-state? Likely no. Does the presence of continuous and uninterrupted self-governance by Indigenous nations or tribes or bands somehow exist outside the presence of the settler-colonial nation-state? Of course not. However, thinking (and living) beyond the limits of the nation-state can do something else. What would happen if we collectively imagine true sovereignty—or something else that better describes Indigenous autonomy and self-determination? I believe that it is up to us—and the ancestors and spirits and rocks and land and water, among others—to prefigure something else.

Debenjigejig, Indigenous Sovereignty

In my utopian desire to prefigure better and more just ways of being in this world, I consistently turn to the ways that Xicanx (Indigenous Mexican-Americans) and Wiisaakodewininiwag (Otepemisiwak or Métis or Michif) communities have imagined away the border since its very inception. These communities have consistently asked if borders must exist. In a similar way, can't we collectively imagine a non-colonial ontology where borders are not needed? I see the creative imagining of a noncolonial way of being as central to the work I do. If we cannot imagine a way of living beyond the limitations of the nation-state (or any imposed limitation), we are doomed to not only destroy Shkaakaamikwe, but also annihilate ourselves in the process.

At various points in time, my paternal ancestors travelled the vast expanses of Mikinaak-minis, using the rivers and lakes as pathways. Because they so intimately knew both *aki* (land) and *nibi* (water), settlers employed them—as was common of Wiisaakodwininiwag at the time—to serve on survey expeditions and as translators. While geopolitical borders meant little to First Nations people and their Halfbreed cousins, the segmentation and privatization of land ownership was paramount to colonial agents and the system they imposed.

Mapping and ownership over the land, as an abstract and inanimate object, was what settlers so greatly desired. Inversely, kinship and land-use was (and still is) far more important for Indigenous communities. These are very disparate ways of relating to the land and distinct ways of being in the world. Each respective relationship—one based on ownership, the other on usage and relationality—forms the core of two conflicting modes of sovereignty and the polities that then emerge from them.

As has been frequently noted, Indigenous communities were (and still are) stewards of the land and territories were commonly shared—a concept that Western nation-states and their settler-colonial administrators cannot comprehend. Indigenous territoriality was not a monolithic and individual claim. Alliances and confederacies were (and are) common across Mikinaak-minis. Although we shouldn't pretend as if war and conflict never occurred, we should also recognize that how we understand sovereignty (that is as a form of Westphalian sovereignty) and its unique form of territoriality is a colonial imposition. If decolonization, anti-colonialism, and the non-colonial are not simply metaphors, as Eve Tuck and K. Wayne Yang write, then we need to imagine modes of understanding Indigenous "sovereignty" beyond dominant juridical and political systems. For me, this begins with imagining something else.[14] As an artist, that is what I do.

"All space is public, all land is indigenous."
Dylan Miner

Currently, at least according to Wikipedia, there are five ongoing border disputes, with many more historical ones, between Canada and USA. The very presence of a Wikipedia page titled "List of areas disputed by Canada and the United States" reflects this ongoing problem of how contemporary nation-states imagine their boundaries.[15] Isn't this border supposed to be a non-conflictive one? Unfortunately, the Canada-USA border, like all geopolitical borders, is violent and conflictive. However, the structures and discourses circulating around the Mexico-USA border are even more violent. The Canada-USA border masks its violence better than the border located twenty-five-hundred kilometers to the south. Contemporary "crises" have their origin in continual colonialism and capitalism, there is no denying this.

The Canada-USA and the Mexico-USA borders share many similarities with other geopolitical borders. But even when borders are not militarized or viewed as conflictive, the border—by its very presence— enacts a certain power over individuals and especially over Indigenous and migratory peoples. As an indigenist—that is, someone who takes Indigenous issues as their utmost priority—I am particularly concerned with the violent imposition of geopolitical boundaries and the nation-states that impose them. With the ongoing impact of climate change on Indigenous communities, as well as the eminent threat of armed violence and the economic clash of capitalism, Indigenous capacities to self-determine are quickly being further and further eroded.

In July 2015, the Haudenosaunee Women's lacrosse team withdrew from the Federation of International Lacrosse U19 World Championship held in Edinburgh, Scotland.[16] In 2010, the Haudenosaunee Men's team—commonly known as the Iroquois Nationals—also withdrew from the World Lacrosse Championships in Manchester, England.[17] On both occasions, European governments failed to recognize the legitimacy of Indigenous passports, asking instead that each player submit either a Canadian or U.S. passport in conjunction with their Haudenosaunee one. On both occasions, Indigenous sovereignty was challenged and, in the face of global transnational migration, Indigenous presence was denied. Inversely, in 2015, the Haudenosaunee Confederacy stamped the passports of members of the English national lacrosse, welcoming them to Onondaga territory for the World Indoor Lacrosse Championship.[18]

We are in the midst of a never-ending settler-colonial barrage against Indigenous peoples and their abilities to self-govern, maintain Indigenous political and economic structures, and travel in traditional and contemporary ways. Border and immigration policies across the continent are indicative of this. Since the initial arrival of Europeans to this continent, immigration and Indigenous sovereignty have been irreducibly linked. In many ways, it has not been Indigenous peoples who have made this so, rather it emerges from the settler-colonial logics of Manifest Destiny and Canadian Confederation. While many Indigenous communities are fundamentally linked by and through seasonal and other migration patterns, the cementing of geopolitical boundaries between different nation-states significantly impedes this ability, if not ending it completely. Two decades after Propagandhi taught me to sing along to "Fuck the Border," I am inclined to, once again, reflect upon these words and their ongoing relevance today. Shall we continue to uncover ways to resist the border and its imposition on each of us?

Over the course of the three years, I created a series of projects coming from an Indigenous understanding of the Canada-USA border. These were commissioned by curator Srimoyee Mitra for an exhibition cycle at the Art Gallery of Windsor titled *Border Cultures*. In 2013, for the

"No Borders, Indigenous Sovereignty," posters created for *Border Cultures* exhibition. *Dylan Miner*

first *Border Cultures* exhibition, I created a series of screen-printed posters, in addition to an installation and mobile screen printing units with Indigenous and Latinx youth on both sides of the border. The posters, printed in the art gallery during the exhibition's opening, included the text "Gaagegoo Dabakaana[n]" and "Debenjigejig."

As is common when I work on a project, I asked an elder how I would say a particular English-language idea in Anishinaabemowin. As a language-learner, I still need to make direct translations, knowing the futility of this task, but also acknowledge the power in my attempts to move beyond my colonial language usage. These posters communicated "No Borders" and "Indigenous Sovereignty." While a small and seemingly insignificant act, on some level these collective actions sought to undermine the power of the border and imagine a world without it.

In an art gallery, geographically located on the Detroit River on the Canada side of the settler-colonial border, a small group of Indigenous, settlers, and arrivants collectively printed posters in Anishinaabe language text that called for the dissolution of borders and assertion of Indigenous sovereignty. Working and acting collectively, we were struggling for a world without borders and where Indigenous sovereignty was not limited. Now, a few years later as I continue to imagine ways of being in this world, I think I had better ask an elder how to say "No fences, no borders. Free movement for all."

Notes

1. The North American Indian Association of Detroit, established in 1936, is perhaps the oldest Indian center in the United States.
2. Jürgen Osterhammel, *Colonialism: A Theoretical Overview* (Princeton, NJ: Markus Wiener, 1997), 1.
3. Ibid., 17.
4. Patrick Wolfe, *Settler Colonialism and the Transformation of Anthropology: The Politics and Poetics of an Ethnographic Event* (London: Continuum, 1999), 165.
5. Aníbal Quijano, "Coloniality of Power, Eurocentrism, and Latin America," *Nepentla: Views From the South* 1 (3) (2000): 533–580.
6. Jean-Paul Sartre, "Colonialism is a System," in *Colonialism and Neocolonialism* (New York: Routledge, 2001 [1964]), 9–19.
7. Sartre, 17.

8. As Chickasaw literary scholar Jodi A. Byrd writes, arrivants is a term that she borrows "from African Caribbean poet Kamau Brathwaite to signify those people forced into the Americas through the violence of European and Anglo-American colonialism and imperialism around the globe." Jodi A. Byrd, *The Transit of Empire: Indigenous Critiques of Colonialism* (Minneapolis: University of Minnesota Press, 2011), xix.

9. Aimé Césaire, *Discourse on Colonialism,* trans. Robin D.G. Kelley (New York: Monthly Review Press, 2000 [1955]), 41.

10. Glen Coulthard, "Subjects of Empire: Indigenous Peoples and the 'Politics of Recognition' in Canada," *Contemporary Political Theory* 6 (2007): 439.

11. Julian Brave NoiseCat. "Rand Paul Thinks 'Lack Of Assimilation' Is Native Americans' Problem," *Huffington Post,* September 3, 2015. www.huffingtonpost.com/entry/rand-paul-assimilation-native-americans_us_55e8986fe4b0b7a9633c4edc

12. Idle No More is an ongoing Indigenous social movement that began in late 2012. The movement, named by three Indigenous women (Nina Wilson, Sylvia McAdam, and Jessica Gordon) and one settler ally (Sheelah Mclean), in response to anti-Indigenous and anti-environmental policies of then Prime Minister of Canada, Stephen Harper. Idle No More became a loose set of pro-Indigenous activities in Canada and the US, as well as throughout the Fourth World.

13. Frantz Fanon, "On National Culture," in *Wretched of the Earth* (New York: Grove Books, 2004 [1963]): 145–80. EZLN stands for Ejército Zapatista de Liberación Nacional (Zapatista Army of National Liberation).

14. Eve Tuck, K. Wayne Yang, "Decolonization is Not a Metaphor," *Decolonization: Indigeneity, Education & Society* 1, no. 1 (2012): 1–40.

15. See en.wikipedia.org/wiki/List_of_areas_disputed_by_Canada_and_the_United_States

16. Sam Laskaris, "Passports Rejected: Haudenosaunee Women's LAX Withdraws from World Championships," *Indian Country Today,* July 20, 2015. indiancountrytodaymedianetwork.com/2015/07/20/passports-rejected-haudenosaunee-womens-lax-withdraws-world-championships-161139

17. Thomas Kaplan, "Iroquois Defeated by Passport Dispute," *New York Times,* July 16, 2010. www.nytimes.com/2010/07/17/sports/17lacrosse.html?_r=0

18. Sarah Moses, "Team England arrives on Onondaga Nation to get passports stamped," *Syracuse.com,* September 13, 2015. www.syracuse.com/news/index.ssf/2015/09/team_england_arrives_on_onondaga_nation_to_get_passports_stamped.html

PART TWO

EL MOVIMIENTO IN THE NORTHERN BORDERLANDS

CHAPTER 3

Democratizing Washington State's Yakima County: A History of Latino/a Voter Suppression since 1967

Josué Q. Estrada

In 2015, the nation commemorated the fiftieth anniversary of the Voting Rights Act (VRA). The act enabled previously disenfranchised African Americans greater access to the vote and provided a legal recourse to challenge election schemes that diluted racialized minorities' voting power. In Washington State, starting in 1967, Mexican Americans in Yakima County called for the enforcement of the VRA to end literacy tests that prevented them from registering to vote. And in 2012, Latinos in the largest city of the county—the City of Yakima—used the act to contest the at-large election system, which prevented over 40 percent of the population from having a voice on the city council. The *Montes v. City of Yakima* lawsuit led to the creation of seven single-member voting districts and was the catalyst for a historic election in November of 2015 that resulted in three Latinas being elected to the city council. This was a remarkable feat considering that no person of Latino descent had ever been elected to this office. Yet to democratize Washington's Yakima County, Latinos had to mobilize and use the VRA to fight racism, political marginalization, and resistance by a community that failed to recognize Latino voters as an integral part of their fabric.[1]

To better comprehend the struggles of Latinos in both Yakima County and the City of Yakima, this study first examines the late 1960s political mobilization efforts to secure the franchise for Mexican Americans unable to read and speak English. Despite a lawsuit filed against Yakima County by the Mexican American Federation—an entity calling for Mexican American electoral representation—the test remained in place until 1970. During this period, I argue that Mexican American voter suppression by way of literacy tests was maintained and sustained as a result of national, state, and local factors. At a national level, the VRA of 1965 suspended literacy tests only in the South but not across the country. On a state scale, bureaucrats argued that the state's literacy test was a *requirement* and not a test. And in Yakima County, the county auditor and deputy registrars deliberately enforced the literacy test to suppress the Mexican American vote, a tactic that strictly targeted people racialized as non-white.

A second aim is to understand how Latinos in Yakima County continued to face voter suppression after literacy tests were declared unconstitutional throughout the country in 1970, and in spite of having access to bilingual voting information beginning in 1976. I claim that between 1970 and 1975 the lack of bilingual voting materials absolutely contributed to the dilution of the Latino vote. In addition, the transformation of the Mexican American Federation (MAF) to the Commission on Mexican American Affairs in the early 1970s altered the organization's priorities. The commission no longer focused primarily on voter registration or in addressing racism in Yakima County. And even when the VRA of 1975 mandated that the county provide bilingual ballots, the bureaucrats reluctantly obliged but failed to hire full-time bilingual voting assistants, or to drastically change the county's voting culture to integrate Latino voters. These issues, I argue, severely hindered and discouraged Latino participation in local government and manifested themselves in the *Montes v. City of Yakima* lawsuit in 2012. The court case determined that historical discrimination and the at-large election process weakened Latino political involvement and contributed to their lack of representation on the Yakima City Council.[2]

The history of Latino voter suppression and racism in Yakima County is important for several reasons. First, people tend to connect literacy tests to African Americans in the South. In fact, literacy tests were used in Washington State against Mexican Americans. In Washington State, literacy tests were deemed constitutional until 1970. And up until at least 1972, some Mexican American residents of Yakima County continued to believe that literacy tests were still in place.[3] Only after 1973 were voter pamphlets available in Spanish to explain the voter registration changes and regulations. Literacy tests were not a region- or race-specific tool to restrict the franchise. Therefore, examining Latino voting rights in the state allows for an analysis of the limitations to the VRA of 1965 with regard to national enforcement, and provides an important perspective to comprehend how literacy tests operated outside of the South. Even with language rights such as multilingual ballots secured by the 1975 amendments to the VRA, inadequate enforcement measures enabled Yakima County to continue to skirt its responsibilities. Language rights were liberal guarantees that failed to address the racism embedded in city governments such as Yakima County but contributed to racial liberalism. Daniel Martinez HoSang in *Racial Propositions* argues that racial liberalism uses liberal language (such as rights, opportunity, tolerance, and freedom) to sustain rather than displace white supremacy.[4] Most importantly, this study illustrates how disenfranchised Latinos were not only challenging literacy tests and their continued political marginalization, but also the very definition of an American citizen. Latinos were democratizing Washington State by defining citizenship in their own terms and rousing the state, Yakima County, and the City of Yakima to recognize their distinctive racial, cultural, and multilingual identity.

The story of Caesario Jimenez, one of the four plaintiffs in the Mexican American Federation lawsuit in 1967, provides a good entry point to examine the history of Latino voter suppression in Washington State. In 1909, a year before the Mexican Revolution, Jimenez was born in Hondo, Texas, located an hour west of San Antonio. His family relocated to Mexico when Jimenez was only three. In Mexico, he attended school up to the fourth grade, raised a family of his own, and lived in the country for about 47 years. In 1959, facing financial difficulties he returned to Texas to find employment while his family remained in Mexico. Once across the border, he connected with a relative who informed him of the availability of jobs in Washington State. By the spring of 1961 Jimenez was working in the hop industry and had a company home provided by the Golding Hop Farm in Toppenish, Washington. From March to October, Jimenez labored in the state and during the winter months he returned to Mexico.[5]

In his court testimony, Jimenez expressed that the government should help workers for the overall welfare of the community, and that he should not be denied the right to vote because of his inability to read and speak English. By stating that the government needed to support workers, and by taking a stand against the powers that prohibited him from the franchise, Jimenez was calling attention to the struggles of the agricultural working class and the discriminatory voting practices in Yakima County. For Jimenez, being an American citizen was to have the right to speak out against injustices in his community.

Jimenez's story also reveals the labor demands that pulled workers to Yakima County, and the Texas-to-Washington State migrant stream connection. Pacific Northwest historian Erasmo Gamboa notes that starting in the 1900s, Yakima County's investment in irrigation projects and the land rich in minerals "made possible extraordinary high yields of a variety of crops."[6] Growers planted numerous fruits and vegetables. Hops and sugar beets—the most economically profitable—were labor-intensive crops that required an ample seasonal workforce. Therefore, as Yakima County growers began to increase their acreage, they also needed to recruit more seasonal workers.

To meet their labor demands, growers recruited seasonal workers from various ethnic and racial backgrounds. Gamboa writes that Yakima County "became one of the most important users of seasonal farm workers in the West."[7] From 1890 to the 1930s, white migrant workers from the Midwest and Southwest, indigenous migrant laborers such as the Blackfoot and Sioux, along with Yakama Natives, were the most dependable workforce.[8] During the early 1900s, Japanese workers also toiled and permanently settled in the Yakima Valley.[9] Then, in the 1920s, "Filipino laborers were brought into the Valley by labor contractors."[10] Also in the 1920s, the first Mexican migrant workers arrived from Colorado, Wyoming, Montana, and Idaho to the area.[11] In these states, people of Mexican descent worked for sugar beet companies like Amalgamated Sugar and Utah-Idaho Sugar, which recruited them to work in their plants in Washington.[12]

By the 1940s, Yakima County had received national recognition as a top agricultural producer, yet a shortage of agricultural laborers created serious problems for the county's growers.[13] This was caused by a number of reasons. First, growers started to perceive indigenous people as an unreliable labor force.[14] Second, anti-Asian exclusion laws had expelled many Japanese and Filipino agricultural workers from the area. And third, the World War II (WWII) economy pulled many white migrant workers from Yakima County into higher paying industrial employment opportunities in Portland and Seattle.[15] The labor crisis was further exacerbated by a wartime demand for increased agricultural production.

In response to the labor shortage, growers formed the Yakima Emergency Harvest Committee, which became instrumental in the recruitment of Mexican contract laborers to Yakima County.[16] Starting in 1942, through a bilateral diplomatic agreement between the United States and Mexico known as the Bracero Program, workers were allowed to enter the country. Between 1942 and 1947, approximately 4,658 braceros toiled in the fields of Yakima County.[17] However, after 1947, the U.S. government was no longer willing to cover the transportation costs for braceros to work on Washington farms. And since the growers could not afford the estimated cost of $163 per worker, the importation of braceros become economically unfeasible.[18] In the Southwest, the Bracero Program lasted until 1964 since transportation costs were not a factor. While short-lived in the Yakima area, the program for the first time brought a significant number of Mexicans to the Pacific Northwest. Braceros played an important role in the county's economy and agricultural production, and were critical laborers on the domestic front to win the war.

No longer able to secure braceros, Yakima Valley growers shifted their focus to the recruitment of Mexican American migrant workers from the Midwest and Southwest, especially Texas Mexican laborers like Caesario Jimenez. For the growers, these laborers were an ideal and exploitable workforce because, unlike braceros, they had no pre-conditions of employment. Therefore, growers did not have to provide a set wage, housing, meals, or transportation costs. Additionally, these workers, according to the Washington's Emergency Farm Labor Supply Program, were "in plentiful supply in other agricultural areas in the nation," and labor specialists urged growers to recruit workers from Texas.[19]

Once Yakima County growers recruited and tapped into this work-force, they were able to absorb them into the economy as agricultural production continued to expand.[20] Furthermore, before and during WWII, migrant Mexican workers from Texas had begun to arrive in the Yakima area. Texas Mexican migration to Washington was expedited by factors in Texas that forced many to leave such as racial discrimination, extreme poverty, and depressed wages caused by Mexican contract laborers and undocumented immigration from Mexico.[21] As a result, starting in the 1940s, Texas Mexicans settled in the Yakima Valley at a higher rate than Mexicans from other states.

Mexicans from Texas were not only migrating to but settling in Wash-ington, and they were transforming the environment. Historian James Gregory in *The Southern Diaspora* writes: "Migrations make history not merely through the movement of bodies but because of the consumer and political choices that the newcomers exercise and because of the new forms of enterprises that commercial, cultural, and political activists introduce."[22] In other words, migrants relocating to Yakima County were bringing with them new ways of thinking about citizenship, community, and political engagement. Marc Rodriguez in *The Tejano Diaspora: Mexican Americanism and Ethnic Politics in Texas and Wisconsin* describes this complexity in migration. He demonstrates how the political activism that developed in South Texas after the WWII also migrated to the Midwest as "translocal politics," and became especially influential in Wisconsin's labor movement.[23] Among the Texas-born Mexicans who migrated and settled in Washington were important leaders including Caesario Jimenez, along with Sam Martinez, who founded the Mexican American Federation, and Guadalupe Gamboa, who co-founded the United Farm Workers Cooperative in Washington State. These organizations were to become critical to the early Mexican American voting rights movement in Washington.

By the 1950s, Yakima County was being transformed by Mexican Americans from places like the Rio Grande Valley along the Texas-Mexico border, who began to permanently root themselves in larger numbers than in previous decades. For a variety of reasons, they left the migrant stream and made Washington their home. For this time period, an accurate number of Mexican Americans in the county is difficult to ascertain. However, the U.S. Census data does reveal a dramatic increase in the foreign-born population of Mexicans (see Table 1). Their settlement along with those not recorded was in direct relationship with agricultural growth and production. Likewise, the diversification of crops provided employment for longer periods and permanent year-round work.

Table 1
Foreign-Born Mexican Population in Yakima County,
Washington State (1940-1970)

	Yakima County		
1940	1950	1960	1970
93	929	3,717	6,266

Source: United States Census, Washington State Characteristics of Population, 1940, 1950, 1960, and 1970.

During the 1950s, the Mexican American population in Yakima County had not reached a critical mass to exert political pressure on local governments. In addition, there was no organized political effort to mobilize the community. While Mexican Americans transferred their Tejano/Mexicano culture to Washington, the most prominent brand of political activism advanced by the League of United Latin American Citizens (LULAC) in Texas did not emerge in the county until the late 1960s.[24] Founded in South Texas during the late 1920s, LULAC promoted assimilation and integration to achieve upward mobility. In *Walls and Mirrors: Mexican Americans, Mexican Immigrants, and the Politics of Ethnicity*, David Gutierrez writes that LULAC advocated for Mexican Americans to speak English and "encouraged Mexican American citizens to register, pay their poll taxes, and vote..." as a way to prove that they were loyal American citizens.[25] This organization was made up predominantly of middle-class Mexican Americans and therefore was not likely to appeal to the agricultural working-class. The workers migrating to Washington's Yakima area embraced their culture and Spanish language because cultural retention was significant to the formation of community in a region outside the Southwest. To an extent then, Texas Mexicans in Yakima County rejected LULAC's assimilationist model. This may explain why this organization failed to emerge in the area during the 1950s. But with no critical mass or a political organization, it was unlikely that Mexican Americans could overcome the greatest barrier to their political mobilization—literacy tests.

Washington's literacy tests required individuals to read and speak English in order to register to vote. As a result, denying the vote to Mexican American citizens with limited English skills meant their political activism through electoral politics was nonexistent. For many Mexican Americans settling in Washington, the inability to read and speak the English language stemmed from attending segregated schools in Texas with no bilingual education, frequent work-related moves that resulted in academic inconsistencies, and socio-economic factors such as poor health and nutrition.

Local and state impediments to Mexican American political enfranchisement were further complicated by national efforts that paid little to no attention to the struggles of the Mexican American electorate. In the western United States, American citizens with limited English skills were generally barred from the franchise and in the 1950s, their plight went unnoticed by the U.S. Commission on Civil Rights addressing voter suppression in the rest of the country. Starting in 1957, when the commission was formed, it collected 382 sworn complaints from people restricted from registering to vote or whose ballots had not been enumerated. The grievances were confined to rural areas in the South: Alabama, Arkansas, Florida, Georgia, Louisiana, Mississippi, North Carolina, Oklahoma, South Carolina, Tennessee, Texas, and Virginia.[26] As a result, when the commission released their report in 1961, its emphasis was the African American electorate along the southern "Black Belt."[27] And rightly so, at the time African Americans were the largest racialized minority and their access to the franchise had been severely hampered even after states ratified the Fifteenth Amendment in 1869.[28] However, since the commission received no "evidence of racial discrimination in voting in any of the other 37 States," this meant that Washington's literacy test was not contested.[29]

While no official complaints of racial inequalities to the franchise were generated in the U.S. West, a complaint against the test was being raised by Puerto Ricans in New York, who challenged the idea that discrimination in voting was solely a black and white issue. In 1959, the grievances of Spanish-speaking Puerto Rican voters (albeit only three of the original 382 complaints) were received by the commission. Nonetheless, two years later, the commission hesitated to pursue this matter stating that "It raised a complex and difficult problem, but one not strictly within the scope of the Commission's authority."[30] In effect, the commission offered no recommendations to address the racial and language discrimination faced by American citizens with limited English proficiency.

The U.S. Commission on Civil Rights, along with the Civil Rights Act of 1964, was instrumental in pressuring Congress to pass the VRA of 1965. The most crucial components of the VRA were Sections 2 and 5. The language of Section 2 established a suspension of literacy tests and devices that denied or restricted people's right to vote in select states. Section 5 required that no jurisdiction could be able to implement a voting change without prior approval by the federal government.

For African Americans in the South, the VRA of 1965 was a landmark act that immediately increased their number of registered voters. With no literacy tests or other restrictive devices, Alexander Keyssar in *The Right to Vote*, explains the registration of African Americans in Mississippi "went from less than 10 percent in 1964 to almost 60 percent in 1968; in Alabama, the figure rose from 24 percent to 57."[31] In the South, the overall registration of African Americans reached a high mark of 62 percent.[32] However, the VRA was not a panacea and had several limitations.

The VRA addressed the complaints of the Puerto Rican people who no longer were subject to literacy tests, but failed to protect other Spanish-speaking groups across the country since it only mentioned one ethnic group. Also, the VRA did not require states to begin to provide bilingual voting information.[33] Overall, the VRA of 1965 failed to address that English-only elections were a form of voter suppression that affected not only Puerto Ricans, but also Mexican Americans in places like Washington State.

In Washington, the VRA had no impact on literacy tests and they continued to be used to disenfranchise Mexican American citizens. It is important to note that at a state level, the State Board Against Discrimination asked Attorney General John J. O'Connell to give an opinion on whether Washington's literacy test was in violation of the 1965 VRA. On

June 15, 1967, O'Connell responded by claiming, "Except for persons who come within the Puerto Rico provision, the Washington State literacy requirement remains in effect. However, the manner of testing for literacy is now controlled by federal law, as will be hereinafter."[34] O'Connell wrote that literacy tests in the State of Washington had not "been prohibited outright by federal legislation" and made a case that if the state had a test it was appropriate. Literacy tests had been suspended in states where fewer than 50 percent of the voting age residents were registered and Washington was not identified. Federal standards required that everyone be given a test in writing. In Washington, O'Connell stated that not all persons were tested but only in cases where "the registration officer 'is not satisfied' with the applicant's sworn statement" and the person's ability to read and speak English.[35] And lastly, he cited *Louisiana v. United States,* claiming that the state clearly adopted a literacy test to "purposely disenfranchise Negroes, it being understood that the registration officers would use their discretion for that purpose."[36] To demonstrate that Washington was supposedly more righteous, O'Connell declared that Washington had no "tradition of discrimination against minorities in voting" and would prohibit literacy tests as required by the federal government.[37]

By emphasizing that literacy was a *requirement* versus a test, claiming that Washington's test was non-discriminatory, and proclaiming that Washington apparently had no history of racial discrimination in voting, state bureaucrats undermined the VRA and at the same time emboldened local officials and country registrars to continue to suppress the Mexican American vote. But in the late 1960s, a number of factors aligned that moved Mexican Americans to revolt against literacy tests, the white local establishment, and demand that they be recognized as full citizens in Yakima County.

When placed within a national discourse, literacy tests in Washington were not exceptional, they were merely modeled after other states. Yet, their application appears to have been inconsistent and sporadic.[38] It was not until 1967, with the political mobilization of Mexicans Americans, that literacy tests came to be aggressively enforced. That year, the emergence of both the United Farm Workers Cooperative (later called the United Farm Workers Union) and the Mexican American Federation played a vital role in enforcing the VRA of 1965. By the time these organizations came to fruition, a critical mass of people of Mexican descent had settled in Yakima County. In total, they represented roughly 5.5 percent to 8.2 percent of the County's population.[39] Additionally, a great number of migrant agricultural workers continued to arrive and settle in the state. In fact, in 1966, Washington ranked fifth in the employment of migrant laborers, with Yakima County hiring the largest number, 41 percent of whom were Mexican American.[40] This labor flow enabled area growers to expand their farmlands with migrant and seasonal farm workers, who continued to be economically exploited and politically marginalized.[41] The United Farm Workers Cooperative and the Mexican American Federation became advocates for farm workers. On one hand, the United Farm Workers Cooperative concentrated on workers' health and living conditions as well as unionizing efforts. On the other hand, the Mexican American Federation worked to promote civic engagement through electoral politics. Although the organizations had different objectives, one service that benefitted both entities and the farm workers they served was legal assistance.

In March of 1968, the United Farm Workers Cooperative "requested the assistance from the American Civil Liberties Union (ACLU) of Washington in organizing a legal assistance program for farm workers in the Yakima Valley."[42] The ACLU's Yakima Valley project aided an estimated one hundred farmworkers, mostly with issues related to automobiles.[43] In addition, the project initiated a number of lawsuits including *Mexican American Federation v. Naff*, which pushed for the enforcement of the VRA to end literacy tests.

The ACLU-supported case immediately propelled the nascent Mexican American Federation (MAF) and its stalwarts into the spotlight. In 1967, the MAF was started by forty Mexican Americans from Washington State. The founders established a state-wide organization with a presence in Yakima County but also Puget Sound, Moses Lake, Tri-Cities, and Bellingham-Lynden.[44] The MAF encouraged Mexican Americans to vote, run for elected office, and take positions on political issues to influence local and state governments. Furthermore, a paramount goal of the MAF was to "dispel forever the apathy of the Mexican-American voters of Washington and of the nation."[45] While focused on registering voters, in 1968 the MAF also organized and financed the political campaign of Ernie Aguilar. Although unsuccessful, Aguilar's run for a seat in Yakima County Commissioner's Office received an estimated 12,000 votes, but more importantly, it represented a glimpse of MAF's organizing potential.[46] Supporting candidates was important for the MAF, but a top priority was the "registration of all Mexican American people eligible to vote in the state of Washington."[47] The epicenter for the voter registration drives was Yakima County, where the MAF estimated that nearly 4,000 Mexican Americans could be registered.[48] Yet, the county was also the site of most resistance to Mexican Americans' electoral activism.

In early March of 1968, MAF leaders Sam Martinez and Ricardo Garcia began their efforts to mobilize the Mexican American electorate and met with Yakima County Auditor Eugene Naff, who was shocked by their request to appoint Spanish speaking registrars.[49] Naff responded to Martinez and Garcia stating that it seemed ridiculous to appoint "Mexican registrars…if this was the case we probably should have Negro, Indian, Filipino, and Japanese registrars if we were to go by ethnic group."[50] In addition, Naff acknowledged that he was aware of the 1965 VRA but stated, "I still don't see, however, how anyone who can't read English can figure out how to vote on a ballot…I believe it is privilege to register to vote."[51] Despite the remarks by Naff, Martinez and Garcia demanded a firm answer but no agreement was reached. As a result, a follow-up meeting was scheduled.

On March 15, the second meeting was more intense and described by the local newspaper as a standoff where "recriminations and sparks crackled."[52] The MAF leaders continued to insist that Mexican American registrars were necessary and presented names of qualified people for Naff to potentially appoint. Naff resolutely said no. His reasoning was that he did not want to discriminate against other groups. Naff then bluntly stated, "Do you think you've really got a problem? Do you think anyone is being deprived of the right to vote because he can't register?"[53] In a last attempt to make Naff change his decision, Martinez argued that the voters he was "talking [about were] American citizens…and I am asking that no barriers be placed before these people."[54] Naff responded that the MAF should register Mexican Americans. In the end, a frustrated Naff commented that for twenty-five years he had been registering voters and "I've never had any trouble until you [Martinez] came in and started this."[55] Until the early 1970s, Naff continued to resist the appointment of Spanish-speaking registrars.[56]

After these meetings, the situation intensified as deputy registrars began to administer literacy tests specifically to Mexican Americans in Yakima County. Furthermore, bilingual interpreters were prohibited from assisting Spanish-speaking voters. As a result, on September 11, 1968, four Mexican Americans, the MAF, and the United Farm Workers Cooperative, with legal support provided by ACLU, filed a class action lawsuit against the county claiming that Washington's literacy tests violated the VRA of 1965.

The plaintiffs in their deposition statements vociferously expressed that they were American citizens. For example, Simon Ramos, born in Bay City, Texas and resident of Toppenish, Washington, since 1946 stated, "I am a citizen and I have the right to vote. The first time I try to act like a citizen, they throw me back. I don't feel too good."[57] Expressing a similar feeling was Jennie Marin, born in Grand Junction, Colorado, and resident of Toppenish since 1957, who said, "I feel bad about not being able to vote. Not quite a citizen. Maybe even cheated a little. I have a son who served four years in the Navy and I'm proud of him. I feel I have a right to be a full citizen."[58]

Despite these individuals' appeals to be recognized as citizens of Yakima County and the ACLU's argument of targeted racial discrimination against Mexican Americans, on May 2, 1969, a panel of three judges ruled against the plaintiffs and MAF. The judges collectively agreed that "A simple inquiry by the registrar of the applicant in this form, 'Can you speak and read English?' is not a test and could not conceivably result in discriminatory practices."[59] The verdict was a setback, yet the ACLU quickly appealed the decision. However, before the ALCU's rebuttal reached the courtroom, the issue of literacy tests was surprisingly resolved.

In August of 1970, U.S. Attorney General John Mitchell, who viewed voting rights as a national issue and advocated for the extension of the VRA, requested that Governor Dan Evans ban literacy tests in Washington State. Governor Evans agreed. The *Seattle Post-Intelligencer* estimated that 8,000 Mexican and Native Americans would be enfranchised.[60] In the Yakima area, the ACLU calculated that 1,500 Mexican Americans would be able to register to vote. Additionally, Washington's Secretary of

State encouraged election officials to employ bilingual deputies, though he did not require them to do so.[61] The timing was critical because in some cities such as Wapato the Mexican American population by this time was more than 40 percent (see Table 2).

Table 2
Mexican American Population in Selected
Cities of Yakima County (1970)

City	Total Population	percent Mexican American
Yakima	45,588	3.0
Wapato	2,841	40.5
Toppenish	5,744	25.8
Sunnyside	6,751	25.4
Grandview	3,605	17.5
Mabton*	953	56.0

Adapted from: Erasmo Gamboa, "A History of Chicano People and the Development of Agriculture in the Yakima, Valley, Washington" (master's thesis, University of Washington, 1973), 89. *Note: Mabton's population in 1968 from Dan Hannula and Ray Ruppert, "The Agri-Revolution: Just One Mexican-American Holds Office," *Seattle Times*, July 22, 1968.

The southern states saw a clear increase in the number of registered voters after literacy tests were barred, however, this does not appear to have been the case in Yakima County. While county voting registration records are not available for people of Mexican descent, candidacy-filing documents support this argument. According to political scientist Matt Barreto, there is a direct correlation between Latino candidates running for elected office and voter registration numbers.[62] Barreto argues that Latino candidates mobilize the Latino electorate, which results in greater voter turnout. Therefore, it can be inferred that with no upsurge in Spanish-surname candidates running for office, there was no significant increase in the number of registered voters. The county records show that only two cities (Granger and Mabton) saw a real change in the number of people with Spanish surnames running for elected office between 1970 and 1975 (see Table 3).[63] This suggests that there were other barriers impacting the community's ability to mobilize and obtain political advances by way of electoral politics.

Table 3
Spanish Surname Candidacy Filing Information (1970-1975)

Year	City Council (location)	School Board (location)
1970	0	0
1971	3 (Granger)	3 (Mabton)
1972	1 (Selah); 1 (Mabton)	1 (Wapato); 2 (Mabton); 1 (Grandview)
1974	0	0
1975	3 (Granger)	3 (Granger); 1 (Mabton); 2 (Toppenish); 2 (Sunnyside)

Source: Yakima County Auditor's Office (1970-1975), "Candidate Filing History," Elections Results/History. www.yakimacounty.us/vote/english/Candidate_FilingHistory.htm.

The continued struggle of Mexican Americans to achieve full citizenship and political representation after literacy tests were eradicated can be attributed to various factors. First, once the Mexican American Federation was transformed into the Commission on Mexican American Affairs (now called the Commission on Hispanic Affairs), they no longer had a strong presence in Yakima County, and their goals did not specifically address the registration of voters.[64] Second, while the United Farm Workers Cooperative continued to register Mexican American voters, there was no other entity that specifically focused on voter education, registration, or financing campaigns of Mexican American candidates. And finally, states and counties across the nation were not required to provide bilingual voting information or oral assistance. This was a serious issue for Washington's Spanish-speaking population since changes related to voter registration and residency requirements were not disseminated in a language they understood.

Although the *Mexican American Federation v. Naff* case did not officially end literacy tests in Washington, the MAF's activism was crucial to their eventual elimination. The organization called attention to the language and racial barriers confronted by Mexican Americans in Yakima County.[65] And it is important to note that the MAF's activism represented one important aspect of the political movements by Mexican Americans in Washington.

While the MAF and United Farm Worker Cooperative were formed to address the needs of farm workers, after 1967 the social, student-led, and community groups that formed were not farm worker-based or located in Yakima County. In Seattle starting in 1968, a number of organizations came to fruition, including Seattle's El Club Latino, which promoted cultural events; student-centered organizations such as the United Mexican American Students and the Brown Berets at the University of Washington; Equal Opportunity for Spanish Speaking Americans, which provided basic education and job placement services to Latinos relocating to Seattle; and El Centro de la Raza, which provided community services to the city's Latino population.[66]

The rise in political activism along with steady population growth on the west side of the state definitely influenced the transformation of the MAF to the Commission on Mexican American Affairs. This conversion involved the merger of Eastern Washington (rural agriculture) and Western Washington (urban non-agriculture) politics, which exposed the sharply divergent issues and needs of each location. Still, perhaps more controversial was the state's formation of the commission that incited tremendous opposition by government officials and residents, particularly from Yakima County. At the helm of this tremendously challenging political task was Governor Dan Evans.

In 1971, Governor Evans appointed to the commission numerous individuals from across the state including professionals, farmworker activists, student leaders, and former members of the MAF.[67] The functions of the commission were:

1. Identifying and defining issues concerning the rights and needs of Washington State's Hispanic community;
2. Advising the Governor and state agencies on the development of relevant policies, plans and programs that affect Hispanics;
3. Advising the legislature on issues of concern to the state's Hispanic community; and
4. Establishing relationships with state agencies, local governments, and members of the private sector.[68]

Notably absent from the aims of the commission were voter registration and education, matters upon which the MAF was founded. From the outset, the commission faced criticism. For instance, Yakima County

Republican Senator Perry B. Woodall was "incensed by the appointment...of a brown beret, or member of a militant Chicano group."[69]
Governor Evans defended all his appointments and stated that he sought
representation from "The right, left, the middle, the bottom, and the
top..."[70] His statement did not satisfy Republicans from the county
and in 1972, the Lower Valley Men's Republican Club protested to
dismantle the commission. Senator Damon Canfield, another Yakima
County Republican, claimed the problems stemmed from Governor
Evans selection of "radicals" and had, since the forming of the commission, opposed their inclusion.[71] By the end of the year, Governor Evans
had received numerous letters from Yakima County officials cautioning
him against appointing "revolutionary" commissioners."[72] Due to the
mounting pressure and Governor Evans' own dissatisfaction with the
commission, he stated that certain commission members in the "agriculturally oriented Yakima Valley [were] too militant."[73] The result of this
friction reached a climax in 1973, when Ricardo Garcia stated that he was
given an ultimatum to "quit or be fired" as the commission's executive
director. Garcia had been a founding member of the MAF and a driving
force behind the political mobilization of Mexican Americans in Yakima
County.[74] The *Seattle Times* reported that "conservative elements in the
Mexican-American community, who opposed his strong support of the
United Farm Worker Union," and many complaints by "Yakima Valley
legislators," led to his removal.[75] Ultimately, the transition of the MAF
to the Commission on Mexican American Affairs stifled and hindered
the earlier advances of the Mexican American vote in Yakima County.

After the MAF was no longer a vehicle for Mexican American voter
mobilization, college and high school students in the county organized
voter registration drives. For example, in 1970, students from Granger,
Washington, successfully acquired funds from the United Farm Workers
Union (UFW) to organize a project called El Año del Mexicano (Year of
the Mexican). The main objective was to introduce Chicanos in Granger
to the democratic process and encourage participation in local government
on the school board and city council.[76] Students in other Yakima Valley
cities also engaged in these efforts. For example, Ermelindo Escobedo,
in his final years at Wapato High School (1971 and 1972), remembered
how he, along with roughly ten other students, knocked on doors to

encourage and assist Mexican Americans to register to vote.[77] Student efforts such as these indicate that young people were eager to engage in civic politics. While they may not have been able to vote, students took action to inform the Mexican American community of the potential power available through electoral politics. And in the early 1970s, these sporadic voter registration campaigns provided an outlet for young Mexican Americans to participate in civic politics and attempted to fill the void left by the MAF. In spite of their labor, it was limited to a small population and could not be sustained over a long-term period.

Meanwhile the UFW continued to work in the Yakima area, but aside from the union no other organizations formed to target the Mexican American electorate until 1983.[78] Despite their continuous presence in the county, the UFW's limited staff and changing priorities hampered the organization's ability to focus exclusively on voter registration and education. Still, the UFW did execute successful drives to reach Mexican American voters. In 1972 for example, the UFW traveled throughout the Yakima Valley and set up booths, knocked on doors, and conducted voter registration rallies, registering an estimated 3,500 to 4,000 people.[79] The success of these campaigns depended on bilingual registrars who were appointed reluctantly by Yakima County Auditor Eugene Naff.[80] Through this process, the UFW learned that Mexican Americans felt intimidated by the registration process and required "a lot of explanation on the part of the registrars."[81] The investment required by the UFW was tremendous and put a strain on the union's small staff and therefore, registration campaigns were not continuous or as successful.

The lack of information in Spanish and bilingual assistants were among the reasons Mexican Americans in Yakima County did not experience the same level of success after literacy tests were suspended as African Americans did in the South. Without bilingual materials, they were not informed of voter registration changes, residency requirements, pertinent voting issues, voting locations, candidate filing information, or election results. As a result, a portion of the Mexican American electorate was not aware of essential changes that affected their right to vote. For example, during the UFW's 1972 voter registration drive, organizers realized many were unaware that literacy tests were no longer allowed or that the residency requirement had changed from ninety to sixty days.[82]

The lack of bilingual registrars further prevented Mexican Americans from the franchise, particularly on Election Day. After literacy tests were barred, some interpreters were able to register voters and assist them through the process. Still, student activist Escobedo recalled that on Election Day students were not allowed inside the election booths where Mexican Americans cast their votes. Problems then did arise and to overcome these challenges, students educated and coached voters on the complex English-only voting procedures. The registration process was intensive and at most, each student could help roughly ten to fifteen people.[83]

After Mexican Americans in Yakima County were no longer subject to literacy tests, they faced additional barriers in comparison to African Americans in the South. With a dearth of local and state entities to mobilize, register, and educate Mexican American voters, and no bilingual voting materials or assistance, their electoral power continued to be suppressed. And while the UFW and local students attempted to provide these services, their efforts had limitations.

In January of 1975, the U.S. Commission on Civil Rights published a report called the "The Voting Rights Act: Ten Years After." Their findings acknowledged that the "registration of Spanish-speaking voters throughout the United States [lagged] behind that of blacks and well behind that of whites."[84] The term "throughout" was a misnomer since the research was heavily reliant on data from the Southwest. The investigation revealed that only 46 percent of the Mexican American population reported themselves as registered, compared to 65.6 percent of blacks and 73.4 percent of whites.[85] The report called attention to the barriers faced by American citizens with limited English language skills, a group referred to as "language minorities." The term was a racially liberal concept that attempted to eliminate race but focus on cultural differences. In other words, Mexican Americans were not denied the franchise because of race, but because of their Spanish-speaking culture. Ultimately, Congress made a case that language minorities such as Spanish-speaking Americans deserved the right to bilingual ballots, but never fully acknowledge that racial discrimination had been at the core of Mexican American voter suppression.

To address the cultural challenges facing citizens with limited English proficiency, Congress in 1975 extended the VRA of 1965 and included Section 203, which required counties with more than 10,000 residents, or over 5 percent of the population, with limited English skills, to provide bilingual "registration or voting notices, forms, instructions, assistance, or other materials or information relating to the electoral process, including ballots."[86] Nevertheless, in a similar fashion to the VRA of 1965, the revised VRA was plagued with enforcement issues that became evident in Yakima County.

By 1976, Yakima County was "designated by the Director of the Census as a jurisdiction subject to the requirement of Section 203 for persons of Spanish heritage."[87] And according to former Yakima County Auditor Bettie Ingram, Yakima County provided voting ballots in Spanish from 1976 to 1982.[88] Ingram stated that the County did not want to "risk having their elections thrown out in court and face other sanctions, including stiff fines."[89] The impetus to provide bilingual ballots was not so much to assist Spanish-speaking voters but for Yakima County to avoid penalties from the federal government.

Although the county provided bilingual ballots, by refusing to hire bilingual registrars it failed to comply with Section 203. In fact, a full-time bilingual coordinator was not hired until 2004.[90] In the meantime, Spanish speakers who had trouble understanding the ballot or instructions had no one to help them cast their vote. Clerks at the polls were sometimes those who not long before had prevented Mexican Americans from registering to vote. Jennie Marin, a plaintiff in the *Mexican American Federation v. Naff* case, stated that after she was not allowed to register to vote, Maurine Seefeldt—the Toppenish County Clerk—tore her form and threw it in the waste basket. Martin stated that "[Seefeldt] was kind of rude about it, and I got kind of mad. I hate to go pay my water bill now because I have to see her."[91] Despite the availability of Spanish ballots, with no bilingual personnel to act as mediators in the registration process, individuals such as Ms. Marin were perhaps no more likely to vote than before.

It can be argued that, since 1976, Yakima County had not been in full compliance with Section 203 of the VRA. With no bilingual assistance or a drastic change in Yakima's voting culture to integrate Spanish-speaking voters, Latino participation in local government was hindered and discouraged. Moreover, white candidates did not feel obliged to address the concerns of the population and so they bothered little to reach out to the Latino community.

Furthermore, in Yakima County, after the 1975 VRA, there were no political organizations that focused specifically on Latino voter education and registration efforts until 1983, when the Hispanic Democratic Caucus was formed.[92] The following year, El Concilio for the Spanish Speaking of King County (El Concilio), partnered with the Texas-based Southwest Voter Registration and Education Project (SVRP) in an attempt to form a Pacific Northwest Voter Registration and Education Project to target Mexican American voters, specifically in the Yakima Valley. These efforts saw mixed results. For instance, the Pacific Northwest Voter Registration and Education Project never became a reality. According to SVREP president, Antonio Gonzalez, the funds to sustain the project were exhausted and El Concilio and other local constituents were unable to secure monies to continue this work.[93] Former El Concilio director Ricardo Sanchez observed that SVREP representatives after visiting the area were discouraged that the number of potential Mexican American voters was less than expected. Therefore, no real change came out of this work. On the other hand, the Hispanic Democratic Caucus was the first organization that worked within a political party to organize voter registration and education campaigns. However, by the late 1980s, due to funding and internal strife the organization disbanded.

At the state level, only in 1994 did the Commission on Hispanic Affairs establish a voter education and registration project. Utilizing the slogan, *Su Voto Es Su Voz* (Your Vote is Your Voice), this campaign was the "first non-partisan, statewide voter registration and education effort aimed at Hispanics."[94] Curiously, the start of this effort was in Spokane, not Yakima County.

The combination of the county's unwillingness to hire bilingual poll workers as well as dearth and delay of voter education and registration efforts thwarted the mobilization of Latino voters. However, in 2002, the U.S. Department of Justice stepped in to enforce the VRA, ordering Yakima County to hire bilingual registrars to assist at polling locations and provide voting information in Spanish.[95] Almost immediately, they observed how Yakima County officials complained about the cost of translating materials, mailing bilingual ballots, and hiring bilingual workers; how the newly enforced requirements supposedly further divided the community; and witnessed remarks by Yakima residents who stated: "They knew when they came across the border that the language was English…I don't believe that's right. That [sic] not what I fought for during World War II;" and "Let 'em go the old-fashioned way to become a citizen…Let them study our language and study our constitution and then let them become citizens."[96] The resistance and rhetoric reflected the racism and nativism that fueled prior attempts to deny Latinos the vote.

In 2004, the Justice Department released a report stating the county had made progress but found that "hostility to bilingual election workers and Spanish-speaking voters continues to be an issue in Yakima County."[97] In addition, the Justice Department officially sued Yakima for violating the VRA. However, in its last act of defiance the county claimed that it did "not admit to the allegations" but they would comply with the recommendations of the Justice Department.[98] Yakima's historical resistance to the incorporation of the Latino electorate, the intense media coverage highlighting its opposition to the Justice Department, and its refusal to admit wrongdoing, defined the county as hostile, confrontational, and apathetic to the needs of Latino voters.

The history of Latino voter suppression and racism is important and complex, especially in the Washington State. Here, the disenfranchisement of Mexican Americans through literacy tests was inconsistent but clearly evident when the Mexican American Federation began to organize the electorate. Grassroots movements by the MAF and the United Farm Workers Cooperative moved Mexican Americans to challenge voter suppression and racism in Yakima County, and fight to be acknowledged as full citizens and incorporated into the political fabric of the county. And although the Voting Rights Act removed all tests and devices that had previously disenfranchised racialized minorities in the South, racists in Yakima County resisted the VRA. At times, enforcement required intervention by the federal government as it did in Yakima County. Still, Latinos continued to face barriers after literacy tests were abolished that weakened their ability to participate in electoral politics and impacted their representation in city government.

The complexity of this study lies in how congressional mandates like the Voting Rights Act are enforced at various levels of government. At a national level, in the 1960s, there was never an urgency or a concerted movement to bring Latinos into the fold as voters. Only with the 1975 amendment to the VRA was there an intentional effort to address Latino voter suppression. The gains by Latinos with regards to the vote can be seen as incremental but not substantial. It appears that as soon as one barrier was overcome another was erected in its place. And while literacy tests were eventually abolished, the lack of bilingual ballots presented new problems. Then, barriers involving at-large election schemes diluted the Latino vote, but also compartmentalized this population into a special interest, one that the City of Yakima paid little attention to as evidenced in the *Montes v. City of Yakima* lawsuit.

There is empirical evidence that Latino voter turnout is considerably lower than that of whites and African Americans.[99] The reasons often cited are that a large portion of the Latino population are not naturalized citizens, many are undocumented and unable to vote, and voter apathy. This work has argued that structural factors, enforcement of the VRA, lack of voter registration and education efforts, and racial discrimination have contributed to Latino voter suppression. Just as crucial, this study has demonstrated how local rural governments have operated to exclude the Latino voter while undermining the authority of the federal government. It reveals how Yakima County's government and white residents have challenged and resisted the political incorporation of Latino voters. Since 1967, Latinos have been democratizing Washington State, striving to be acknowledged as full citizens, and insisting that their voices and demands are recognized.

Notes

1. In this essay, I will use the term Mexican American to describe people of Mexican descent who reside in the United States. I use Latino as an umbrella term to describe people of Latin American origin and of Mexican background who live in the U.S. or territories regardless of their citizenship. Additionally, I use the term Texas Mexican to describe people who were born or resided in Texas regardless of citizenship status. To better understand the multifaceted dimensions within each group, and how their experience has varied in the U.S., see David

G. Gutierrez, *Walls and Mirrors: Mexican Americans, Mexican Immigrants, and the Politics of Ethnicity* (Berkeley: University of California Press, 1995).

2. *Rogelio Montes and Mateo Arteaga v. City of Yakima et al.*, Complaint CV-12-3108-TOR, U.S. District Court, Eastern District of Washington (2012).

3. Jesus Lemos, "A History of the Chicano Political Involvement" (master's thesis, University of Washington, 1974), 101.

4. Daniel Martinez HoSang, *Racial Propositions: Ballot Initiatives and the Making of Postwar California*, American Crossroads (Berkeley: University of California Press, 2010).

5. *Mexican-American Federation v. Eugene Naff, Yakima County Auditor*, U.S. District Courts, Eastern District of Washington, Yakima, Civil Case Files 1967–1970, 2454–2457, Box 361, National Archives and Records Administration (NARA), Seattle, WA.

6. Erasmo Gamboa, *Mexican Labor and World War II: Braceros in the Pacific Northwest, 1942–1947* (Austin: University of Texas Press, 1990), 2. See also Erasmo Gamboa, "Under the Thumb of Agriculture: Bracero and Mexican American Workers in the Pacific Northwest, 1940–1950" (PhD diss., University of Washington, 1984).

7. Gamboa, *Mexican Labor*, 4.

8. Erasmo Gamboa, "A History of Chicano People and the Development of Agriculture in the Yakima, Valley, Washington" (master's thesis, University of Washington, 1973), 25–26. In the 1930s, a significant number of white migrant workers from the Great Plains began to settle and work in fields of the Yakima Valley, displaced by soil erosion and drought. And by the 1940s, white and Mexican/Mexican American migrant families lived as neighbors in a Yakima Valley community called Crewport. See Mario Compean, "Mexican American and Dust Bowl Farmworkers in the Yakima Valley: A History of the Crewport Farm Labor Camp, 1940–1970," in Jerry García and Gilberto García, eds., *Memory, Community, and Activism: Mexican Migration and Labor in the Pacific Northwest* (Michigan: Julian Samora Research Institute, Michigan State University, 2005).

9. For additional information regarding the Japanese in the Yakima Valley see Thomas H. Heuterman, *The Burning Horse: Japanese-American Experience in the Yakima Valley, 1920–1942* (Cheney, WA: Eastern Washington University Press, 1995).

10. Gamboa, "A History of Chicano People," 33.

11. See Erasmo Gamboa, "Mexican Migration into Washington State: A History, 1940–1950." *Pacific Northwest Quarterly* 72, no. 3 (1981): 121–31; and Gamboa, *Mexican Labor and World War II*, 8.

12. For more on sugar beet production companies see Leonard J. Arrington, *Beet Sugar in the West: A History of the Utah-Idaho Sugar Company, 1891–1966* (Seattle: University of Washington Press, 1966).

13. Gamboa, *Mexican Labor and World War II*, 2.
14. Marta Maria Maldonado, "Harvesting the Fruits of Color Blindness: Racial Ideology in Employers' Discourse and the Everyday Production of Racial Inequality in Agricultural Work," (PhD diss., Washington State University, 2004).
15. Gamboa, *Mexican Labor and World War II*, 23.
16. Gamboa, "Mexican Migration into Washington State," 122.
17. Ibid., 124. In total, between 1942 and 1947, 220,200 Mexican braceros entered the U.S. and approximately 47,000 of these workers were sent to the Pacific Northwest. See also Erasmo Gamboa, "Braceros in the Pacific Northwest: Laborers on the Domestic Front, 1942–1947," *Pacific Historical Review* 56, no. 3 (August 1987): 378–98.
18. Gamboa, *Mexican Labor and World War II*, 122.
19. Gamboa, Mexican Migration into Washington State," 127.
20. The transition from braceros to Mexican American laborers was also facilitated by the sugar beet companies that had established migrant streams from states like Colorado, Montana, and Wyoming starting in the 1920s.
21. See Josué Q. Estrada, "Texas Mexican Diaspora to Washington State: Recruitment, Migration, and Community, 1940–1960" (master's thesis, Washington State University, 2007).
22. James Gregory, *The Southern Diaspora: How the Great Migrations of Black and White Southerners Transformed American* (Chapel Hill: University of North Carolina Press, 2005), 168.
23. Marc S. Rodriguez, *The Tejano Diaspora: Mexican Americanism and Ethnic Politics in Texas and Wisconsin* (Chapel Hill: University of North Carolina Press, 2011).
24. 1968 LULAC chapters were established in two lower Yakima Valley towns. See NonProfitFac.com-Tax Exempt Organizations, www.nonprofitfacts.com//WA/League-Of-United-Latin-American-Citizens-47012-Lulac-Council.html.
25. David G. Gutierrez, *Walls and Mirrors: Mexican Americans, Mexican Immigrants, and the Politics of Ethnicity* (Berkeley: University of California Press, 1995), 78.
26. United States Commission on Civil Rights. *1961 Commission on Civil Rights Report*. (Washington, DC: U.S. Government Printing Office, 1961), 21.
27. Ibid., 19.
28. In 1870, the landmark amendment was ratified by Congress and stated that, "The right of citizens of the United States to vote shall not be denied or abridged by the United States or by any State on account of race, color, or previous condition of servitude." This constitutional modification was intended to the enfranchisement African Americans. See U.S. Constitution, amend. XV, § 1.
29. United States Commission on Civil Rights, *1961 Commission on Civil Rights Report*, (Washington, DC: U.S. Government Printing Office, 1961), 21.
30. Ibid., 18.
31. Alexander Keyssar, *The Right to Vote: The Contested History of Democracy in the United States* (New York: Basic Books, 2000), 212.

32. Ibid.

33. The federal law was immediately challenged by New York legislators in *Katzenbach v. Morgan*. In 1966, the court ruled that New York's literacy tests were invalid since these citizens were educated in American schools but instructed in Spanish. See *Katzenbach v. Morgan*, Supreme Court of the United States, 384 U.S. 641 (1966).

34. John J. O'Connell, *Opinions* (1957–1968). Attorney General's Office 1967 No. 21 (June 15, 1967). www.atg.wa.gov/AGOOpinions/opinion.aspx?id=8938#. Ut9ZWRDTnIW.

35. Ibid.

36. Ibid.

37. Ibid.

38. This also appears to be in the case in California. See Roger Daniels and Eric F. Petersen, "California's Grandfather Clause: The 'Literacy in English' Amendment of 1894," *Southern California Quarterly* 50, no. 1 (1968): 51–58.

39. According to the Yakima Valley Council for Community Action (part of the War on Poverty, Office of Economic Opportunity) and the MAF, these organizations estimated that the Mexican American population ranged from 8,000 to 12,000. See Tom Chambers, "A Second Look at Literacy Tests," American Civil Liberties Union (ACLU) of Washington, 1942–1996, Accession No. 1177-005, Special Collections, University of Washington Libraries; and United States Census, Washington State Characteristics of Population, 1960.

40. Tom J. Chambers, "The Excepted People: The Migrant Workers in Washington State" (Seattle: Washington State Council of Churches, 1969). ACLU of Washington 1942–1996. Accession No. 1177-005. Special Collections, University of Washington Libraries.

41. For example, total farm acreage increased from 1,884,694 in 1959 to 2,099,942 in 1964. See Charles E. Ehlert, "Report of the Yakima Valley Project" (Seattle: American Civil Liberties Union, 1969), 7. ACLU, 1942–1996, Accession No. 1177-005, Special Collections, University of Washington Libraries, Seattle.

42. Ehlert, "Report of the Yakima Valley Project," 73.

43. Ibid.

44. Mexican-American Federation Puget Sound Newsletter, 1968–1970, Box 7, Folder 11, Tomás Ybarra-Frausto Papers, Accession No. 4339-001, University of Washington Libraries, Seattle.

45. Ibid.

46. Ehlert, "Report of the Yakima Valley Project," 73.

47. *Mexican-American Federation v. Eugene Naff, Yakima County Auditor.*

48. Don Hannula and Ray Ruppert, "The Agri-Revolution: Just One Mexican-American Holds Office," *Seattle Times*, July 22, 1968.

49. "Mexican-Americans Seek Spanish Speaking Registrars," *Yakima Herald Republic*, March 8, 1968, 8. Sam Martinez was instrumental in the founding of the MAF

and in the *Mexican American Federation v. Naff* case. See Mary Hersey, "Mexican American Federation: Its Goals, Structure, Leader," *Our Times: A Catholic News Report for Central Washington* 10 (1968): 1–3.

50. "Mexican-Americans Seek Spanish-Speaking Registrars," *Yakima Herald Republic*, March 8, 1968, 8.
51. Ibid.
52. "Spanish-Speaking Elections Registrars? No, Says Naff." *Yakima Herald Republic*, March 16, 1968, 2.
53. Ibid.
54. Ibid.
55. Ibid.
56. In March of 1972, it took a thirty-five-member delegation to force Naff to appoint Spanish-speaking registrars. "Spanish-Voter Signup Set," *Seattle Times*, March 31, 1972.
57. *Mexican-American Federation v. Eugene Naff, Yakima County Auditor*.
58. Ibid.
59. Ibid.
60. Hilda Bryant, "New Voters May Change Yakima Area," *Seattle Post-Intelligencer*, August 21, 1970; "State to register 'illiterate' votes," *Seattle Times*, August 22, 1970. In the U.S., all literacy tests were barred by *Oregon v. Mitchell* (1970). The case ruled that even if literacy tests were administered in a non-discriminatory manner, Congress had the authority to ban education provisions or "other devices" related to the franchise. See *Oregon v. Mitchell. Supreme Court of the United States*, 400 U.S. 112, 133, 1970.
61. Bryant, "New Voters May Change Yakima Area."
62. Matt Barreto, "Sí Se Puede! Latino Candidates and the Mobilization of Latino Voters," *American Political Science Review* 101, no. 3 (2007): 425–41.
63. In Granger, the rise in candidacy numbers may be attributed to population density, a 1969 visit by Union Farm Workers President César Chávez, and voter registration drives conducted in the early 1970s. In Mabton, the increase in candidacy figures could be related to the town's Mexican American population, which was nearly 50 percent, and that it was the only city in the Yakima County to have an elected Mexican American mayor. He may have galvanized the Mexican American electorate in the rural town.
64. There is no indication that the Commission had a strategic goal to increase the number of Mexican Americans voters in Washington, or specifically in the Yakima Valley.
65. By the 1970s and 1980s, the increased immigration of Latinos apart from people of Mexican descent to the Westside contributed to the name change of the commission.
66. Larry Rumley, "Plight of Mexican Americans," *Seattle Times*, August 9, 1970.

67. Margaret Miller, "Community Action and Reaction: Chicanos and the War on Poverty in the Yakima Valley, Washington" (master's thesis, University of Washington, 1991), 88.

68. 2011-2012 Washington State Latino/Hispanic Assessment Report, Washington State Commission on Hispanic Affairs. Olympia: Washington, 2012. http:// cha.wa.gov/wp-content/uploads/2014/06/ChaReport2012_English_web.pdf

69. "Evans' G.O.P Critic Criticized," *Seattle Times*, February 25, 1971.

70. "Evans Appointees Defended by Active Mexicanos Aide," *Seattle Times,* March 2, 1971.

71. "Evans: Dissatisfaction Cited in Yakima Valley," *Seattle Times,* October 6, 1972.

72. Miller, "Community Action and Reaction," 88.

73. "Evans, Rosellini in Different Areas," *Seattle Times*, October 27, 1972.

74. "Mexican-American Director Resigns," *Seattle Times*, December 3, 1973.

75. Ibid.

76. Lemos, "A History of the Chicano Political Involvement," 62.

77. Ermelindo Escobedo, interview with author, February 15, 2014.

78. In 1983, the Hispanic Democratic Caucus began to work with voters in the Yakima Valley. The political group was able to register roughly 500 Mexican American voters. See Dick Clever, "Hispanic voter drive is aimed at future clout," *Seattle Times,* February 19, 1984; and Craig Troianello, "Flexing their Muscle: Hispanics Help Put Some of Their Own in Office in Yakima County," *Yakima Herald Republic,* February 24, 1984.

79. Lemos, "A History of the Chicano Political Involvement," 101.

80. "Spanish-Voter Signup Set," *Seattle Times*, March 31, 1972.

81. Lemos, "A History of the Chicano Political Involvement," 101.

82. Ibid.

83. Ermelindo Escobedo, interview with author, February 15, 2014.

84. United States Commission on Civil Rights, *1975 Commission on Civil Rights Report* (Washington, DC: U.S. Government Printing Office, 1975), 57.

85. Ibid.

86. Voting Rights Act Amendments of 1975, Voting Rights Act, Section 203, Public Law No. 94-73.

87. *United States of America v. Yakima County, Corky Mattingly, Yakima County Auditor, et al.* CV-04-3072-LRS, Eastern District of Washington, Yakima Division, 2004.

88. Yakima County stopped producing bilingual materials because after 1982 the U.S. Census Bureau "numbers showed that ballots were no longer required here and Spanish voting went away." However, Census data in reality demonstrated an increase of the Spanish/Hispanic population. In 1980, the "Spanish origin" population in Yakima County represented 17.7 percent of the total population and 12.3 percent were of voting age. And by 1990, Yakima County's total "Hispanic" figures increased to 23.9 percent and the number eligible to voters

also surged to 13.1 percent. See Tom Roeder, "Yakima County Had English, Spanish Ballots 20 Years Ago, *Yakima-Herald Republic*, August 11, 2002; United States Census, 1980 Census of Population, General Population Characteristics (Washington, DC: U.S. Census Bureau, 1980). Available at a shortened link: http://www.census.gov/prod/www/decennial.html; United States Census, 1990 Census of Population, General Population Characteristics (Washington, DC: U.S. Census Bureau, 1990), www.census.gov/prod/cen1990/cp1/cp-1-49.pdf.

89. Roeder, "Yakima County Had English, Spanish Ballots."
90. Lázaro Cárrion, "Voting Rights of Latinos in Yakima and Enforcement by the State," The State of the State for Washington Latinos, Whitman College, 2008, walatinos.org.
91. *Mexican-American Federation v. Eugene Naff, Yakima County Auditor.*
92. *Yakima Herald Republic,* February 24, 1984.
93. Antonio Gonzalez interview with author, December 15, 2013.
94. Rachael Konrad, "Project Aimed at Registering Hispanic Voters," *The Spokesman-Review* (Spokane, WA), April 12, 1995.
95. Using the 2000 Census, the Justice Department estimated that over 30,000 or roughly 12.3 percent people did not speak English well in the county. See Tom Roeder, "Bilingual Election Ballots Mandated: Demographic Changes in Yakima County Trigger Change Under Voting Rights Act," *Yakima Herald-Republic,* August 3, 2002.
96. Roeder, "Bilingual Election Ballots;" John Iwasaki, "Bilingual Ballots Draw Protests," *Seattle Post-Intelligencer,* October 18, 2002.
97. "County Makes Progress in Helping Spanish-Speaking," *Seattle Post-Intelligencer,* October 25, 2004.
98. *United States of America v. Yakima County, Corky Mattingly, Yakima County Auditor, et al.* CV-04-3072-LRS, Eastern District of Washington, Yakima Division, 2004.
99. Mark López and Ana González-Barrera, "Inside the 2012 Electorate," Pew Research Center: Hispanic Trends, June 3, 2013. www.pewhispanic.org/2013/06/03/inside-the-2012-latino-electorate.

CHAPTER 4

The Struggle for Xicana/o Studies in the Northern Borderlands: War of the Flea in [Azt]lansing Michigan

Ernesto Todd Mireles

"If we can't read about our history, then you cannot read about yours."
—*Rosa Linda Salas, Tlataoni, MSU MEXA, 1998–1999*

During the 1990s, as an undergraduate student at Michigan State University (MSU), it was my privilege to witness and participate in the historic struggle for Xicana/o studies. African liberationist Frantz Fanon wrote eloquently about colonized people gaining control of their destinies. The struggle at MSU, and others like it in communities across Aztlán are skirmishes in the five-century-old battle to end settler colonialism in the Americas and reclaim the cultural, political, and intellectual destiny of the people of Aztlán. Fanon's powerful critique of the role of the indigenous intellectual, both traditional and organic,[1] in creating a new national culture to replace the colonial structure stated "there is simply a concentration on a hard core of culture which is becoming more and more shriveled up, inert, and empty." His words are more relevant than ever.[2] This national liberation struggle is one where, as indigenous intellectual Taiaike Alfred, a Kanien'kehaka Mohawk, in his book *Wasase: Indigenous Pathways of Action and Freedom* writes, "warriors battle against the political manipulations of their innate fears and repel the state's attempts to embed complacency inside of them. They counterattack with a lived ethic of courage and seek to cause the reawakening of a culture of

105

freedom."[3] The MSU students—my comrades—organizing and fighting "the state's attempts to embed complacency inside of them" found voice within their demands for Xicana/o[4] studies.

The first Xicana/o studies programs across the country were created in the social upheavals of the 1960s and 1970s. By the 1990s, dozens of Xicana/o studies programs were established, functioning, and thriving in institutions of higher learning across Aztlán.[5] For Xicana/os living outside of California and the Southwest watching the struggles that exploded around Propositions 187 and 209,[6] along with the January 1, 1994, Zapatista uprising in Chiapas, Mexico, in opposition to the implementation of the North American Free Trade Agreement (NAFTA), it was a time for serious reflection and commitment to the Xicana/o national struggle. The Zapatistas were at that time the most publicized indigenous response to capitalism and colonialism in the Americas. These struggles and their international dimensions had a profound impact on Xicana/o students across the country. This chapter examines how the news of these resistance movements influenced Xicana/o students at Michigan State University.

Documents gathered through Freedom of Information Act requests and personal student archives contrast the Xicana/o studies politico-cultural movement of the 1990s to its direct predecessor at MSU mainly through the application of militant bottom-up organizing and anti-authoritarian direct action tactics. These ideas and their implementation were still unique in the Xicana/o student movement of the 1990s. Direct action tactics aligned within a Third World organizing framework of heightening contradictions, along with the arrival of specific faculty, were key catalysts in the establishment of Xicana/o studies at Michigan State University. This moment of reawakening, fueled by direct action, can be framed within specific watershed moments that created cohesion and momentum for the students and community. For the Xicana/o and non-Xicana/o community, a deeper commitment to social justice and a widening cultural-politico perspective evolved quickly from a Xicana/o-centric perspective to a broader visualization of indigenous identity.

Heightening contradictions is an organizing strategy that prepares communities to participate in confrontational tactics. By exposing the irreconcilable differences between the oppressor and the oppressed, organizers educate the community with the aim of involving them in cultural-politico confrontations to win demands. This preparation is predicated on education and the development of critical thinking skills. Across the world, insurgents and liberation fighters use this educational tactic to heighten and dramatize differences between themselves and their colonialist oppressors. It is the basis of Mao Tse Tung's famous "war of the flea" described by Robert Taber (1964) in his book of the same title. "The flea bites, hops, and bites again, nimbly avoiding the foot that would crush him. He does not seek to kill his enemy at a blow, but to bleed him and feed on him, to plague and bedevil him, to keep him from resting and to destroy his nerve and his morale."[7] Metaphorically speaking, the heightening of contradictions is the breeding of the flea.

Any discussion about the political and cultural gains at Michigan State University in the 1990s must take into account the terms of tactic and strategy. How did the strategies and tactics of the Xicana/o movement in the 1960s and 1970s inform or shape the actions of Xicana/o militants both on and off campus in the 1990s and beyond? At MSU, the frame of heightening contradictions was widened with the inclusion of environmental activists and white anarchists, along with their knowledge of direct action tactics. This collaboration with forces outside the small Xicana/o and Latina/o community also speaks directly to a sense of entitlement to higher education on the part of the Xicana/os of the 1990s. It is also important to keep in mind that in terms of creating a Xicana/o studies program it wasn't until the 1990s that the Xicano/Latino population at MSU reached a critical mass with sufficient numbers to carry out a direct action campaign needed to build enough pressure on the university to force the administration's acquiescence.

On September 9, 1994, La Onda Latina (LOLA), a statewide network of Xicano and Latino students, organized a conference. White student activists at MSU agreed to teach the Xicana/o and Latina/o students the fundamentals of direct action protest and tactics. Nicole Newton, the director of MSU's Women's Council, produced an instruction manual titled "Don't Get Caught" that outlined practical information for organizing large protests, forming affinity groups, and interacting with the police, along with information on the arrest process, grand juries, and being contacted by the police and the FBI. This training, association, and conversations with more seasoned activists had a profound impact on Xicana/o students at MSU and many of those involved with LOLA. It allowed them to begin thinking about the contradictions of a settler education and self-determinative solutions for Xicana/os, and how to organize around direct action campaigns within the Xicana/o and Latina/o community to make those solutions a reality.

Edward L. Katzenbach Jr., who served as the deputy assistant secretary of state under President John F. Kennedy, in his influential essay on the military theories of Mao Tse Tung, enumerated the three tangibles of warfare. First are "the weapons systems…instruments of war that have given a sole possessor a moment of military supremacy. Second, there is the supply system, logistics in the broadest sense…Third, there is manpower." Katzenbach writes that Mao chose to develop his revolutionary theory focusing on the three intangible aspects of warfare—space, time, and will:

> The basic premise of this theory is that political mobilization may be substituted for industrial mobilization. Mao's military problem was how to organize space so that it could be made to yield time. His political problem was how to organize time so that could be made to yield will, that quality which makes willingness to sacrifice the order of the day…Mao's real military problem was not that of getting the war over with, the question to which Western military thinkers have directed the greater part of their attention, but that of keeping it going.[8]

Students at MSU focused on the intangibles of war. Their prolonged fight for the "space" of Xicana/o studies gave these students the time over the course of a decade to build the will of their fellow students to remain in the fight. Today, within the Xicano movement, organizers and activists suffer from unrealistic expectations about the role of reform and revolution in a Xicana/o national liberation struggle. Space + Time = Will is an important equation from Katzenbach's analysis of Mao's guerrilla theory that could help shape the Xicana/o movement with realistic expectations of what constitutes protracted struggle during this historical episode.

Divestment is a non-violent tactic that creates a process for removing material, cultural, and political support from someone, something, or some idea unacceptable to you. In the 1980s, MSU was one of the first major universities to divest from South Africa. In doing this, MSU took a moral and financial stance against South African apartheid, paving the way for other universities and corporations to do the same. Today with the electoral elimination of affirmative action through state proposals, society faces a similar question around issues of tacit support for inequality and how to resist injustice. In his book, *Why We Can't Wait*, Dr. Martin Luther King Jr. stated about non-violent direct resistance:

> When, for decades you have been able to make a man compromise his manhood by threatening him with a cruel and unjust punishment, and when suddenly he turns upon you and says: "punish me. I do not deserve it. But because I do not deserve it, I will accept it so that the world will know that I am right and you are wrong"... You know that this man is as good a man as you are; that from some mysterious source he has found the courage and the conviction to meet physical force with soul force.[9]

These ideas—Mao's "war of the flea" and Martin Luther King's "soul force"—provided the theoretical basis for non-violent direct action at MSU during the 1990s, and inspired the depth of commitment assumed by the students to face continual confrontation, the burden of punishment, and the obligation to bear it under any circumstance.

Direct action and militant non-violence are the overarching lessons of the 1990s at MSU for Xicana/o students. Although the first evidence of this lesson was discovered by accident, it became quickly apparent the greater the amount of pressure brought to bear on an issue the more incentive there is to resolve that issue. Because universities and their administrators often work hard to project a very liberal and caring image, heightened levels of tension can and often do force a faster resolution to the matter. The job of the students then becomes exposing the contradictions between opposing groups. These practices must be based on the fundamental belief in the irreconcilable differences in values, beliefs, and most of all, interests of the two conflicting parties.

THE INITIAL REPORTS

Before the 1990s, several official university reports and studies indicate that the main concerns of Xicana/os and Latinos at MSU from the 1970s to the late 1980s were employment of Xicana/o faculty and staff, and Xicana/o student retention. The reports are summarized in a March 8, 1989, document titled "Report of the Task Force on the Hispanic American

Institute," which identified five central issues impacting the Hispanic community: employment development, education, political empowerment, health and family welfare, cultural awareness and enrichment. The opening paragraph of the report reads in part,

> Since 1977, comprehensive reports have been prepared and submitted to the MSU central administration calling for modest action to improve the participation of Hispanics at all levels of the University community…however, while there appears to have been a serious effort in fashioning reasonable proposals for bringing Hispanics into more meaningful roles in the University, the University response has consistently been silence at best.[10]

Later, the report clearly outlines the need for research faculty at MSU as a vital component for increasing campus participation, "the key missing element is a cadre of research faculty with a demonstrated commitment to orient and coordinate programs to Hispanic issues."[11]

Taken out of context, the above quote might be misunderstood as assigning intent concerning the creation of a Xicana/o studies program. When the authors speak about "programs" they in fact are referring to a number of university and academic programs:

> The limitations among Hispanic faculty and the research interest of non-Hispanic faculty at MSU have precluded a Hispanic focus in University programs directly relevant to our areas of concern. For example, the Cooperative Extension Service, the Institute for Research on Teaching, the Institute for Family and Child Study, the Labor Program Service, the Agricultural Experiment Station, and the National Center for Research on Teacher Education are some of the programs and research centers which could be mobilized to attend more to Hispanic interests in their research and service agenda. Once again, the key-missing element is a cadre of research faculty with a demonstrated commitment to orient and coordinate programs to Hispanic themes.[12]

The authors of the report put forward the traditional rationale of building Xicana/o presence on campus by increasing faculty positions in existing departments. Their stated goal was not to create a new department that would oversee the development of a Chicano studies program but to make their specific departments more responsive to Xicana/o/Latinos at MSU.[13] This is very different from the later demands of activists in the 1990s who wanted a dedicated Xicana/o studies faculty to lead and orient Xicana/o students for greater academic success within that specific discipline.

Another important aspect of the reports submitted leading up the 1990s was the conciliatory language used on the part of the Xicana/o and Latina/o community to convey their sense of engagement in the process of change. Consider this excerpt from the Task Force Report: "A more cynical view might interpret the regression which has occurred over the past decade in most areas of university participation as hostile to the inclusion of Hispanics…We trust the sincerity of the commitments which have been made to us to go beyond the rhetoric of the past decade and to begin to implement the many recommendations which have been made over this period."[14]

Another prominent thread present in the pre-1990s reports was the constant comparison with African Americans on campus. The use of African Americans in these reports as benchmarks for measuring the progress of the Xicana/o and Latina/o population on campus shifted in the 1990s as an increasing sense of Xicana/o nationalism and Indigeneity took hold among the students. The shift in the type of language used to engage the university provides one of the most dramatic ways of understanding the fundamental differences between the two eras and their approach to activism and campus organizing. In terms of creating programs or studies, the situation at MSU before the 1990s was in many ways one dictated by numbers.

The culmination of the activism during this period was the creation of the Julian Samora Research Institute in 1989.[15] This accomplishment cannot be downplayed or underestimated in its achievement. Clearly, the Xicana/o and Latina/o population at MSU had not reached a critical mass dense enough to make demands from the "street." It also shows the demand for Xicana/o studies was unique to the movement of the 1990s.

WHITENESS, MSU, AND THE XICANADA

The implicit lessons of my early life were resistance and survival in an overwhelmingly white world. I am half Mexican and no one (not even those who loved me) ever let me forget this fact. I have lived my life with white people, eaten with them, called them mother, grandmother, and uncle. I know them in a way they do not know themselves. I understand how they think because I think the same way. I am one of you and of my own free will, I choose to be the other. This was my first lesson in contradiction.

Michigan State University casts a long shadow in Lansing, and growing up in that shadow I believed MSU was somehow different—a utopia of knowledge and learning. I learned, as we all do during our primary indoctrination, that education is the great equalizer. I believed that when I became educated the world would see me the same way I wanted to see it, with greater understanding and clarity. I did not understand how wrong I was.

I was stunned by first day at MSU by the explosion of white skin and blue eyes. It was not that I had never seen so many white people before, I grew up in Michigan; it was the deficiency, the absolute absence of other Xicana/os and African American people that crippled me as I struggled my way around campus. Just a few short miles from my childhood and the familiar streets of Black and Brown Lansing, Michigan, I realized something was drastically wrong with my utopia.

Between 1992 and 1993, a core of Lansing locals had come over from Lansing Community College (LCC) and we formed along with Rudy Hernandez (then a young graduate student from Detroit, now a professor of sociology at the University of Michigan, Flint) the nucleus of a discussion group about MSU and the space Xicana/os occupied on campus and in society. Members of this original group were: Anthony Spangler, Rainer Delgado, Magda Sanchez, Stephanie Rios, Francisco Lopez, Paulo Gordillo, and myself. We had several common denominators in that we were in our mid-twenties when we came to MSU (slightly older than most undergraduates), we had all attended community college together, and as residents of Lansing had recently lived through the community fallout from the brutal killing of Cipriano Torres Jr. on November 4, 1991, by Lansing Police Department Officers.[16] I met Rudy the year before while I was working on a local Xicana/o community newspaper named *El Renacimiento*. I was still at community college with dreams of becoming a newspaper reporter. Rudy quickly became one of my main initiators into the La Xicanada (the Xicano community); through the 1990s, he literally kicked down the doors of Michigan State's admissions office for me and many others.

It was 1993, and at MSU the Coalition of Hispanic Student for Progressive Action (CHISPA)[17] was the only student group for Xicana/o and Latina/o students. Rudy suggested we form a new student group and in doing so introduced us to Movimiento Estudiantil Xicana/o de Aztlán well known across the country as MEXA (but entirely new to us) and we, trusting Rudy unconditionally, declared ourselves MEXistas.

M. PETER MCPHERSON AND THE GRAPE BOYCOTT

Early in 1992, these newly minted MEXistas compiled along with the Asian Pacific Student Organization and CHISPA their first list of demands, which they delivered to interim MSU president Gordon Guyer. Number seven of the thirteen demands reads, "MSU [must] instate a Chicano/Latino Studies Center (similar to Wayne State University's)... This program will do its own recruitment, retention and teach its own curriculum."

Central to that list of demands was the creation of a Xicana/o studies program at Michigan State. One of the sub-demands was for the recognition of the United Farm Workers (UFW) grape boycott. This becomes important later with the October 1993 arrival on campus of new MSU President M. Peter McPherson, former director of USAID under Ronald Reagan, a group executive vice president at the Bank of America in San Francisco, and rumored to be the grandson of the first president of Michigan's farm bureau. He was white, rich, privileged, and from a farming background, the perfect foil for a bunch of cockroaches in revolt.[18]

We harassed him, followed him from meeting to meeting. Confronted him at places he never dreamt we would dare. It was brutal and he was not ready for it. As a rich and powerful man, he was used to being obeyed instantly and not challenged. Shortly after his arrival, McPherson started meeting with leaders from student-of-color groups.[19] When it was our turn, we delivered him our thirteen demands. As he was reading the list, he suddenly stopped. "Xicana/o studies? What do you do with a degree in Xicana/o studies?" McPherson asked us with a laugh. "What kind of job can you get with that?" I asked him back, "What kind of job do you get with an English degree? The point is you do with a degree what you want to do with a degree." As we pressed him further on the subject of Xicana/o studies McPherson said, "I think ethnic studies programs tend to balkanize campuses." At the time, I was not even sure what he meant by that. Later, when we understood his meaning we took every opportunity to repeat his assertion to anyone who would listen.

Through the end of 1994, we pounded McPherson with protest after protest. Always in the forefront of our demands were Xicana/o studies and the UFW grape boycott. We had stumbled unwittingly on issues that not only heightened contradictions but also created an almost insurmountable ideological chasm. These two issues allowed us the freedom to educate the community about the plight of farm workers, pesticides, and self-determination through education in the classroom and protest in the streets. As the university administration reacted in defense of its own interests, the contradictions became more evident.

One particularly noteworthy action occurred Friday, February 11, 1994, the day that Dolores Huerta was visiting MSU.[20] MEXistas and their allies had been sending McPherson boxes of grapes every hour with notes reading, "These grapes were watered with the blood of migrant workers," and similar statements.

The day culminated with close to one hundred Xicana/o students and their white allies taking over the president's office and demanding to speak with him. Although he first refused, eventually he relented, asking us to join him in the board of trustees meeting room adjacent to his office. In we went; as we filled up the room McPherson took the seat at the head of the table, Dolores Huerta directly to his right, and the university-appointed advisor to Latino students Luis Alonzo Garcia directly to his left.

It was ugly. McPherson tried to defend what was in our eyes indefensible and he was clearly angry at being challenged. Dolores also criticized McPherson; that was beautiful.[21] The white kids in the room also challenged the president. But the *coup de grace* came when after about an hour of verbal bantering he began some long ramble about Native Americans, reservations, and manifest destiny. Across the table Anthony Spangler, a Lansing native and MEXA member, stood abruptly in the middle of

McPherson's last monologue, took a couple of bags of leftover grapes and slammed them down on the board of trustees table.

The room got loud, people started to move. McPherson called for order but the noise level in the room rose dramatically as RAZA and their allies stood and began to shout. Julie Salazar, a Xicana from the barrio of South West Detroit, and Cindy Cerda, another Xicana from Chicago, began ripping open the bags Spangler had hurled on the table and throwing grapes in all directions. The crowd reacted as crowds often do: chairs started to tip over as people stood, and this space, this center of European hegemony broke into bilingual pandemonium while Salazar, Cerda, and other Xicanas threw handfuls of grapes at President McPherson. For me the room froze. All around me people were shouting and throwing grapes. McPherson started pounding the table yelling, "Get her down!" I turned to see Salazar towering, both figuratively and literally, over the room, her laced Timberlines stomping grapes on top of the board of trustees meeting table like a Xicana/o version of an *I Love Lucy* episode gone wild. It all happened in about thirty seconds.

Minutes later in the hallway a second drama unfolded as Luis Garcia scolded some of the students about their behavior. In what was a prophetic moment, Francisco Lopez, a student at Lansing Community College, went up to Garcia and confronting him said, "Whose side are you on?" "What, what do you mean?" Garcia responded. "From where I was sitting," said Lopez to the low murmurings of the crowd. "It looked like you were with the man."[22]

Fanon tells us the colonizer equates the colonized to animals; makes them beasts of burden in order to justify their murderous exploitation. Fanon writes that the colonized, "knows that he is not an animal; and it is precisely at that moment he realizes his humanity and begins to sharpen the weapons with which he will secure its victory."[23] We walked out of that boardroom victorious. The edge on our intellectual machetes was starting to sharpen. The situation had just gotten a little wild but that is expected when "two forces, opposed to each other by their very nature," meet.[24] As Fanon warns, decolonization is a process that begins with an intellectual rejection of the dominant colonizer paradigm and moves toward a physical challenge of that same system. It "sets out to change the order of the world, is, obviously, a program of complete disorder."[25] That was the winter of 1994, things were just getting started, and unknown to us, help of a sort was about to appear on the scene.

Ethnic Studies at Michigan State

Any account of the struggle for Xicano studies at MSU would be incomplete without discussing the efforts of Dr. Refugio I. (Will) Rochin, who was hired in the summer of 1994 as the first permanent director of the Julian Samora Research Institute (JSRI). Rochin came from the University of California, Davis, where he had started and directed along with others one of the country's more successful and enduring Xicana/o studies program. A professor of agricultural economics, Rochin also served on the California State Board of Food and Agriculture, and the board of the Rural California Housing Corporation, a non-profit builder of low-income housing for farm workers and others in rural communities.

A veteran of the Xicana/o studies struggles of the 1960s and 70s, Rochin immediately grasped the political situation and hit the ground advocating for Xicana/o studies as a component of ethnic studies. Rochin became the director of JSRI on September 1, 1994. He arrived at a critical time on campus. He was thrust by MSU administration, and his own history and personal beliefs, into the center of the fight for Xicana/o studies. Because of the upsurge in Xicana/o student activism after the grape-throwing incident and the ongoing direct-action organizing of the MEXA students, the demand for Xicana/o studies was becoming a rallying cry on and off campus. Far from trying to distance himself, Rochin immediately began trying different administrative ways to capitalize on the momentum created by Xicana/o students.

An interesting glimpse into his advocacy for Xicana/o studies can be found in an October 3, 1995, memo to then-Provost Lou Anna Simon (now MSU president) and the dean of Social Sciences, Kenneth Corey. Rochin, as part of his ongoing argument for the creation of a Latino studies program at MSU wrote, "Understand that I am firmly committed to Xicana/o/ Latino studies and 'multiculturalism' because it is in my blood."[26] In a November 10, 1995, memo to Simon, Corey laid out the agenda for the November13 meeting:

In order to address and meet the expressed educational needs for our students, we want your mandate to have JSRI develop and implement an undergraduate specialization in Latino/Xicana/o Studies…

In order for JSRI to have a reasonable chance of successfully realizing its current and proposed expanded mission, JSRI should be authorized to appoint in the Institute, tenure and tenure stream faculty, and JSRI should be authorized to offer credit instruction and programming.

In order for JSRI to be successful therefore, it needs to be empowered to function across the mission of teaching, as well as research and outreach. Scholarly holism is essential.[27]

As the documents show, certain factions within the university were interested in creating an ethnic studies program, or as Rochin wrote in an email on November 13, Simon "acknowledge[s] the interest of [MSU professor] Chris Vanderpool and Ken Corey in establishing a specialization in ERGI [Ethnicity, Race, Gender and Inequality]"[28] and praises them for the work they had done up to that point.

The problem for Rochin was between his push for Xicana/o studies and a greater role for JSRI against Simon's reluctance to create "new programs which would draw 'political' opposition."[29] This struggle between Simon's reticence toward Xicana/o studies and Rochin's advocacy came to center stage during the meeting mentioned above when Simon tells Rochin plainly that she "did not want JSRI to become a department."[30] This statement by Simon is important in that Rochin was advocating for the creation of a Xicana/o studies program with faculty lines that would lead to the creation of Xicana/o studies department within JSRI. Simon set clear boundaries for Xicana/o studies and Rochin at MSU by making sure the merger between the two did not take place. (Some believe she is carrying on her legacy of limiting ethnic studies today as MSU president).

Rochin was clearly attempting to capitalize on the promises made by McPherson in the spring of 1994 and the momentum created by the aggressive activism of the MEXA students and their white allies. In a letter written to then-President McPherson on March 2, 1994, concerning their understanding of an earlier meeting, student activists from MEXA wrote, "the University has agreed to create some type of program for

Chicano/Boricua studies within the year. Especially in the area of hiring the faculty responsible for implementing the curriculum."[31]

McPherson responded on March 29, 1994 with a two-page letter addressing the concerns raised by the MEXA students, noting,

> We support the establishment of an ethnic studies program that would include Chicano/Boricau (sic) courses…As to an exact time line, none was given, however, Provost Simon has indicated that it would take from 12-15 months before significant progress would be achieved. However, the Provost is prepared to immediately invest resources in partnership with the colleges and departments to achieve this goal. Such resources may include some additional faculty hires and faculty support to begin this curricular development.[32]

Less than a year later, Simon, told Rochin (who had clearly demonstrated his experience at UC Davis), "that the problem for the specialization was leadership; someone to assume the responsibility for developing the specialization."[33] She went on to "caution against approving high profile initiatives which were not developed through traditional processes."[34] This conversation certainly is in part a reference to the activism of MEXA and Xicana/o community activists.

By the fall of 1995, Vanderpool, Corey, and Rochin had accomplished a significant amount of work along with others[35] in establishing the feasibility of ethnic studies (in which, under their model, Chicano/Latino studies would be a component) at MSU. For unknown reasons Simon remained consistently against the idea of JSRI under Rochin's direction as the spearhead for the ethnic studies movement at MSU.

Later in the email, Rochin expresses his concern that the intent of his proposal will be altered radically. He again echoes his belief that "students of Raza need computer experience and a way to address issues of Hispanic communities through research and investigation."[36] His concern for students and the efforts they were putting forward at the time is also reflected in his earlier statement, "I am now wondering about the curriculum for Chicano/Latino students. They have made a plea for support and have gotten nowhere in terms of courses in the catalog."[37]

Even though it was clearly his intention to act aggressively to create an ethnic studies program or at least the Chicano/Latino component of it, Rochin received heavy criticism from the MSU MEXistas. After he released his first proposal in November of 1995, he received letters from MEXA student organizers questioning the direction of his proposal. In part, they wrote, "as we were not given a role in your formulation of a draft proposal for 'an Ethnic Studies Specialization' …we [MEXA Students] feel as if we need to create our own role as a resource in putting together this area of study."[38]

The three-page letter goes on to outline three major concerns on the part of the MEXistas and begins this by acknowledging the unique role Rochin occupied at MSU during those times they wrote, "It is obvious Michigan State University looks to you to represent the Chicano/Latino opinions and needs on campus. But since you are in fact representing student opinion we would like to bring your recommendations into line with student needs and concerns."[39]

Perhaps the most striking aspect of this letter is the tone. Unlike their correspondence with Anglo administrators, the MEXistas spoke openly of wanting to find a common ground with Rochin to promote Chicano/Latino studies. The students continued, "obviously we cannot force our requests in this letter be followed word for word, but we do expect you will consider them and will be willing to go over these with us…we feel this is the least you can do, as we obviously should have a voice in this issue and you have not promoted this thus far."[40]

Rochin responded, assuring the MEXA students his proposal was a "draft to begin discussion with faculty and students on campus."[41] He went on to tell the MEXistas that "[he] is serving as a coordinator for 'ethnic studies'…that the true responsibility for 'ethnic studies' is the faculty."[42] What is interesting about Rochin's continued insistence (through most of his documents, emails, and memos) upon centering the responsibility of creation on the faculty, is the statement in the draft about faculty at MSU up to that point: "JSRI…identified only one Latino professor who is teaching a specific course on Chicano/Latino status and culture, Professor Joseph B. Spielberg in Anthropology. While there are currently and literally a handful of Latino professors with tenure line academic appointments, the fact of the matter is that their courses are more mainstream and not of the genre referred to as ethnic studies."[43]

In fact, white faculty working on ethnic studies at MSU had also identified this very same lack of minority faculty as one of the major blocks to establishing any type of program. In an April 7, 1994, memo to Dean Corey, Larry Robbins of the anthropology department spelled out this dilemma: "I am especially concerned about this [development of ethnic studies] in relation to the composition of our faculty. We only have one minority faculty member, Professor Spielberg. We have never had an African American faculty member in anthropology...I think the addition of an African American, who is linked to the ethnic studies program...would be a very exciting development."

The development of a core faculty would remain a problem for Xicana/o/Latino studies until well into the first decade of the new century.

The continuing policy of the provost (now president) Lou Anna Simon to act as a gatekeeper not only toward Xicana/o studies and the students demanding these classes, but tenured Xicana/o faculty with legitimate academic requests for ethnic studies programs, exacerbated the deeply contradictory nature of the relationship between Xicana/o students, their allies, and the universities administration. This hard line position against Xicana/o studies on the part of the university moved the Xicana/o community to a different level in terms of their methods of resistance and how to express those ideas.

Hunger Strike/Brown Berets

The year 1996 at MSU and the greater Lansing area brought significant challenges and change. First, three men, two Mexicans and one African American, were killed by the police.[44] Additionally, a raid on a local community center resulted in hundreds of arrests.[45] Massive gentrification in the barrio of North Lansing and the reversal of the name of Chavez Avenue back to Grand Avenue was still fresh in everyone's mind.[46]

Feelings were running high and Xicana/os in Lansing were mad. On campus, multiple MEXA protests were successful beyond our wildest dreams. Under the direct tutelage of longtime activist Apaxu Maiz, the group was coming together as a tough cadre of organizer/activists dedicated to the idea of Xicana/o nationalism.[47] In the 1960s, Maiz had organized Brown Beret chapters around the state, with the exception of the Detroit chapter. He is the author of two self-published books *Xicana/o: An Autobiography* and *Looking for Aztlán*. The murder of Cipriano Torres Jr. in Lansing had a profound impact on the Chicano community and it was during this episode that many of us first became associated with Maiz. More than once, tactical disputes in the 1990s were settled with the statement "Apaxu says…" It seems impossible to overstate his importance to the Xicana/o student movement at MSU in the 1990s. He unquestionably served as the source of courage Xicana/o students needed in the beginning to confront first the university, then the police, and later the local political structure. His unwavering nationalism, activist experience, and ability to communicate his beliefs and experiences in a blunt yet sophisticated manner, along with what was being learned from white environmental activists, created a thriving combination of theory and practice.

In early 1996, we were looking for a way to bring attention back to the grape boycott. The idea for a hunger strike came from Mark Anthony Torres, who would later become the Tlatonai[48] for MEXA de MSU. In the beginning, the idea was met with some resistance and healthy skepticism. After much discussion, we began to research the feasibility. Two community members Fenis Ibanez and Rose Castilla (later members of the Brown Berets de Aztlán) did the initial research. We learned immediately that there is little written about hunger strikes. Most of the literature centered on the hunger strikes of Irish political prisoners protesting British prison conditions. Each of those individual hunger strikes ended in the death of the striker.[49] Through this research, we realized that we had more time than we originally thought to be on a hunger strike. Everyone was in reasonably good health and we figured we could go at least two weeks without any real damage. So it was decided among ourselves that Maria Zavala, Mark Anthony Torres, Daniel Soza III, Andres Guerrero, Matthew Martinez, and Jose Romero Jr., would drink only water for an indeterminate amount of time (privately agreed upon not to exceed two weeks) and in doing so follow in the non-violent traditions of Jesus, Gandhi, Tolstoy, Dr. King, and of course César Chávez.

The hunger strike began at dawn on February 13, 1996, with a sunrise ceremony honoring the four directions, a practice we would keep over the next seven days. The strike also coincided with President

McPherson's third state-of-the-university address.[50] It was a concerted attempt to redirect media attention away from him and toward the issue of the grape boycott. It was moderately successful and another example of how we were coming to understand the power of media in publicizing our political agenda.

The hunger strike lasted for seven days. At the end of those seven days, it became apparent to us that McPherson was not going to yield. We had to find a creative way to pressure the university into some type of compromise—mostly because we had been reckless and over-confident by making the fast an all-or-nothing proposition. We sent Mark Torres to the hospital.[51] Mark's father and mother were longtime activists with the United Auto Workers and had both endured the brutal conditions of the U.S. agricultural fields in their younger days. When McPherson called them about their son, they promptly told him they were behind Mark all the way. Mark returned from the hospital declaring his intention to stay the course.

The hunger strike brought the white progressive community out in force to support the fasting MEXista. This was our first glimpse of the intra-Latino campus rivalry that would become so crippling later, as many of the Xicana/o and Latina/o students stayed conspicuously absent from activities supporting the hunger strike. The main support staff behind the effort to keep the seven hunger strikers alive was a young couple, Amy Cairns[52] and Kimberly Hauze. Veterans of the peace and justice movement, they turned the Centro de la Raza in the basement of Wilson Hall into a fast headquarters, sending out press releases and maintaining schedules for everyone involved. To maintain the integrity of the fast, all of the strikers lived in El Centro and after classes returned there immediately, accompanied by a volunteer. During those seven days, none of student protesters were ever alone. The end of the hunger strike came quickly.

Two white students, Jason Wade and Peter Nitz, were scheduled to begin indefinite hunger strikes. When this became known the university was ready to make a deal. We did not get the grape boycott but we did get a mechanism for removing grapes from the dorms and we got "No Grapes Day" every March 31. It does not seem like a lot, and maybe for a week of going hungry it is not, however, the greatest victory came from the sense of purpose. Our personal determination to create change at

Movimiento Estudiantil Xicano De Aztlan hunger strikers (left to right) Daniel Soza III, Maria Zavala, Mark Anthony Torres, Matthew Martinez, Jose Romero, (not pictured, Andres Guerrero) hold a press conference in El Centro de la Raza located in the basement of Wilson Hall, MSU, to announce Torres' decision to continue the hunger strike after he returned from the hospital.

MSU was renewed and strengthened. The hunger strike ended the grape boycott movement at Michigan State University. From there forward Xicana/o students turned their attention exclusively to Xicana/o studies.

"IF WE CAN'T READ ABOUT OUR HISTORY THEN YOU CAN'T READ ABOUT YOURS"

Our next action, the book checkout, was the most dramatic of the three watershed events. The action was a combination of all the skills we had learned over the past eight years. The book checkout took the demand for Xicana/o studies from wishful thinking to serious consideration.

As a large research university, MSU has strict rules about privacy in research. Workers at the library do not have the right to ask your intentions concerning books or deny you a book. At that time, the number of books any student could check out during a semester was unlimited. The stage was set. MEXA members descended upon the library and started checking books out by the hundreds. The library staff was livid. They wanted us to stop. The director of the library stomped around huffing and puffing, demanding explanations, alternately threatening and cajoling but to no avail. Like other actions, it always amazed me when what

Detroit Brown Beret Joaquin Ramos, Tomas Soria, Jennifer Thompson-Torres, Rosa Salas, and David Khilji stand guard while MEXA speaker Marcelina Trevino-Savala delivers the initial statement to the press on the purpose of library action.

we had planned actually worked. Brown Berets from Detroit (of which I was a member at the time) came and provided security for the students checking out the books. Dr. Lee June, retired vice president of Student Affairs, walked by laughing. "Good one," he said as he whisked through. "Totally within the rules." June kept walking. We had won again.

The books were stacked on the floor in front of the checkout station in a rectangle about four feet tall, three feet wide, and fifteen feet long. It was mighty pile of books. Of the thirty or so students participating, we were divided into several groups. One group brought the books down from the stacks and piled them neatly on the floor. Another group took turns checking out books. Others then carried them out to the U-Haul we rented and the Brown Berets loaded them into the truck. All in all, we took over 5,000 books from the library that day and as we were shutting the door to the U-Haul, surrounded by panic-stricken librarians and dumbfounded news reporters, someone asked us the reasons behind our actions. "If we can't read about our history, then you cannot read about yours," responded Rosa Salas one of the Tlataonis for MSU MEXA.

This action was the last straw.[53] The next week we followed the book checkout action with "Operation Zero."[54] The library checkout idea belonged to Rudy Hernandez. He originally came up with the idea early in 1994 along with the "Operation Zero—We refuse to be used." In this action Xicano students would go to the registrar's office and officially change our ethnicity to white with the university's registrar. Since how you choose to identify yourself ethnically is a matter of personal choice and has no legal ramifications it stands to reason the only entity that benefitted from minority students was Michigan State. Since the university refused to make even the smallest concession in the form of Xicano studies, why should MSU benefit from the presence of students to boast about their diverse student body? Personally, I thought this was a beautiful idea and we tried to implement it with varying degrees of success. Like most good ideas I saw Operation Zero as smart and to the point. However, the drama of the book check overshadowed the foundational philosophy of non-compliance and divestment represented by Operation Zero.

In the midst of all this activity, Dr. Theresa Meléndez, a recent arrival from the University of Texas El Paso (UTEP), was working to successfully create the structure for the current Xicana/o studies undergraduate specialization. Dr. Meléndez, like Dr. Rochin, was a product of the turbulent struggles to create Xicana/o studies. Unlike Rochin, Dr. Meléndez had participated directly in student-led struggles at San Francisco State University and the University of San Diego as part of the Zapata Lumumba Collective.

We needed the break. Up to that point, none of the faculty at MSU had provided us the moral and personal support Meléndez brought to the struggle for Xicana/o studies. Rochin had done his part in pushing forward a version of this Xicana/o studies specialization, but in the end, he wanted his creation to dovetail into the ethnic studies program when it came to fruition. The internal documentation is very clear on this development—our Hispanic teaching faculty, with the exception of Rochin and Meléndez, had ignored the idea of ethnic studies. For some it may have been apathy, for others a disbelief in the likelihood of success and for many a desire to protect their careers. Like so many events in life, timing is paramount. We could have gone on forever and I am sure despite the promises and documents, MSU in the 1990s was counting on graduation to silence student voices, and continued inaction by present faculty.

There is no question Meléndez is the faculty hero of this story. She paid the price for her collaboration with MEXA rabble-rousers, as she was ultimately denied tenure. The MSU administration did not count on the fact she saw service to her community as the greater calling; they quickly learned the error of their ways. Meléndez simply would not back down and it was her resolve to continue that carried the day.

The new Xicana/o and Latina/o studies undergraduate specialization immediately grew to well over one hundred participants. By 1999 what we had been clamoring for had arrived, and just in time, because after eight years of struggle, morale was running low. Even the younger students who had participated in the early protests of the 1990's were graduating. Many had run a marathon and sacrificed a speedy undergraduate education for something most would never experience—enrollment in a Xicano studies program. The program began to grow administratively and more importantly as a fixture in the minds of the MSU Xicana/o/Latino community at MSU. The Xicana/o and Latina/o studies undergraduate specialization served an important purpose: There are those in our community who lack an ability to imagine success. It was impossible for them to see how we could create a Xicana/o studies program from the ground up. The responsibility of struggle is too much for most students, staff and faculty, but once it is there, and usually in the interests of their own careers, they become an integral part of its structure. Nothing co-opts a movement more than its own success.

CONCLUSION

Rudy Acuña writes in his decisive book on the state of Chicano studies, *Sometimes There is No Other Side: Chicanos and the Myth of Equality* (1998), "The threat of Chicano history is its political dimension," a dimension that could provide, when allowed or encouraged, an oppositional paradigm to white hegemony. Acuña reminds his readers that it is human nature "to participate in history." Xicana/os are and should be the creators of their history and the "acquisition of historical consciousness means learning the 'discipline of memory'…identifying your personal and community interests." Acuña warns, "A false collective memory facilitates subordination."[55] It is this call to intellectual action that characterizes Acuña's writing on Chicano studies and creates the context within which he situates the real purpose of the discipline. Drawing from Thomas Kuhn's *The Structure of Scientific Revolutions*, Acuña explains the necessity of understanding paradigms and their importance to the struggle for Xicana/o studies when he writes, "Kuhn...popularized 'paradigms,' the theory that in every field of study the established order sets structural guidelines that influenced the thinking and actions of its scientists and social scientists. The concept holds in this context, existing paradigms restrict the growth and expansion of the new and competing models."[56]

It is only through physical, social, or intellectual struggle that existing paradigms can be eradicated. Since struggle of any kind is not unique to any one group of people or scholars, it is safe to say identification with oppositional paradigms within Xicana/o studies is not generational but situational. The generation of the 1960s was not inherently more radical or challenging then subsequent generations. Examining the record of oppositional paradigm politics at MSU in the 1990s clearly bears this out. The choice both generations of students made to fight for Xicana/o studies was made based on their situation. Others chose a different path. Fanon discussed this internal conflict between colonized people when he wrote, "The last battle of the colonized against the colonizer will often be that of the colonized among themselves."[57] Certainly, the political crisis of a colonized people moving toward national liberation, while building political structures to facilitate that change, is the inevitable violent outcome of drawing borders and deciding on some level, who is in and who is out.

Fanon describes the phases of intellectual development native or colonized people must pass through before they arrive at the moment of national liberation:

> The first phase, the native intellectual gives proof that he has assimilated the culture of the occupying power...second phase we find the native is disturbed; he decides to remember what he is...Sometimes this literature of just-before-the-battle is dominated by humor and allegory; but often it is symptomatic of a period of distress and

difficulty…the third phase, which is called the fighting phase, the native having tried to lose himself in the people and with the people, will on the contrary shake the people.[58]

The portrayal of Xicana/os politically, in mass media, academic literature, grassroots activism, and intellectualism helps to shape our vision of our community and is becoming increasingly important as our community struggles and maneuvers itself through the minefield of decolonization. There is a growing understanding within the Xicanada that our goal is not to struggle with white Americans about reform or whether we belong in Anglo society as a part of a greater American multiculturalism, but facilitating an internal dialogue that awakens the people to their own destiny. This is the ultimate destiny of Xicana/o studies.

Xicana/o/Indigenous scholars working within a frame work of national resistance are clearly situated within the context of Fanon's work when he writes, "at the beginning the native intellectual used to produce his work to be read exclusively by the oppressor, whether with the intention of charming him or of denouncing him through ethnic or subjectivist means, now the native writer progressively takes on the habit of addressing his own people."[59] The Xicana/o and Indigenous scholars are once again "addressing" their own people, moving toward a period of intellectual development in opposition to their colonization that Fanon calls the "literature of combat, in the sense that it calls on the whole people to fight for their existence as a nation."[60]

Mainstream Chicana/o scholars continue to turn away from the reality of the Xicano nation by using liberation rhetoric strictly in terms of identity, literature, and literary criticism. The role of the intellectual and the nation in creating culture and resistance is important writes Fanon, "Because the nation by its manner of coming into being and in the terms of its existence exerts a fundamental influence over culture. A nation which is born of the peoples' concerted action and which embodies the real aspirations of the people while changing the state cannot exist save in the expression of exceptionally rich forms of culture."[61]

This is the core concept so many scholars fail to comprehend—nation and culture go hand in hand. They are dynamic processes that move the people toward their goal of liberation. The fate of our people, the struggle of our Meso-American Xicana/o nation is not summed up by the lives of a few men and women held up by this system as examples of individualistic attainment but by the collective actions and accomplishments of us all. I believe the true lessons students of color and Xicana/o communities can take away from this story are summed up in the words of Sun Tzu, the Chinese sage of war, "The art of war teaches us to rely not on the likelihood of the enemy not coming, but on our own readiness to receive him; not on the chance of his not attacking, but rather on the fact that we have made our position unassailable." All who undertake the creation or defense of a Xicana/o studies program would do well to remember his advice.

Notes

1. "Organic intellectual" is a term coined by Marxist writer Antonio Gramsci, who was imprisoned by Benito Mussolini. This person is an intellectual that develops from the working class (not a traditionally trained academic) who uses their ability to motivate and guide the working class in what Gramsci called the "war of positions," an ideological battle/war between the proletariat and the bourgeoisie.
2. Frantz Fanon, *The Wretched of the Earth* (New York: Grove Press, 1963), 238.
3. Taiaike Alfred, *Wasáse: Indigenous Pathways of Action and Freedom* (Toronto: University of Toronto Press, 2005), 29.
4. "It must be remembered the word MeXicana/o (meh-shee-cano) was given birth by the Spaniards in the 16th century in attempt to pronounce Mexicatl (me-shee-cottle). During this time period the letter X was pronounced with the *sh* or *ch* sound...it is becoming common practice to use the letter *x* to spell Chicano as Xicana/o. Very simply it stresses the historical and emotional connection to MeXicana/o and it *screams* of Indian pride and rebirth." Apaxu Maiz, *Xicano: An Autobiography* (East Lansing: Sun Dog Publishing, 1995), 52.
5. Traditionally Aztlán is defined as the Southwest United States.
6. Passed by California voters in 1994, Proposition 187 required public workers to turn in illegal or suspected illegal immigrants. Proposition 209, the California Civil Rights Initiative, was passed by California voters 1996. It amended the state constitution to prohibit state governmental institutions from considering race, sex, or ethnicity in the areas of public employment, public contracting, and public education, and was the first electoral test of affirmative action policies in the United States. *en.wikipedia.org.*
7. Robert Taber, *War of the Flea: The Classic Study of Guerilla Warfare,* (Lincoln, NE: Potomac Books, 2002).

8. E. L. Katzenbach Jr., "Time, Space and Will: The Politico-Military Views of Mao Tse Tung," in *The Guerilla and How to Fight Him* (Quantico: Marine Corp Gazette, 1962), 11–19. Katzenbach uses the word yield here as you would talk about a harvest—we planted four acres and it yielded three metric tons. Mao needed time and China is big, so he traded space for time—some people call it retreating. Mao retreated until he was ready and the time that was yielded allow him to increase will. This idea has become the basic formula for revolutionary warfare or what experts now are calling asymmetrical conflict.

9. Martin Luther King Jr., *Why We Can't Wait* (New York: Signet Classics, 2000).

10. C. Caguiat, G. Cornell, R. Gonzalez, J. Marinez, J. Figueira-McDonough, R. Navarro, L. Nelson, D. Rivera, J. Spielberg, (chair), M. Thullen, J. Dahomey, F. Kaptizke, *Report of the Task Force on the Hispanic American Institute*, Michigan State University, 1988.

11. Ibid.

12. Ibid.

13. Ibid.

14. Ibid.

15. The Julian Samora Research Institute (JSRI) is committed to the generation, transmission, and application of knowledge to serve the needs of Latino communities in the Midwest. The Institute has current research/outreach initiatives targeting the needs of the Hispanic community in the areas of economic development, education, and families and neighborhoods. A database is also being developed to serve as a resource on and for Hispanics. JSRI has organized a number of publication initiatives to facilitate the timely dissemination of current research and information relevant to Latinos. See jsri.msu.edu

16. Cipriano Torres Jr. was shot dead by three Lansing Police department officers in the parking lot of the Motel Six on the corner of Washington and Business Loop 496.

17. By the end of 1993 CHISPA had become Culturas de las Razas Unidas (CRU) partially in response to the creation of MEXA. This effort was spearheaded by Chris Delgado, a Puerto Rican student who worked diligently on advancing the Latino student agenda while he was at MSU.

18. Many years later after the second invasion of Iraq and the downfall of Saddam Hussein, McPherson would be called upon to provide the technical expertise in restructuring the economy of that shattered country.

19. J. Haake, "Hispanic Groups Ask for Representation," *The State News* (Michigan State University), January, 31, 1994, 3.

20. J. Haake, "Chicanos Deliver Grapes, Demands," *The State News* (MSU), February 11, 1994: 1.

21. To see parts of this meeting on YouTube, search "MEXA 1994 Grape Boycott." The video created by MSU students Maria Zavala, Robert Patino, and Francisco 'Tenoch' Lopez, is in four parts.

22. Luis Garcia went on to become (and still is) the director of MSU's College Assistance Migrant Program. My own experience with Garcia is mixed. To illustrate the dynamic and controversial nature of Xicana/o politics in the 1990s at Michigan State University one story stands out. I was visiting Garcia in his office one day and he asked if there was something I wanted to tell him. He then told me a friend of his who worked for the Lansing Police Department had called to tip him off that I was being targeted as a drug dealer and that my house (which I shared with several other MEXistas) was going to be raided soon. He asked me point blank if I was selling drugs. I told him no. We continued our conversation and Garcia reassured me that he would call his friend in the police department and tell him I was not a drug dealer. Nevertheless, I should probably take it easy on the activism and lay low for a while, Garcia said. I was so freaked out by the whole thing I went and told my mentor, Apaxu Maiz. He told me not to worry about it and asked me if it was okay for him to talk to Garcia about this. A few days later, I stopped by Garcia's office again and discovered him and Apaxu sitting there; Apaxu had his boxing gloves in his coat pockets. Apaxu said, "We were just talking about you son, come in and sit down." Apaxu looked at Garcia and said to him, "Tell him what you just told me." Garcia balked but told me he had made up the whole thing about the police. He had never gotten a call and there was no one asking if I was a drug dealer. He tried to tell me how I had to understand that all this political activity was very dangerous and he just did not want to see me caught up in something. I learned from that and other incidents that no matter how hard authorities try to convince you of your own insignificance—they are watching.

23. Fanon.

24. Ibid.

25. Ibid.

26. Refugio I. Rochin, memo to Lou Anna Simon and Kenneth Corey, October 3, 1995.

27. Kenneth Corey, memo Lou Anna Simon; November 10, 1995.

28. Refugio I. Rochin, memo to Robert Aponte, Ken Corey, and Chris Vanderpool, November 13, 1995.

29. R. Rochin, 1995, personal communication,

30. Ibid.

31. Ernesto Todd Mireles, letter to M. Peter McPherson, March 2, 1994.

32. M. Peter McPherson, letter to Ernesto Todd Mireles, March 29, 1994.

33. Rochin, email to Aponte, Corey, and Vanderpool, 1995.

34. Ibid.

35. It would be a mistake to not mention the contributions of Professor Linda Jackson during the 1990s in preparing the groundwork for an ethnic studies specialization at MSU. She was the author of at least two reports, one from September 1994 titled "An Ethnic Studies Specialization at Michigan State

University: Criteria for Course Inclusion," and another to Dean Corey on April 1995 titled "Report on Discussion with the Faculty and Administrators about an Ethnic Studies specialization at MSU."

36. Rochin, email to Aponte, Corey, and Vanderpool, 1995.
37. Ibid.
38. Maria Zavala, letter to Refugio Rochin, 1995.
39. Ibid.
40. Ibid.
41. Rochin to Maria Zavala, December 11, 1995.
42. Ibid.
43. Refugio I. Rochin, Draft, Ethnic Studies Specialization Proposal, Michigan State University, 1995, 14.
44. The three men killed were Cipriano Torres, Jesse Tijerina (the uncle of Rose Castilla, a MEXA member and Brown Beret), and Rex Bell. Torres was shot to death by the Lansing police a few years earlier but the emotion surrounding what was seen as an "execution" was still fresh in the minds of the community.
45. Local officials claimed that Latin American Cultural Center director Juan Beltran was running a "Blind Pig." This was the first attempt by members of MEXA de MSU to organize in the Lansing community. There were 120 people arrested and with everyone requesting a trial by jury, the court system became so backlogged that the Ingham County prosecutors dismissed the charges for everyone but Beltran. He was found guilty and placed on probation.
46. Eleanor Templeton, "Vote May Rename Chavez Avenue," *The State News* (MSU), 1.
47. Xicana/o nationalism has long been the subject of intense debate within Xicana/o activist circles. The student activist at MSU would define Xicana/o nationalism as a belief in Xicana/os as a unique grouping of people with a common heritage and belief system. They did not believe that a land base was necessary for the creation of a national grouping. Examples of these stateless nationals are present here in the United States are the Amish and the Mormons. Their own twist reflecting the strong anarchist tendency present at the time was the term Anarcho-Nationalist, which was in use for a while during the late 1990s and early 2000s.
48. The Nahuatl word Tlataoni means "speaker." It was the title/honorific of the ruler of the Mexica.
49. The ten IRA hungers strikers who died in 1981 were Bobby Sands, Francis Hughes, Raymond McCreesh, Patsy O'Hara, Joe McDonnell, Martin Hurson, Kevin Lynch, Tom McElwee, Kieran Doherty, and Mickey Devine.
50. Heather Johnson and Rachel Perry, "McPherson Reviews Successes: Activists' Hunger Strike to Continue 'Until We Win,'" *The State News* (MSU), February 14, 1996, 1.

51. H. Johnson, "Fasting Hospitalizes One Activist, Spurs Protest," *The State News* (MSU), February 19, 1996, 1.

52. Cairns has spent years working in the peace and justice movement, specifically with the Michigan Peace Team, which trains individuals to be observers at demonstrations around the world. Cairns has worked with observers all over this continent and in middle of the Palestinian/Israeli conflict.

53. Mary Sell, "Protesters Check Out Books to Prove Point," *The State News* (MSU), February 19, 1999, 1.

54. Mary Sell, "Students Battle for a Full-Degree Program," *The State News* (MSU), February 25, 1999, 1.

55. Rodolfo Acuña, *Sometimes There is No Other Side: Essays on Truth and Objectivity* (Notre Dame: University of Notre Dame Press, 1998).

56. Ibid.

57. Fanon, *Wretched of the Earth.*

58. Ibid.

59. Ibid.

60. Ibid.

61. Ibid.

CHAPTER 5

El Movimiento in Washington State: Activism in the Yakima Valley and Puget Sound Regions

Oscar Rosales Castañeda

The Chicana/o movement in Washington State sought many of the same goals as the national Chicana/o movement of the 1960s and 1970s. Namely, the assertion that ethnic Mexicans and other Latinos were deserving of dignity, respect, and civil and human rights as a community. The Southwest has long had a history of social action and engagement by way of participation in mutual aid societies, labor unions, and political organizations that sought a greater voice for the community. What set the Chicana/o movement in Washington apart from the Southwest was that, given its geographic isolation on the northwest Pacific Coast of the United States, the movement appears to have evolved without local precedent, with many organizations of differing social and political ideologies developing simultaneously as activism mushroomed. Likewise, in contrast to the Midwest, the internal migration to Washington was a newer phenomenon and did not have as strong a presence until well after the end of World War II. In the absence of numerical critical mass, the movement relied upon a network of activist organizations from throughout the state to attain social justice for the ethnic Mexican community in rural eastern Washington and the urban Puget Sound region. This paper will argue that it is this symbiotic relationship between the regions, east-west, rural-urban, that allowed the movement to flourish and empower a socially and economically marginalized community to claim a voice in determining its own destiny.

In his analysis of the movement in Washington State, Jesus Lemos posited the broader discourse on the foundations of "La Causa" within the scope of activity in the Southwest.[1] "Throughout the entire United States, Chicanos are organizing to overcome the racial discrimination, economic exploitation, and political disenfranchisement that have victimized them for centuries. In some places, such as Southern Texas, the Movimiento was dominated to a large extent by the activities of La Raza Unida Party.[2] In other places, the Movimiento was dominated by other activities such as those of the Crusade for Justice in Denver, Colorado." Furthermore, he noted that in Eastern Washington activity revolved around local activity for farm workers' rights to a point where, to many participants, the drive for unionization was synonymous with the movement.[3] "To support the Movimiento is to support the effort of United Farm Workers Association (UFWA) and vice-versa."[4]

In addition to the eventual fusion of farm labor activism and El Movimiento, the early rumblings of a movement in Washington State came to the fore in the wake of the tumultuous 1960s, a time when many factors contributed to the opportunity structures (external conditions in place that empower collective action and influence the evolution of social movements) and critical mass that fomented the conditions necessary for said collective project in seeking social and economic parity. In Washington's Yakima Valley, justice for farm workers would come first in the form of federal "War on Poverty"[5] programs, as a means of bringing a voice to those on the margins of society. Likewise, the War on Poverty's Yakima Valley administrative entity, the Yakima Valley Council for Community Action (YVCCA), was instrumental in training Chicana/o leadership that would soon organize independently of the YVCCA and usher in the organizational framework of El Movimiento.

In her study of the War on Poverty's impact on subsequent organizational efforts within the Chicana/o community, Margaret Miller noted, "[t]he War on Poverty was joined by concurrent movements to effect social change. These included the Catholic *cursillo* movement, farm worker unionization, Brown Beret activities, and the reinvigoration of Chicano cultural pride as a more general result of the Chicano movement. This convergence of struggles lent a sense of urgency to Chicano participation in the Yakima Valley Council for Community Action. The period also proved to be fertile ground for the growth of a wide array of community-based organizations which survived even in the wake of the War on Poverty."[6] As Miller asserts, while the hierarchical administrative structure slowly began reaching the population most in need, a movement from below that sought equity emerged. Out of these efforts surfaced a collection of enthusiastic, committed activist-organizers who transferred their skills to employment with Office of Economic Opportunity (OEO) programs in the Yakima Valley.

Other arguments have contended that, in addition to the YVCCA, the Catholic *cursillo* movement[7] in the Yakima Valley preceded War on Poverty efforts. One organizer, Ricardo Garcia, even noted that *cursillo* activity existed around 1964–65, while others contend that *cursillismo* did not necessarily make an impact until 1967. Needless to say, the evolution of the *cursillo* in confluence with YVCCA activity provided activists the skills for furthering their efforts. The purpose of the *cursillo* itself was to engage participants in community action in a way that allowed for participation not only within the church, but also within the community at large, by stressing strength in unity and action to better the lives of others. At the peak of this activity, both with the *cursillo* and involvement within the YVCCA, organizers helped establish community centers throughout the valley to aid those who were most in need. Also by this time, the student movement was in full swing in many places across the country. In 1966, two students from Yakima Valley College (YVC), Guadalupe Gamboa and Tomas Villanueva, both of whom were employed by the YVCCA as young organizers, undertook a trip to California to meet the leadership of the United Farm Workers Organizing Committee (UFWOC).

Inspired by the UFWOC's grape boycott, Gamboa and Villanueva traveled to Delano at the invitation of a union organizer who had come to Washington in search of migrant workers involved with previous strike activity in 1966. Both Villanueva and Gamboa were profoundly influenced by this gathering in California, where they met with UFWOC leader César Chávez. Gamboa recalled: "It was pretty amazing the first time that we saw him. Actually, the thing that made the most impact on me was, well, in addition to César and his charisma, was the impact that he had obviously had on all the workers there...They stuck together. It was an incredible transformation, and it had a really lasting impact on me. It showed the possibilities of what could be done."[8]

UFW Co-Op, Mexican American Federation, and Community Activism

Upon returning to the Northwest, Gamboa and Villanueva continued community organizing work. Gamboa finished his coursework at YVC and transferred to the University of Washington. Meanwhile, Villanueva stayed in Central Washington and helped spearhead initiatives that included the eventual founding of a farm workers clinic in the Yakima Valley and the creation of the United Farm Workers Co-operative (UFWC) in Toppenish, Washington, which was modeled after some of the programs initiated by the early National Farm Workers Association (NFWA, a precursor to the UFWOC) in Delano.[9]

The UFWC is credited as being one of the first activist Chicano organizations in Washington State.[10] Founded amid several War on Poverty efforts in the valley, Tomas Villanueva recalled that the UFWC was "completely non-governmental...Everybody viewed the United Farm Workers Co-op and the United Farm Workers Service Center kind of as the counterpart of the UFW in California."[11] Villanueva also noted that the local John Birch Society was very strong, as was a group called Taxpayers of America, who opposed the farm worker center. Despite encountering resistance from politically right-wing members of the larger community, the UFW Co-op was instrumental in advocating for workers' rights, serving as a community center, facilitating Chicana/o student enrollment at the University of Washington (UW), and laying the groundwork for struggles around workers' rights, civil rights, and educational access.

Another prominent group that emerged from the town of Granger during this time was Northwest Rural Opportunities (NRO). An advocacy organization funded by the state, NRO was an entity that, though not having the same organizational dynamic as the UFW Co-op, nonetheless advocated for farm workers' rights. Primarily organized by Mexican Americans, the group's objectives were to provide access to social and health services to the migrant community, as well as granting migrants a voice in advocating for the betterment of social conditions as a whole. The NRO outlived the UFW Co-op as well as other entities and was instrumental in the eventual founding of Radio KDNA (one of the first non-commercial Spanish-language radio stations) in 1979. NRO would continue much of its work until the organization's demise in the early 1980s.

Another organization that emerged with the UFW Co-op in 1967 was the Mexican American Federation (MAF),[12] which represented a new direction in Mexican-American community organizing. In previous decades, most associations were social and cultural in nature. MAF was one of the first groups to advocate for community development and political empowerment in the Yakima Valley. The organization established chapters in many areas with significant ethnic Mexican populations throughout the state. Historian Jerry García noted, "The initial organization of the MAF was divided into five areas: Puget Sound, Moses Lake, Tri-Cities, Bellingham-Lynden, and the Yakima Valley."[13] However, by 1970, after El Año del Mexicano, a project that sought political development for the Chicana/o community, MAF overextended its resources, and with organizers moving on to other projects, MAF eventually dissolved, and its core was soon restructured into the Washington State Commission on Mexican American Affairs in 1971. It was these two organizations—the UFW Co-op and the MAF—that invited the Washington State chapter of the American Civil Liberties Union, based out of Seattle, to initiate a legal assistance program.[14]

ACLU Summer Project of 1968

Recognizing the need for legal representation for farm workers and their families, the UFW Co-op called upon the American Civil Liberties Union to organize a legal assistance program in the Yakima Valley in the summer of 1968.

Charles Ehlert, author of the program report, noted that in "the cycle of poverty in which farm workers and their children are locked... governmental neglect and discrimination are both causes and effects of one another, and operate to continue the cyclical blight of poverty in their lives." The UFW Co-op brought in the ACLU, in Ehlert's words, because, "farm workers [were] not able to obtain justice and decent lives for themselves and their children through the normal political process."[15]

ACLU staff attorney Michael Rosen organized the program with borrowed typewriters, law books loaned from the University of Washington Law School, and a house in Toppenish loaned from St. Ignatius Church. He enlisted the aid of five law students—Jim Marsten, Gerry Bopp, John Goodall, Nick Mathias, and Tom Chambers. As a result of various lawsuits filed through the ACLU, Yakima County was forced to take measures to ensure Chicanos were afforded equal voting rights through removal of the English literacy requirement, as well as other rights, such as fair wages and adequate housing, that had previously been out of the reach of this community.[16]

The report issued by the ACLU illustrated the importance of the work activists were undertaking. According to Ehlert, a United States Department of Agriculture study ranked the economic status of the rural population of Yakima County among the lowest two-fifths of rural populations of all counties in the United States, taking into account a composite of factors, including dependency rates, amount of income, length of schooling, and condition of housing. Yakima farm workers suffer from low wages, lack of job security, poor health, high mortality and injury rates, inadequate nutrition, education, and housing, discriminatory exclusion from the benefits of social welfare legislation enjoyed by others, and a lack of political power."[17] At this time, the situation for farm workers in the valley was dire as Yakima County reported 39 percent of the population living below the poverty level.[18]

In addition to lack of opportunities within the larger society, farm workers in the Yakima Valley also risked injury in performing job duties. "While the average life expectancy for a person in the United States is about 70 years [according to 1970 figures], a child born to a Chicano migrant family has a life expectancy of only 38 years. Death at time of birth among the migrant newborn is 36 percent; this due solely to the lack of medical attention during birth."[19]

The Chicana/o Youth Movement: Formation of UMAS and the UW Grape Boycott

The fall of 1968 was defined by social upheaval at the national and international levels.[20] Universities at this time were hubs for socio-political activity, providing the critical discourse needed for seismic shift in the larger society. Moreover, the year 1968 also witnessed the first large group of Chicano students to arrive at the University of Washington in Seattle. The new student presence at the UW owed a great deal to the Black Student Union's (BSU) militant efforts to promote campus access and diversity. On May 20, 1968, BSU members occupied the offices of University of Washington President Charles Odegaard.[21] The group organized a four-hour sit-in where they voiced their demands for making the university more relevant to people of color by improving the recruitment of minority students, doubling black enrollment, increasing funding for minority student programming, and creating black studies courses. The BSU laid the foundation for the recruitment of students from throughout the state, including Mexican Americans. According to Jeremy Simer,[22] "this connection between the BSU and Chicano students would later be strengthened by collaborative efforts on campus."[23] Of the thirty-five students recruited in 1968, most were from the Yakima Valley, the area with the largest concentration of ethnic Mexicans in Washington State.

Chicano students at the UW, few as they were, were inspired by activity on campus. They already possessed an understanding of the plight of farm workers as well as of the perceived repressive, race-prejudiced apparatus.[24] Soon after setting foot on the UW campus, thirty-five Chicano students, led by Jose Correa, Antonio Salazar, Eron Maltos, Jesus Lemos, Erasmo Gamboa, and Eloy Apodaca, among many others, formed the first chapter of the United Mexican American Students (UMAS) in the Northwest. Modeled after the group that was founded at the University of Southern California in 1967 as well as the UW Black Student Union, UMAS at UW worked to establish a Mexican American studies class through the College of Arts and Sciences.

In addition, UMAS took the lead in a campaign to halt the sale of non-union table grapes at the University of Washington. Working alongside other activist organizations such as the BSU, Students for a Democratic Society (SDS), members of the Associated Students of the University of Washington's Board of Control, the Young Socialist Alliance, Black and White Concern, and the Student Assembly (precursor to the ASUW Student Senate), the coalition first petitioned the dormitories to stop selling grapes in their eating facilities, and quickly secured an agreement. But efforts to persuade the Husky Union Building (HUB) to cooperate proved more challenging.[25] Nevertheless, after a protracted struggle against the HUB, conservatives, and the UW Young Republicans, on February 17, 1969 the UW Grape Boycott Committee[26] was victorious as the HUB officially stopped selling grapes.[27]

The victory made the University of Washington one of the first campuses in the United States to remove grapes entirely from its eating facilities. Even more notable was the organization's skill at building coalitions among other undergraduate groups,[28] especially the Black Student Union. As the *University of Washington Daily* reported, "UMAS ha[d] the full support of the BSU." According to the *Daily*, the alliance was tangible as BSU allowed a representative from UMAS in their meetings and UMAS reciprocated the courtesy by inviting three BSU officers to attend a UMAS conference in Toppenish. As the paper reported, "The two groups give each other mutual help—time, effort, funds and active support."[29] The alliance would be instrumental in the evolution and development of Chicana/o student organizing on campus and would foster further activist collaboration in later years. At the national level, the grape boycott organized by the UFWOC achieved success in 1970 when the union finally won a contract, ending a five-year strike in Delano.

THE YOUTH MOVEMENT SPREADS THROUGHOUT WASHINGTON

In addition to the grape boycott and the push for Chicano studies, UMAS also called a conference in Toppenish in December of 1968 to encourage the creation of Chicano youth groups at the high school and college levels. Likewise, with the assistance of UW faculty, UMAS created in Granger in 1969, La Escuelita (The Little School), a Chicano cultural center, which in turn led to the creation of the *calmecac* project, a program that taught history and culture to Chicano youth in Eastern Washington.[30] Through this early stage, access to education and a resurgent pride in culture were imperative for the creation of an oppositional consciousness to combat racism, institutional neglect, and other adverse conditions in Washington State.

The student movement soon spread to other campuses across the entire state. Following the example of UMAS, Chicana/o students organized at Yakima Valley College to form a chapter of the Mexican American Student Association (MASA) in 1969. MASA, like UMAS, had its roots in southern California, originating out of East Los Angeles College. Later in 1969, Chicana/o students who made their way to Washington State University via the High School Equivalency Program (HEP), organized another MASA chapter at WSU Pullman.[31]

In 1969 the Chicana/o student movement reached a new apex, with activity at a fever pitch. Chicano youth took to the streets, accessed colleges for the first time in significant numbers and gravitated toward a more militant Chicana/o ethos. The Chicano Youth Liberation Conference, hosted by Rodolfo "Corky" Gonzalez's Crusade for Justice in Denver, Colorado, set the framework for a youth-initiated Chicano Power movement. The conference produced one of the key documents of the period, El Plan Espiritual de Aztlán, which rejected the earlier stance of moderate, assimilationist Mexican-American organizations and instead advocated a separate, third political space, away from both the political mainstream and the white-dominated student Left, which initially ignored the concerns of students of color. The conference also urged cultural regeneration, the rejection of assimilation into the dominant society, and called for Chicano self-determination. This emphasis on cultural nationalism would be a critical early facet of the movement, before broader implications of activism *sin fronteras* (without borders) and Marxist-Leninist leaning Chicana/o groups transformed the Movimiento discourse in later years.[32]

THE EVOLUTION INTO MOVIMIENTO ESTUDIANTIL CHICANO DE AZTLÁN (MEChA)

Beyond the immediate concern of wartime conscription of youth was the question of educational equity, with access to colleges and universities a key element in upward social mobility. As a result of these concerns, the Chicano Council on Higher Education (formed after the East Los Angeles high school walkouts of 1968)[33] organized a conference at the University of California at Santa Barbara.[34]

The conference's resulting document, El Plan de Santa Barbara, articulated a master plan for curriculum, services, and access to higher education in the Chicano community. It soon became the blueprint for the implementation of Chicano studies and Educational Opportunity Programs throughout the West Coast, including the University of Washington, and outlined the role of the university in community and social justice issues. Moreover, the conference transformed the way Chicana/o students organized themselves. The delegates agreed to merge the many student activist organizations[35] under the umbrella of El Movimiento Estudiantil Chicano de Aztlán (the Chicano Student Movement of Aztlán—MEChA). MEChA soon became the primary vehicle for Chicana/o student activism on campuses throughout the United States.[36]

In the fall of 1969, UW UMAS officially adopted the name MEChA de University of Washington.[37] This reflected a shift in consciousness with students rejecting the term "Mexican-American" in favor of the label "Chicano." Over the next two years, Yakima Valley College and Washington State University would follow suit. Throughout the 1970s, numerous MEChA chapters arose in Washington State, including groups at Columbia Basin College, Seattle Central Community College, Central Washington University, The Evergreen State College, Western Washington University, A.C. Davis High School in Yakima, and others. In April of 1972, students organized the first statewide MEChA Conference at Yakima Valley College. The conference resulted in the creation of a statewide board authorized to facilitate communication between all MEChA chapters in Washington about activities at the state level. Chicanos near the Spokane area waited until 1977 to organize at Eastern Washington University, and it wasn't until 1978 that the organization affiliated with MEChA.[38]

The Chicano movement focused considerable attention on educational issues, including access to higher education. The Vietnam War and the draft raised the stakes for young Chicanos. Because of the availability of student deferments, access to higher education often had literal life-or-death implications for Chicano youth who were at risk of being conscripted. Anti-war protest activity had wide reach across the nation, including Seattle. Former UW student activist Ricardo Martinez remembers the spontaneous demonstration that erupted the day after the Kent State shootings in May of 1970. "I was actually involved in the very first freeway march." During a demonstration on the UW campus, he remembers students yelling "let's take it to the freeway," as a mass student contingent slowly made its way to Interstate 5. "We took over the freeway. It must've been 10,000 people that marched, stopped all traffic, [and] marched down to the federal courthouse."[39] The Chicano anti-war demonstrations would reach their peak at the National Chicano Moratorium in Los Angeles, in August 1970, which attracted perhaps as many as 30,000 participants. The largely peaceful march would end with massive police repression, as Los Angeles County Sheriff Deputies made an arbitrary decision to disperse the crowd by shooting canisters of tear gas and wielding nightsticks to attack demonstrators who didn't clear out of Laguna Park. According to historian Lorena Oropeza, "For these participants, the tragedy of August 29, 1970, symbolized above all the repressive and brutal nature of American society, the unwillingness of the 'power structure' to countenance real change. Nevertheless, the moratorium was more than a lesson in defeat, a crystallization of injustice. Through the anti-war campaign, activists had organized one of the largest gatherings of Mexican-origin people in the history of the United States."[40]

The Brown Berets in Seattle and the Yakima Valley

Throughout the period, activism on campuses was mirrored by activism in the community, and the Brown Berets emerged as a key organization linking students to communities and to young people who were not enrolled in college. Brown Beret chapters formed in both Yakima and Seattle and by 1970 had attracted over two hundred members. Originally founded in California, the Brown Berets gave a new and refocused look to the movement in the late 1960s.[41]

The Brown Berets evolved from a Los Angeles-based youth group called the Young Citizens for Community Action (later the Young Chicanos for Community Action). The group had a more moderate, reformist orientation and participated with the Community Service Organization, which facilitated access to speakers and politicians who instructed the youth in the ways of practical political organizing. With the assistance of the Episcopal Church of the Epiphany in Lincoln Heights, the group also secured funding for a meeting space. Even with political backing, the YCCA clashed with local police over their constitutionally protected rights to peaceably assemble.

When police began harassing youth at a coffeehouse in East Los Angeles, Young Chicanos for Community Action responded by organizing protests at nearby sheriff stations. Young leaders such as David

Sanchez viewed harassment as symptomatic of the larger problem of police violence directed at the Chicano community and advocated a more militant stance. In January of 1968, the YCCA adopted a new image and uniform, becoming the Brown Berets. According to historian Ernesto Chavez, "Law enforcement abuses had transformed them from moderate reformers into visually distinctive and combative crusaders on behalf of justice for Chicanos."[42] By 1969, *La Causa*, the Brown Berets newspaper, reported that the Berets had approximately twenty-eight chapters throughout the West Coast and Midwest. Two of these chapters were in the state of Washington.[43]

SEATTLE CHAPTER: UW STUDENTS AND URBAN YOUTH

The Brown Beret organization in Washington State was comprised mostly of motivated, militant university students and youth from Seattle's Chicano community. Former Brown Beret Rogelio Riojas recalls that the Seattle chapter was a "group of men and women that wanted to work at the community level."[44] Much like the groups in Southern California, the UW Brown Berets donned their distinctive headgear and military fatigues as a symbolic statement that they were willing to go to war for their communities, bringing attention to the fight at home in the barrios against racial discrimination, poverty, and police brutality. The Brown Beret chapters sought to do this primarily through implementing programs dealing with food, housing, unemployment, and education. Following the lead of the Black Panther Party, they instituted breakfast programs and community clinics. However, as noted earlier, the fight against police violence and racial discrimination served as the key catalyst in the evolution of the group. The Brown Berets' uncompromising stance on these issues attracted Chicana/o youth to the organization. Referring to instances when the Brown Berets acted in defense of students being harassed or intimidated by bigoted peers, former student activist Pedro Acevez recalls, "I perceived them as a positive. [Sometimes] the muscle of the Brown Berets came in handy."[45]

The UW Brown Berets most likely originated in Granger, Washington, and drew members from throughout the Yakima Valley. The group was then transplanted to Seattle as students from Central Washington were recruited to the University of Washington in the late sixties and early seventies. According to Pedro Acevez, it was Carlos Treviño, Roberto Treviño's brother, and Luis Gamboa, who first "came up with this Brown Beret thing."[46]

The Brown Berets initiated or participated in a number of programs targeted at the specific needs of the local community. According to Jesus Lemos, "in the winter of 1970, the Seattle chapter organized a 'Food for Peace' drive to gather food, clothing and money in order to make and distribute Christmas baskets to Chicanas/os in the Yakima Valley who were in the most need."[47] The UW chapter engaged in other activities including the creation of a legal defense fund for Chicano activists and support of UFW activities such as the grape boycott. As Riojas recalls, "we were raising money for UFW, going to Olympia, and helping [in the] community."[48] The Brown Berets financed most activity through collection drives, and requesting funds from sympathetic staff and faculty at the university.[49]

In an article in the *Seattle Times*, members of the Brown Berets also articulated the reasoning behind their economic justice projects. "The Chicanos have left their children a heritage of poverty from the beginning...Now the Brown Berets (a nation-wide movement) are trying to do something about it," noted Armando Mendoza. Member Carlos Treviño added, "the Brown Berets on campus are trying to encourage Chicano youngsters to finish high school and to look toward college if they have the aptitude. They urge unionizing of farm workers, and they 'believe in César Chávez.' They believe also that Chicano children should have milk and toys and a bed to sleep in, just as your children do."[50]

THE YAKIMA VALLEY BROWN BERETS: CONTESTING THE POWER STRUCTURE

The Yakima Valley chapter, the first of the two major Brown Beret chapters to emerge in Washington State, had a profound impact on the collective consciousness of people in the valley. Their continued insistence on demanding that authorities treat ethnic Mexicans with respect proved their greatest asset. This non-student arm of the youth movement was part of the committee that invited César Chávez to the lower Yakima Valley in December of 1969, and even coordinated his security detail while he was in the area. According to Lemos, "In the early part of 1970 they organized a five-mile march to the welfare office in Yakima to protest the abuse of Chicanas/os who were often ridiculed and treated with great disrespect and insensitivity by the welfare authorities."[51]

The Yakima Brown Berets also played a supportive role in La Escuelita in Granger and were involved with other organizations in the El Año del Mexicano project of 1970, which sought an increased political role for Chicanas/os. It was perhaps the Brown Berets' participation in La Escuelita that led to the program's demise by way of lack of funding. According to historian Margaret Miller, *calmecac* participants felt a strong affinity with the struggles of El Movimiento and many were active in the UW Brown Beret chapter. Fears circulated that innocuous *calmecac* cultural heritage classes had been actually used as forums for militant Brown Beretism.[52]

Upon completion of the El Año del Mexicano project in December of 1970, La Escuelita was shuttered and, due to pressure from growers in the parish, St. Patrick's Church opted not to allow La Escuelita further use of the building. Rather, it opted to support the more conservative Sociedad Mutualista of Granger. Despite the setback, the Brown Berets were a force within El Movimiento that was visible at most major meetings and events, providing security and defending those who were discriminated against, often clashing with authorities.

On the other hand, confrontational tactics utilized by the group placed them at odds with many moderates within the Chicana/o community itself. In fact, by 1970 St. Patrick's Church forbade members from distributing flyers inside the building. Despite a strong yet brief presence, the Yakima Valley chapter of the Brown Berets had trouble maintaining consistent membership as numbers fluctuated and many activists left to help organize with the hop strikes in the lower Yakima Valley. The group became inactive a few weeks after the march on the welfare office in Yakima.[53]

LAS CHICANAS: DEMAND FOR EQUITABLE SPACE WITHIN THE STRUGGLE

Another key group that emerged in the early 1970s was a women's organization called Las Chicanas, which focused on women's issues within the Chicana/o/Latina/o community.[54] Composed primarily of students and staff at the University of Washington, the organization was born in

1970 out of the need to address issues pertinent to women, who struggled against both sexism and racism. The importance of the organization was a reflection of the gendered dynamics of most social movements of this time. At the national level, discord within the Brown Berets (especially the East Los Angeles chapter) was rooted not only in ideological rifts, but also in sexist practices. According to historian Dionne Espinoza, "Chicanas were, at the outset, incorporated into the general activities of the entire membership and they collaborated with men under the presumption of a collective project in the East Los Angeles chapter of the Brown Berets. The organization seemed initially to deploy a unique conjunction of consensus and paramilitary procedures; but when conjoined with cultural nationalism, sexist behavior, segregated practices, and external repression, the organization's project moved toward a single-minded militarism based on aggressive and violent masculinity."[55] As a result, many women in organizations formed autonomous collectives or developed caucuses within groups that would work at keeping organizations accountable to Chicana interests.[56] This dynamic played out as well in Seattle. As student activist Jesus Rodriguez mentions, "Las Chicanas got formed [in MEChA] because, you know, no offense to anyone, but we were pretty chauvinistic, we were machistas."[57]

In 1971 members of Las Chicanas walked out of the Coalition of University Organizations for Women's Rights to call attention to the issue of race, which was often secondary concern for the mainstream women's movement. They later joined the Campus Third World Women's Coalition. However, they eventually decided to meet separately and support other ethnic women's groups when needed. As noted in UW MEChA's newsletter, *La Chispa*, in 1972, Las Chicanas communicated, "In [breaking from Mainstream Feminism], we are not an extension of Women's Liberation. We work in our own way and strive to work by the side of our men in struggle."

This was a response to the conditions that Chicana activists encountered as they were actively organizing against multi-pronged discrimination that included sexism, racism, and classism. This was especially true as many members were also active in MEChA (founded at UW in 1968) as well as in the UW Brown Berets. Rodriguez also mentions, "the Brown Berets that we started…we had women too. *Y les gustaba tirar golpes* (And they liked to fight)." Former UW Brown Beret chair Rogelio Riojas also noted, "We were sexist. But that didn't take away from the women doing their thing. I mean the women were aggressive. They felt they were equal to anyone and they participated as strong as anyone I would say. They were more active than we were. They were really strong. Women were in a leadership role."[58]

Evolution of the Brown Berets in Washington State

On the whole, aside from a few posters, MEChA documents, and photographs, little is known about the Brown Berets in Seattle. According to former activist Adrian Moroles, "much of the Brown Beret activity had to do with [the] anti-Vietnam War movement. Moroles, who arrived in Seattle in 1972, mentions that there is little "in writing [about the Seattle Berets] because it was all informal and secretive type activity. I came in at the tail end after the war was just about over in 1972."[59]

As time progressed, the Seattle Brown Berets solidified as a subgroup under UW MEChA.[60] For the remainder of the group's existence, it was the wing of the Chicano student movement most closely rooted in the community.[61] The Brown Berets, among other groups, also tried to form a wing of the La Raza Unida Party (LRUP) in the state of Washington.[62] The party was an effort to unite Chicanos on both sides of the Cascade Mountains. Despite this effort, LRUP in Washington never grew past its embryonic stage and folded before taking roots in the community. In Seattle, the Brown Berets acted as the "muscle" during many of the demonstrations that MEChA undertook on the UW campus and, much like the Black Panthers, raised concern in conservative sectors of the white community. Along with Las Chicanas, the Brown Berets were also an integral part of the contingent that occupied the old Beacon Hill Elementary School in October of 1972 and demanded the creation of El Centro de la Raza.

El Centro de la Raza

The site of what is now El Centro de la Raza, the Beacon Hill school, sat abandoned by the Seattle school district for some time before the occupation of the building on October 12, 1972. At the time, many of the services provided to Seattle's Chicana/o/Latina/o community were scattered throughout the city. This decentralization made it difficult for many who sought after services to obtain them. The economic conditions at the turn of the decade did not favor many Seattleites. Congress withdrew subsidies for airplane production and the then Seattle-based Boeing Corporation, one of the largest employers in Washington State, laid off sixty-five thousand employees, approximately two-thirds of the total Boeing workforce. The layoffs in turn created an economic ripple effect as an estimated thirty-five thousand additional employees in support industries service jobs were left unemployed as well. According to noted Seattle historian Murray Morgan, "unemployment, low during the sixties, soared to more than 12 percent, double the national average."[63] The situation was so severe Morgan noted, that "a prominent Seattle banker publicly begged the Nixon administration 'to recognize the unique state of emergency and marshal the full resources of the Federal Government toward our recovery.'"[64]

The economic crunch of the early seventies saw many programs sent to the chopping block. The takeover of the Beacon Hill school was a response to the shuttering of the English as a Second Language program for the Chicana/o community at South Seattle Community College. Students and community members affected by the sudden closing of the program were instrumental in planning the takeover. Juan Jose Bocanegra, then a graduate student at the University of Washington, remembers, "we brought in Chicanos from the University of Washington…everyone just popped out of the cars and started walking toward the door…The press started showing at around 9:00."[65]

The effort was orchestrated with three main contingents that allowed for occupying the site while keeping lines of communication open to the community and the city. "We would have a team that would bring food and support, another group dealing with the cops, and another to deal with the city," recalls Bocanegra.[66] The takeover lasted into 1973 as negotiations continued with the Seattle City Council and the Seattle school district, all while demonstrators occupied the old Beacon Hill school and made do without running water or electricity. Ricardo Martinez, one of the UW students involved, recalls his experience: "I remember the first few nights we were there. It was cold! It was really cold, there was no heat, there was no power...The eventual takeover lasted months...We would come and go, and spell each other."[67]

The struggle for El Centro proved difficult. Although the campaign was spearheaded by the Latina/o community, solidarity and support from other communities of color and progressive white allies was instrumental in keeping up the fight with the Seattle City Council. At one point, activists occupied the Seattle City Council chambers in an effort to force city leaders to turn over the building. After a long, drawn-out process, the city of Seattle finally conceded and allowed the use of the property for the creation of El Centro de la Raza in 1973. As former Brown Beret Rogelio Riojas put it, "someone opened the door and we went in and never left."[68]

According to census figures from 1970, the "Spanish-speaking" population in the city of Seattle numbered approximately 10,835 (or 2.04 percent)[69] of Seattle's total population of 530,831.[70] At a time when there was no distinct Chicano "barrio" in Seattle, the creation of a center that housed many of the services that Chicanos lacked was welcomed. El Centro became not only a community center and meeting space, but also a civil rights organization that developed progressive coalitions with activist groups rooted in other ethnic communities, especially Native Americans. According to Ricardo Martinez, "The genesis" of the Beacon Hill takeover "was that the Native Americans had taken over the Daybreak center" at Fort Lawton.[71] These alliances would continue throughout the 1970s and be part of a larger, city-wide Third World coalition.[72]

Much of the social justice work done by El Centro is outlined in its mission statement, which includes "ensuring access to services and advocating on behalf of people regardless of race, color, creed, national origin, gender, level of income, age, ability and sexual orientation."[73] In later years, the organization was also involved in issues of labor, including solidarity with farm workers organizing in the state of Washington and supporting much of the work done in California by César Chávez, Dolores Huerta, and the United Farm Workers Union.

In addition, El Centro also had a bookstore called Libreria Resistencia, initially conceived by poet-activist Raul Salinas in 1973. It would soon develop into a primary outlet for Chicano/Latino literature in the Northwest. The bookstore also carried posters, literary journals, and popular magazines in Spanish, as well as community newspapers and records of traditional music. Another important component was the promotion of bilingual children's books and culturally relevant educational materials.[74] The Centro published a newsletter entitled, *Recobrando*, which as Tomás Ybarra-Frausto noted, "documents and analyzes worldwide peoples struggles and provides a forum to examine and comment on the local socio-political developments within the Chicano/Latino community. It also serves as an important conduit of aesthetic communication. Interspersed in its reportage are photographs, photomontages, and reproductions of socially engaged art of all sorts such as Chicano murals, graphic art from the Taller de Grafica Popular in Mexico, Resistance murals and art work from Chile and especially commissioned drawings and political cartoons."[75]

El Centro also worked in solidarity with international struggles, most notably in Central and South America. Roberto Maestas recalled there was an event El Centro hosted on behalf of earthquake victims in Managua that attracted numerous Nicaraguan exiles living in Seattle, many of whom had escaped the U.S.-backed Somoza family dictatorship.[76] This solidarity with the Central American community continued throughout the 1970s as El Centro helped maintain communication with the Sandinista Movement, which ultimately overthrew the Somoza dictatorship in 1979. In 1983 El Centro de la Raza sent a delegation and a crew from Seattle's KING-TV on a fact-finding mission to Nicaragua. The Sandinista government hosted the delegation for a week as the group talked to people in towns affected by attacks by CIA-backed counterrevolutionary groups.

The creation of El Centro de la Raza was the result of a community coming together to forge space for furthering causes of social justice for Latinos and Chicanos in Seattle.[77] El Centro represented one of the first major attempts in the Seattle area to create community institutions to better conditions for the people. When recalling the creation of the center, Ricardo Martinez remembers "how fun it was being together with a bunch of people doing something that [we] thought was the right thing to do for all the right reasons. [We] were hoping the end results would justify what [we] were doing."[78]

UFWOC and Hop Strikes in the Yakima Valley

The early 1970s brought renewed activity and set forth the modern incarnation of the farm worker movement in the region. By this time the conditions were present that allowed this movement to take hold. Civil rights activism, action taken through War on Poverty efforts, and the genesis of the Chicana/o youth movement in Washington, influenced this activity. Soon after, UFWOC organizers would help organize these efforts, despite working autonomously from the national office in California due to lack of resources. Wildcat strikes (strikes without union support) in the hop fields of the Yakima Valley in 1970 produced the first strike organizing committee, composed of activists Roberto and Carlos Treviño, and University of Washington law student Guadalupe Gamboa.

As Guadalupe Gamboa recalled,

> The first organizing efforts actually took place in the valley, [led by] a couple [of] students, Roberto Treviño and his brother, Carlos Treviño...The Treviños had gone down [to the Yakima Valley]. They were all students at that time at the University of Washington and had been involved in the grape boycott and had heard all about César Chávez. So when they went down, they were drinking and talking to some of their buddies, who were complaining that they were being paid very bad at this hop farm—it was in the fall—and that they were all planning to quit, so they said, "Well, instead of quitting, why don't you organize a strike like they did in California? Ask for better wages." In fact, that's what they did.[79]

As activity increased, "El Año del Mexicano turned its office into the strike headquarters and helped plot strategy for the walkout. Many Chicana/o activists came to help, including Lupe Gamboa, who left an internship at the state Attorney General's Office to become the strike's legal advisor."[80] The group first organized striking workers at Chief Hop ranches in the lower Yakima Valley. The first strike originated in Granger and soon reached the small town of Mabton. As Gamboa noted, "workers from other neighboring farms also came and asked for help, so then we sent organizers there and eventually the hop strike spread to about fourteen or fifteen different ranches. We caught the growers by surprise and they were in the middle of harvest, which has to be done right on time; otherwise the hops lose their value."[81]

Though farm workers overwhelmingly supported unionization (the vote among strikers was 105 in favor of and 3 against unionization), the growers only engaged the group in superficial bargaining and blackballed laborers the following season, refusing to hire many of those who were prominently involved in union activity. Despite this setback, the group was successful in raising the wages paid to workers. Strike activity in the hop fields and was organized around the United Farm Workers Co-op and Service Center because of the center's support for the grape boycott. On weekends, in addition to the strikes, there were hundreds of advocates supporting the César Chávez boycott surrounding the Safeway stores throughout the Yakima Valley. According to Tomas Villanueva,

> At those times we were right in the center of the civil rights movement. There were a lot of things happening, there were a lot of advocates[82]... I remember when the first strike took place, I was on my way to Oregon to visit my brother, whom I hadn't seen for a while and taking my family—we were going to take a couple of days off. I hadn't done it for a long time. But I happened to have left the phone number of where I was going and as soon as I arrived and I got out of the car, my sister-in-law said, "Hey Tomás, there's a phone call for you." I went and they told me, "We just went on strike and these people want you to be here to be with them."[83]

Villanueva stayed only a little while as an organizer. Guadalupe Gamboa, Roberto Treviño, and Carlos Treviño became the official organizers for the campaign. "I didn't want to become an official organizer, primarily because what I wanted to do was run the farm workers union locally and I knew that California was going through a lot of trouble with the agricultural industry and Brother Cesar—I knew his thinking was that he needed to do something in California before he would move to other states and I knew he would like to call if there is an organizer in Washington, He says, 'I need you in California,' or 'I need you in New York. You have to move out,' and I didn't want to do that."[84] Indeed, this was Gamboa's experience as he was sent out to Pennsylvania, Boston, and Canada, for several years. Though taking a step back to do things at the local level, Villanueva still strongly supported, working with them, and helping organize them, but not necessarily as an official organizer with the UFW. "Whatever I was going to do I wanted to do here in the State of Washington. Then in '74 I left. My dad (who is now deceased)—his health wasn't doing too well."[85]

With those strikes over, the union continued, mostly under the direction of Gamboa, and the Treviños, but after a while the effort died down. As Villanueva explained,

> A lot of that had to do with two things: one is that there were a lot of Mexican foremen that did not like the union and they gave the growers good advice on how to stop the union movement. They convinced growers that the best way to get rid of the union (1) was to raise the wages in general and (2) to treat the workers right, and they said that workers loved to have carnitas (barbecues outside) and beer, so it got customary for a little while that they would drink beer and eat carnitas on payday.[86] People started thinking, "We don't need a union. Why should we join a union while the farmers are becoming our friends? They're treating us right. They're even providing us free beer and free carnitas."

The strikes were largely effective at the initial stage because of strategic timing during harvest season, however, there were impediments that stunted organizational growth. According to Yolanda Alaniz and Megan Cornish, "Some ranches required no picketing and others gave in after a few days. But many owners attacked strikers with guns, dogs and fists; the owners preferred to risk their crops and their ranches rather than give in."[87] Also, more conservative Chicanas/os were chosen by farmers to form a company union called the Agricultural Working People's Committee (AWPC), as an "alternative" to the UFW. There were as many as twenty-two members of AWPC and most were labor contractors, foremen, or other supervisory personnel. Often times, "AWPC sent these 'farmworkers' to testify for anti-labor legislation at the state capitol. Supported by local news media, AWPC smeared UFW, accusing it of charging enormous dues and claiming that the jobs of local workers would be taken by Californians with more union seniority. The growers blacklisted UFW leaders and *huelguistas* (strikers). This forced some of the most militant workers to leave the area to find work elsewhere, and intimidated those who remained. The growers also required workers to sign no-strike pledges."[88]

Despite the challenges, the union continued its work, becoming very visible from1970 through 1972. Contributing to the movement's waning were the demands of the UFWOC, with organizers being recalled to California in the summer of 1972 to fight against anti-labor legislation known as Proposition 22. The mobilization to California and overall lack of resources slowed activity in the Yakima Valley. Gamboa was gone for most of the decade as were other organizers, leaving few to sustain local campaigns. As Villanueva recalled, "in my absence, Roberto Treviño stayed here and continued organizing, but, as I understand it, most of the efforts were directed at keeping the boycott going in Washington. It was the lettuce boycott, and then it turned into a grape and lettuce boycott, where they had to go and organize people to go and picket in front of the Safeway stores and in front of Lucky's and the stores that sold the lettuce and the grapes."[89]

Treviño helped maintain a constant UFW presence in the valley. However, because of the shifting emphasis from local activity to the struggle in California, much of the energy tapered off, leaving the movement in a nebulous state, especially as a resurgent social conservative element sought to reclaim power. El Movimiento, though temporarily dormant in the fields, continued elsewhere as institutions were created to consolidate the gains in the 1960s and 1970s. The birth of Radio KDNA was one such notable example. The station would prove instrumental as the union activity was reignited in the 1980s and demographics shifted, with more ethnic Mexicans arriving to Washington State.

El Movimiento: Legacy and Influence

The acute isolation for many Chicanos from other cultural urban centers in the Southwest made the interaction between University of Washington students and the Chicano community of Seattle critical to the process of community building. In fact, the UW Chicano student movement provided the impetus for new community institutions and a new era in the development of the arts and literature in Seattle and throughout the region. This energy would be spearheaded through the efforts of staff and faculty, as well as UW MEChA, the oldest student-initiated Chicano activist organization in the Pacific Northwest.

At the community level, former student activists saw the need to provide services that the community sorely lacked, and sparked the creation of Sea Mar[90] and Consejo Counseling and Referral [91] community health centers in 1978. The two centers initially served the Western Washington Latino community, expanding over time to other low-income communities throughout the state. Sea Mar emulated the farm worker's clinic in the Yakima Valley by offering holistic medical services, while Consejo focused primarily on mental health and chemical dependency. These institutions remain vital in providing access to health care for the Chicano and Latino immigrant communities.

In Seattle, the late 1970s saw the establishment of a chapter of the Center for Autonomous Social Action-Hermandad General de Trabajadores (CASA-HGT).[92] CASA-HGT, was originally founded in Los Angeles in 1968 by Soledad Alatorre and long-time organizer, Bert Corona. The group blended cultural nationalism with Marxist-Leninism, becoming the first Chicano Marxist organization organized by poor and working-class Chicanas/os. The organization started as a mutual aid association that then organized around ridding the local barrios of drugs trafficked in by criminal syndicates, as participants viewed the proliferation of drugs as a neocolonial project. The group also focused on reaching out to both citizen and undocumented immigrant workers. As the group developed, it began organizing workers under the banner *sin fronteras*, an ideology that led the organization toward coalitions with Mexican socialists and the Puerto Rican Socialist Party.

In Seattle, CASA-HGT had many of the same concerns as the Los Angeles chapter, as ethnic Mexicans were also harassed by Immigration and Naturalization Service (INS) authorities and were victims of racial profiling in wake of a wave of anti-immigrant policy. According to former member Ruben Rangel:

> We became affiliated with CASA-HGT and organized a study group under the guidance of Ramon Ramirez. It was a tumultuous time. We held rallies and pickets and sit-ins on many different issues.[93] We began to develop a more radical political perspective on the aims of the Chicano movement. It was a natural progression, for example, in choosing what films to show at a 5 de mayo event, that we began to include an internationalist view: linking our struggle to

the Cuban Revolution, the Young Lords and AIM (American Indian Movement)...It was a conscious decision to refer to ourselves as "Chicano-Mexicano people [sic]" and focusing more of our attention on immigrant rights. One example of this broadening perspective is played out in "Tortilla Curtain" where we examine Chicano prejudice against our own people based on immigration status. Often-times, we were preaching to the choir, in terms of Chicano pride, so our focus shifted to issues of political unity in the face of a common oppression.[94]

This turn toward a more internationalist ideology was a reflection of the changing demographics of the 1970s and was a response to a renewed anti-immigrant backlash. Many organizers came to the conclusion that local and federal agencies never bothered to make the distinction between ethnic Mexicans and Latinos who were citizens, permanent residents, or undocumented immigrants. As such, the simple fact that one "looked Mexican" was enough to make one suspect and worthy of interrogation.

At the national level, the harsh anti-immigrant policies brought forth by the Carter administration,[95] as well as the patrolling of the southern border by the Ku Klux Klan were endemic of a resurgence in conservatism, which prompted many Chicana/o activists to organize in opposition to right-wing nativist sentiment. The conservative backlash was one part "silent majority" revolt, and one part reaction to economic recession of the mid- to late-1970s. The adverse economic conditions made it fashionable to scapegoat groups that resided in the social and economic margins, as politicians used xenophobia to create a rift amongst workers who dreaded having their jobs "taken away" by "non-Americans." The decade witnessed the proliferation of groups advocating "English Only" and "Immigration Reform," such as the Federation for American Immigration Reform (FAIR) and similar organizations financed by conservative think tanks. California also passed legislation such as the Dixon Arnett Bill of 1971, which would sanction employers for hiring undocumented workers. This in turn gave some employers increased control over workers and made undocumented laborers more susceptible to abuses in the workplace. At the national level, proposed legislation called for employer sanctions, a national ID or "work permit" card, the strengthening of the Border Patrol and INS, and the possibility of reintroducing a "guest worker" program.

Resistance to these attacks galvanized a fledgling resistance movement, as the original incarnation of the Chicana/o movement reconfigured and reimagined itself to be more inclusive of the newest wave of ethnic Mexican migration from the south.

In the Yakima Valley the contributions of community activists resulted in the creation of Radio KDNA in 1979.[96] KDNA was the first radio station to dedicate its entire programming to the Spanish-speaking population of Eastern Washington. To this day, the station is nationally recognized for progressive programming that serves to educate people on various issues concerning health, labor, and culture. KDNA is a non-commercial, education-oriented public radio station. Rooted in rural central Washington, many of its listeners are farm workers in the valley, which is why the station describes itself as *la voz del campesino* or "the voice of the farmworker." Much like the organizations that were created in Seattle during the late 1970s, Radio KDNA has been instrumental in advocating for the rights of workers regardless of documented status.

Present-day activism in Washington State owes a great deal to the foundational work initiated by the Chicana/o movement. Many student activists later became seasoned organizers, lawyers, educators, professors, and professionals. Former student activist Santiago Juarez reflected upon his own experience:

> There were issues, and we came with issues. I came in as a grad student in 1971 [at that time we] were fighting for adequate services in the University. We would hang out in the valley, that's where the community was. We were trying to maintain a connection to the barrio...We saw a need and we had a talent. As we grew, we were able to understand the worker struggle. Our analysis became more profound. Borders were created for economic reasons. You have Chicanos working with...Salvadorenos, Nicaraguenses, the quality of organizing changed. No need for Bullshit nationalism. We wanted to understand the world in which we live. In the end we wanted a place where we can grow our people, help our people. Solidarity meant seeing a part of myself in others. As I see myself in you, my relationship to you, and desire to understand you develops.[97]

Notes

1. Jesus Lemos, "A History of the Chicano Political Involvement and the Organizational Efforts of the United Farm Workers Union in the Yakima Valley, Washington"(master's thesis, University of Washington, 1974), x.
2. La Raza Unida Party emerged out of Texas in 1970 and dominated the local elections in Crystal City, TX. The party came out as a direct response to institutional neglect within electoral politics by both the Democratic and Republican Parties.
3. Lemos further explained, "[the fact that] the Union would serve as the vanguard for the Movimiento in Eastern Washington c[ame] as no surprise to most Chicanos. There [was] no other viable alternative organization that [was able to be] used more effectively as a vehicle to make those changes necessary to achieve the social, economic and political equality of the Chicano in Eastern Washington." Lemos, x.
4. Lemos, x.
5. President Lyndon B. Johnson signed off on the "Economic Opportunity Act of 1964," effectively initiating the War on Poverty, and the Office of Economic Opportunity (OEO), whose aim was to alleviate the harsh conditions encountered by many populations that had been previously institutionally neglected. The organization of the Yakima Valley Council for Community Action (YVCCA) allowed for these programs to be administered in the Yakima Valley.
6. Margaret Miller, "Community Action and Reaction: Chicanos and the War on Poverty in the Yakima Valley, Washington," (master's thesis, University of Washington, 1991), 3.
7. As Miller wrote, "[t]he cursillo en cristianidad, translated as workshops in Christianity, sought to inspire Catholics to transform the tenets of Catholic teachings into participatory social action. Cursillistas, both men and women, would spend three intensive days of prayer, song and rededication." Miller, "Community Action and Reaction," 27.
8. Guadalupe Gamboa, interview with Anne O'Neill, April 9, 2003.
9. Lemos, 54.
10. For more on Chicano activism in the Yakima Valley during the 1960s, see Miller, "Community Action and Reaction."
11. Tomas Villanueva, interview with Anne O'Neill and Sharon Walker, April 11, 2003, and June 7, 2004.
12. In addition to MAF, other smaller groups were organized throughout the state. Although many were largely social organizations, one notable exception was the Progressive League of United Mexican Americans (PLUMA), which had chapters in Quincy, Moses Lake, Othello, and Warden.
13. Jerry García, *Mexicans in North Central Washington* (Charleston, SC: Arcadia Publishing, 2007), 90.

14. Consequently, 1968 would be significant as conservative elements in the Yakima Valley, including the Yakima County Commissioners, appropriated a significant part of the YVCCA, effectively neutralizing the entity's effectiveness in procuring rights for those most neglected by the traditional power structure which feverishly attempted to retain its control.

15. Charles E. Ehlert, *Report of the Yakima Valley Project* (Seattle, WA: American Civil Liberties Union, 1969).

16. Some of the lawsuits include: *Mexican American Federation-Washington State v. Naff* (class action brought against the Yakima County auditor that eventually removed the English literacy requirement for voting); *Gutierrez v. Riel* (action against a grower who didn't compensate workers fairly, and changed the way the 'bonus' system was used for paying laborers); and *Buttrey v. Housing Authority of Yakima County* (brought by workers living in a labor camp) among many others.

17. Ibid.

18. U.S. Bureau of the Census, *Census of Population: 1970 Vol 1 Characteristics of the Population, Part 49,* Washington, 322–23.

19. Lemos, 45.

20. See: Elena Poniatowska, *Massacre in Mexico,* trans. Helen R. Lane (Columbia, MO: University of Missouri Press, 1992); Kieran Williams, *The Prague Spring and its Aftermath: Czechoslovak Politics 1968–1970* (Cambridge: Cambridge University Press, 1997); Mark Kurlansky, *1968: The Year that Rocked the World* (New York: Random House, 2005); Kristin Ross, *May '68 and Its Afterlives* (Chicago: University of Chicago Press, 2002); W. J. Rorabaugh, *Berkeley at War: The 1960s* (Oxford: Oxford University Press, 1989); Todd Gitlin, *The Sixties: Years of Hope, Days of Rage* (New York: Bantam Books, 1987).

21. Walt Crowley, *Rites of Passage: A Memoir of the Sixties in Seattle* (Seattle: University of Washington Press, 1995), 255.

22. Simer's work on the formation of UMAS and the formalization of the grape boycott coalition at the University of Washington are, to date, the most comprehensive work done around early Chicano student activism in Seattle.

23. Jeremy Simer, "La Raza Comes to Campus: The New Chicano Contingent and the Grape Boycott at the University of Washington, 1968–69," Seattle Civil Rights & Labor History Project, University of Washington, 2004–2006. depts.washington.edu/civilr/la_raza2.htm.

24. For an analysis of the conditions faced by Chicanos in the Yakima Valley, see: Ehlert, *Report of the Yakima Valley Project.*

25. John Greely, "Hub Board Recommends Stoppage of Grape Sales," *University of Washington Daily,* February 6, 1969, 1.

26. According to Jeremy Simer, on Wednesday, January 29, 1969, students formed a formal grape boycott coalition and a steering committee was chosen from representatives from UMAS, SDS, BSU, YSA, Black and White Concern (BWC), the Student Assembly (precursor to the ASUW Student Senate), members of the

ASUW Board of Control, and the University YMCA Boycott Committee. Simer also notes that Erasmo Gamboa (now a UW professor) was appointed chair of the committee.

27. Simer, "La Raza Comes to Campus."

28. Ibid.

29. "Mexican-Americans Tell Opposition to Grapes," *UW Daily,* January 21, 1969.

30. Lemos, 56–58. According to Margaret Miller, "One of the most controversial federally-funded programs was La Escuelita, or the Little School, a Chicano cultural center. La Escuelita grew out of the efforts of a group of Chicano students at the University of Washington who envisioned a center to reaffirm Chicano cultural pride through a variety of activities. An abandoned building in Granger owned by St. Patrick's Church was donated for La Escuelita and renovated by UW students, community members, For Simcoe Job Corpsmen, and American Friends Service Committee volunteers in August 1969." Miller, "Community Action and Reaction," 81.

31. Gilberto García, "Organizational Activity and Political Empowerment: Chicano Politics in the Pacific Northwest,"in *The Chicano Experience in the Northwest*, eds. Carlos Maldonado and Gilberto García (Dubuque, IA: Kendall/Hunt Publishing Co., 1995), 75–80.

32. According to George Mariscal, "[a]lthough still embedded in a capitalist framework, Third World and even cultural nationalist agendas in the United States promoted what Samir Amin has called a 'social and national' vision that placed the rights and demands of working-class and racialized people at the forefront of political change." See George Mariscal, *Brown Eyed Children of the Sun: Lessons from the Chicano Movement, 1965–1975* (Albuquerque, NM: University of New Mexico Press, 2005).

33. Lorena Oropeza, *Raza Si! Guerra No! Chicano Protest and Patriotism during the Viet Nam War* (Berkeley: University of California Press, 2005), 185.

34. On March 3, 1968, more than 1,000 students aided by members of UMAS and the Brown Berets, peacefully walked out of Abraham Lincoln High School in East Los Angeles, with teacher Sal Castro joining the students in protest of school conditions. The student strike, known as the L.A. Blowouts, would result in over 10,000 high school students walking out by the end of the week. To this day, the event remains one of the largest student strikes at the high school level in the history of the United States.

35. Present at the Santa Barbara conference were the United Mexican American Students (UMAS), the Mexican American Student Association (MASA), the Mexican American Student Organization (MASO), the Mexican American Student Confederation (MASC), and the Mexican American Youth Organization (MAYO), among other organizations.

36. MEChA Chapters formed across the southwest, the north (Washington, Illinois, Michigan, Minnesota, Oregon, etc.), and the east (especially as Chicano students were recruited to Ivy League schools).

37. The original umbrella organization for the UW Chicana/o population and presiding over entities like the UW Brown Berets, Las Chicanas, Chicano Graduate and Professional Students, National Chicano Health Organization, and others. MEChA also helped generate an incredible wealth of cultural work. Notable examples include: El Teatro del Piojo and Teatro Quetzalcoatl; Chicano Calmecac and La Escuelita in Granger, WA; Los Bailadores de Bronze; the UW Centro de Estudios Chicanos, and the journal, *Metamorfosis*. At the community level, the group was also instrumental in hosting Christmas Posadas, poetry readings, Cinco de Mayo Celebrations, "Semana de La Raza," film series' and many others. See "La Historia de MEChA," Internal Document for MEChA Executive Board, 1987, MEChA de UW Archives.

38. García, "Organizational Activity," 75–80.

39. Ricardo Martinez, interview by Oscar Rosales and Edgar Flores, Seattle Civil Rights & Labor History Project, February 8, 2006.

40. Oropeza, 185.

41. Ernesto Chavez, *"Mi Raza Primero!" Nationalism, Identity and Insurgency in the Chicano Movement* (Berkeley, CA: University of California Press, 2002), 44.

42. Chavez, *"Mi Raza Primero!,"* 45.

43. According to Ernesto Chavez' notes, in May 1969 the Beret newspaper *La Causa* reported that the organization had twenty-eight chapters in cities including San Antonio, Eugene, Denver, Detroit, Seattle, and Albuquerque, along with many cities in California (*La Causa*, May 23, 1969); Chavez, 132.

44. Rogelio Riojas, interview, Seattle Civil Rights & Labor History Project, January 19, 2006.

45. Pedro Acevez, interview by Edgar Flores and Oscar Rosales, Seattle Civil Rights & Labor History Project, January 27, 2006.

46. Ibid.

47. Lemos, 57.

48. Riojas interview.

49. Ibid.

50. Don Duncan, "Chicanos 'Make It' to College." *Seattle Times*, November 11, 1970, C16.

51. Lemos, 58.

52. Miller, 81-82.

53. The Brown Beret chapter in the Yakima Valley became inactive in 1970 after a key leader lost credibility in the Chicano community. Despite severing ties to the former leader, the group was unable to regain the community's trust. Lemos, 61.

54. MEChA Newsletter, University of Washington, 1981; *La Chispa,* MEChA newsletter, University of Washington, 1972; Jesus Rodriguez Papers, MEChA de UW Archives.

55. Dionne Espinoza, "Revolutionary Sisters: Women's Solidarity and Collective Identification among Chicana Brown Berets in East Los Angeles," in *Aztlán: A*

Journal of Chicano Studies 26, no. 1 (UCLA Chicano Studies Research Center Press, 2001).

56. Ibid.
57. Jesus Rodriguez, interview by Roberto Alvizo and Cristal Barragan, Seattle Civil Rights & Labor History Project, March 3, 2006.
58. Riojas interview.
59. Adrian Moroles, email communication with author, March 14, 2007.
60. MEChA Newsletter, University of Washington, 1981; *La Chispa,* MEChA newsletter, University of Washington, 1972; Jesus Rodriguez Papers, MEChA de UW Archives.
61. It was later revealed that the Brown Berets were infiltrated and destroyed from within by the COINTELPRO program. The group ceased to exist as a national organization when former founder David Sanchez disbanded the group in 1972. Several chapters continued to exist autonomously to the present day.
62. Rodriguez interview.
63. Murray Morgan, *Skid Road: An Informal Portrait of Seattle* (Seattle, WA: University of Washington Press, 1982), 275.
64. Morgan, 276.
65. Juan Jose Bocanegra, interview by Chris Paredes, Cristal Barragan, and Trevor Griffey, Seattle Civil Rights & Labor History Project, February 2, 2006.
66. Bocanegra interview.
67. Martinez interview.
68. Riojas interview.
69. U.S. Bureau of the Census, Census of Population: 1970 Vol 1 Characteristics of the Population, Part 49, Washington, 231.
70. U.S. Bureau of the Census, Census of Population: 1970 Vol 1 Characteristics of the Population, Part 49, Washington, 40.
71. Martinez interview.
72. For a more detailed examination of Third World coalitions and leftist activism in Seattle, see Alan Aladio Gomez, "'From Below and to the Left': Re-imagining the Chicano Movement through Circulation of Third World Struggles, 1970–1979" (PhD diss., University of Texas at Austin, 2006).
73. For additional information see El Centro de La Raza's website, www.elcentro delaraza.org.
74. Tomás Ybarra-Frausto, "Abriendo Surcos: Chicano Cultural Expression in the Pacific Northwest: A Socio-Aesthetic Chronology (1965-1982) [unpublished manuscript] Box 2, Folder 4, Tomás Ybarra-Frausto Papers, Accession No. 4339-001, University of Washington Libraries.
75. Ibid.
76. Roberto Maestas, interview by Trevor Griffey, Seattle Civil Rights & Labor History Project, February 22, 2005.
77. www.elcentrodelaraza.org
78. Martinez interview.

79. Guadelupe Gamboa interview.
80. Yolanda Alaniz and Megan Cornish, *Viva La Raza: A History of Chicano Identity & Resistance* (Seattle, WA: Red Letter Press, 2008), 298.
81. Gamboa interview.
82. As Villanueva noted, "Back then we managed to get the governor of the state of Washington, Daniel J. Evans, to appoint the first Mexican-American Commission, actually Committee, which later became the Mexican-American Commission and now is the Commission on Hispanic Affairs. It was also very controversial and I thought it was a very good commission when it started, and it was later changed. That's when the Commission all got started, and there was a lot of action in those times." Villanueva interview.
83. Villanueva interview.
84. Ibid.
85. Ibid.
86. Ibid.
87. Alaniz and Cornish, 299.
88. Ibid., 303.
89. Gamboa interview.
90. According to educator and community activist, Adrian Moroles, the name of the health center comes from the contraction of "Seattle and Marysville" which were the original proposed sites for the community clinic. For additional information see: Sea Mar Community Health Centers, www.seamar.org.
91. Consejo Counseling and Referral Services, www.consejo-wa.org/Anniversary.htm.
92. The student wing comprised of a group of students from Los Angeles and Orange County formed El Comite Estudiantil del Pueblo. The group, made up primarily of Chicano Marxists, sought "anti-imperialist solidarity with national and international student struggles, university reform, self-determination against the 'imperial system,' and student-worker unity." The group would later merge with CASA-HGT. The organization would reach all throughout the West Coast, with chapters as far away as Chicago, and as far north as Seattle. Also see Rodolfo Acuña, *Occupied America: A History of Chicanos*, 5th ed. (New York: Pearson Longman, 2004), 353.
93. Ruben Rangel, email communication with author, May 25, 2014.
94. Ruben Rangel, email communication with author, June 17, 2014.
95. Acuña, *Occupied America*, 354-57.
96. Radio KDNA online, www.kdna.org.
97. Santiago Juarez, phone interview with author, June 2, 2014.

CHAPTER 6

Stories of Remembrance and Resistance: María Alanís Ruiz, Chicana Activism, and the Chicano Movement

Norma L. Cárdenas

The Chicano movement is a significant, but often overlooked moment in Oregon history. It is important not only to write the history of the Chicano movement in the Oregon context, but also to write the "Chicana moment" and Chicanas into that history. Bringing Chicana feminism and oral history methods to bear on the Chicano movement challenges the dominant historical discourse that has been delimited by the U.S. Southwest paradigm and decenters its masculinist ideologies. This transnational feminist archival project adds to the growing scholarship on Chicana activist historiography by "retrofitting" the historical record with new perspectives on the development of Chicana feminism in the Chicana/o movement in Oregon. Inspired by Maylei Blackwell's (2011) groundbreaking book, *¡Chicana Power!: Contested Histories of Feminism in the Chicano Movement,* I focus on the rich life history of a Chicana activist in the Chicana/o movement. My aim is to fill the gaps in the masculine hegemonic narratives with a repertoire of remembrance of Chicana political subjectivity and feminist consciousness in *el movimiento* in the context of Oregon. Heeding calls by Vicki Ruiz and Antonia Castañeda for a regional focus means taking a transnational approach to identity formation across local, regional, national, and transnational borders.

Chicanas are often forgotten and excluded in the national historiography, and more so in regional Pacific Northwest history, but are not silent. Scholarship focusing on the Chicana experience in the Pacific Northwest is limited to Yolanda Alaniz and Megan Cornish's (2008) *Viva la Raza*; Elizabeth Salas' (2008) chapter on Chicana *politicas* in Washington State and Latinas in the Pacific Northwest (2006); Lynn Stephen's (2007) work on Mexican immigration and settlement in Oregon; Jerry García's (2003) chapter on Dora Sánchez Treviño and her civic participation in Quincy, Washington; Joanne B. Mulcahy's (2010) book on Eva Castellanoz and *curanderismo* (traditional healing) in Nyssa, Oregon; and Isabel Valle's (1994) *Fields of Toil: A Migrant Family's Journey*, about a year in the life of a migrant family in Walla Walla, Washington. Other treatments of the region's Chicano experience, such as Erasmo Gamboa's (1995) *El Movimiento: Oregon's Mexican-American Civil Rights Movement* and Glenn Anthony May's (2011) *Sonny Montes and Mexican American Activism*, erase Chicana activism during an especially momentous period.

The larger study from which this chapter is drawn focuses on the life history of María Luisa Alanís Ruiz, whose work in the Chicano/a community has left an indelible legacy on the Pacific Northwest. Her contributions to the Chicano/a community include her activism in the farm worker and student movements during the Chicano movement, her work at the Colegio César Chávez, and her co-founding of the Chicano/Latino studies program at Portland State University (PSU), as well as the Portland Guadalajara Sister City Association. This project is truly a collaboration between María and me—a process of shared authority and interest in a narrative in which realities, subjectivities, and identities are co-produced.

As a methodology, I have been collecting oral histories from María since early 2012. She is a repository of historical memory. When prompted with a question, María would narrate her story without stopping, except to ask, "Did I tell you about?" or say, "I have to tell you another story." Comfortably switching between English and Spanish, María would continue offering minute and riveting details. Adding to the archive, I employed ethnographic methods and archival sources such as the Colegio César Chávez and the Valley Migrant League collections as well as newspapers that reveal multiple and contested significations of place, identity, and belonging. A vast majority of archives related to women active during the civil rights era and of those related to the history of Chicana feminism during the Chicano movement are lost, while some are privately held, such as those in María's home office. This chapter is based on my oral history interview with María and all references are to this source.

Telling and writing María's story in thematic vignettes is the most appropriate narrative form to represent her experiences, perceptions, and changes, including migration, subjectivity, and identity. The vignette form also parallels her stories, which are multilayered and multifaceted, as well as her memory, which shifts from recent to more distant pasts. The themes that emerged from the interviews are interwoven and relate how she negotiated, subverted, and developed her identity and consciousness as a Chicana activist. A feminist visionary, María is able to remember and engage in truth-telling as she self-reflects on her regional identity as well as the spiritual moments in her life.

CHILDHOOD—"*TRAVIESA*"

Born in 1948 in Linares, México, María was a slender and sick child who was reluctant to walk until she was three. As a young child, she had typhoid fever that she thinks she may have contracted from a taco cart, and she had to get injections for her delirium. A self-described *traviesa* (troublemaker), María searched for independence, individuality, and adventure. It was a hardship for her father to support the family on his salary in *transportes* (trucking business) while her mother maintained their home in Monterrey. When she was five years old, María was sent to live with her paternal grandmother Micaela (Doña Mica) in Linares for a few years. Despite being a strict disciplinarian, Doña Mica expressed her love through food, making *fritada*, a soup prepared from *cabrito's* (young goat's) blood in *cazos de cobre* (copper pots), and tamales.

A devout Catholic, her grandmother sent María to church and catechism classes. To make her first communion, María had to memorize prayers or she would not be permitted to receive the sacrament. When Doña Mica found out that María had not learned her prayers, it was already too late because she had planned an elaborate celebration to coincide with the baptism of María's younger sister Cristina. María confessed to her grandmother that the nun was being abusive, chasing her in the patio and hitting her with a leather belt. María ultimately learned to accommodate religion to suit her reality, as she would later become the spiritual leader at Colegio César Chávez, reciting the prayer (in Spanish) at demonstrations.

María and her siblings Eduardo, María del Carmen (Carmela), Yolanda, and Cristina Guadalupe (Titina) were all born in Linares, while Mario Salvador was born in Monterrey and José Benito and Francisco were born later in Matamoros. As the second oldest daughter, María navigated the gendered boundaries of her conservative family by refusing the split between public and private spheres and resisting any stronghold of power to control her movement in public. A precocious child, María capitalized on her sociability to win favors from adults, including storeowners and cabdrivers. At age six, she was sent on an errand for *manteca* (pork fat), after which she boarded a taxi and was driven home five blocks to her grandmother who was *mortificada* (mortified). Another time, she fell asleep from heat exhaustion under her bed on the cool concrete floor and could not be found by her family for hours. Such formative childhood experiences fomented María's disposition for risks so that she could live the kind of life she wanted.

Two pivotal junctures in her life revolved around losing both her parents. In February of 1983, her mother succumbed to brain cancer at age fifty-six. After having surgery to remove the tumor, her mother lived for eighteen months with a reduced quality of life. Before dying, her mother asked María for forgiveness, thinking she was too strict, and for "*nunca [me] compro una muñeca [porque] no habia dinero*" (not buying her a doll [because] there was no money). Her mother related the story of crossing a body of water to María, which foreshadowed her crossing into the other world. She lived the last days of her life in a nursing home, which exhausted all of her retirement savings. Finding it too painful to live in the home they shared together, her father moved back to Texas; however, he returned to Oregon in 1991. Having been a smoker for forty years, he got throat cancer and had a tracheotomy. He used an electrolarynx, a hand-held device, but it made his speech incomprehensible to anyone besides his family. In March of 1997, he died at age eighty. Aside from being tasked with making both her parents' funeral arrangements, María has balanced her familial responsibilities with freedom, yet her pain is both visceral and palpable, tinged with the anxiety of remembering and forgetting.

TRANSBORDER MIGRATION—*"HACER MILLIONARIO POR LOS CHIQUILLOS"*

Shortly after her parents married in 1944, her father was recruited as a *bracero*; however he refused to suffer the indignation of disrobing for the physical exam by U.S. immigration and health officials, and was sent back to México. Mexican *braceros* were fumigated with the pesticide DDT at the border. Maria's father eventually became a U.S. permanent resident in 1954 with the financial help of a brother-in-a-law on her mother's side of the family.

After moving from Linares, the family lived in Matamoros, across the border from Brownsville, Texas, from the time María was eleven until she was eighteen. When María was twelve, her sister Cristina fell from a swing and died of an embolism five days later; the Texas state police had to contact her father, who was working at a gas station in Harlingen.

María recalls the challenges of learning to speak English in the United States. Her father paid $8 per month for María to take private lessons in Brownsville, and the family enrolled her in a Catholic school also in Brownsville. Her mother, in particular, pushed thirteen-year-old María to learn English, perhaps thinking María could use the English language to defend herself. Despite her parent's encouragement, María had to contend with the school's racist tracking system. As a Mexican child, she was made to sit at the back of the classroom even though she needed eyeglasses. Fearing punishment from her father, María changed her grades from Fs to As. She was later found out and forced to leave Immaculate Conception Catholic School to help support the family with housecleaning chores and caretaking responsibilities. In fact, her father's low expectations and perception of María's inferior intellect pushed her to academic success later in life. She developed a border identity—a perspective that comes from living between cultures—to fight the disaffection she felt at school and it provided the motivation she needed.

In 1966, when María was eighteen, her father moved his transborder family to Brownsville, Texas. He refused to cross his family *"sin papeles"* (without documentation) to avoid the dangers and trauma that potentially awaited them had they crossed undocumented. After twelve years, he obtained the two letters of support required. Her father had been working in the United States in Illinois, Wisconsin, and Michigan since 1954, the timing of his return visits to Mexico every six to twelve months coinciding with her mother's pregnancies, which resulted in a transborder family.

Tired of working at his current job, and with his eldest daughter (María's sister) suffering from a nervous condition, María's father decided to move the family again. Unfamiliar with social service agencies that might help them, they loaded the station wagon and started the trek north. The car broke down, but by chance they met another family headed to Salem, Oregon, at a gas station. The other family invited them to come along with prospects of working in the fields, which illustrates the power of migrant social networks. The man said, "*se va hacer millionario por los chiquillos*" (he would become a millionaire with the children)—by conscripting the children into farm work. They followed the migration routes from South Texas to Oregon set by earlier migrants in the 1950s.

The family settled in the Eola Village migrant camp in Oregon in 1968, and lived there until 1973 when they moved to Woodburn. Meanwhile, María's older sister, Carmela, was interned at the Oregon State Hospital in Salem and would not fully recover. After having spent a few weeks of vacation with her cousins in Monterrey, Carmela had returned a different person. Her fiancé called off their engagement. In the early years, she escaped the hospital several times, once boarding a bus and arriving at her aunt's house in Monterrey without any money, form of identification, or her medication. Her care and recovery was limited by the lack of bilingual counseling. She was the first person in Oregon to apply and qualify for a HUD-funded residential facility, where she currently lives and María visits frequently.

EDUCATION—"THERE WAS ANOTHER ME COMING OUT"

Both of María's parents stressed the importance of an education, as her father and mother went up to the sixth and third grade, respectively. María understood that education was the means to realize her dreams, albeit reimagined dreams in the new context of the United States. Soon after moving to Oregon, María met Berna Wingert, an organizer for the Valley Migrant League (VML), who was recruiting students from the fields. "*Dejala*" (let her), said her mother, while her father was less supportive. In

March of 1970, Felipe Cañedo and Alfonso Cabrera, graduate students
at the University of Oregon (UO), recruited María and other migrant
workers like her to the High School Equivalency Program (HEP) at the
university. In patriarchal fashion, her father thought she was "[*perdiendo*]
el tiempo" (wasting her time). Another male migrant worker voiced his
disapprobation, "*Pa' que la manda tan lejos, se va regresar embarazada*" (why
are you sending her so far, she's going to come back pregnant). (Ironically,
María would assist the same migrant worker years later with admissions
at Colegio, at which point the man remarked, "*cómo se voltean las mesas*"
[how the tables got turned].) Refusing the gender expectations and sexual
limitations imposed on her, she asserted her right to an education. Her
father was skeptical of her aspirations, but he did not try to undermine
her desire to improve her life chances. Before María even learned she had
passed her General Education Development (GED) test, Felipe Cañedo
had already secured a SESAMEX (Spanish-English Speaking American
Mexican) scholarship for her to study during the summer of 1970 at the
Language Institute at Oregon State University (OSU).

In María's words, the empowering experience was an embodied transformation: "It felt like there was another me coming out." Motivated
by social justice, María was consciously connecting her mind and spirit
to action. She epitomized the transition to college for women as she
courageously negotiated alienation and family expectations. By June,
she was enrolled at the university and living at Callahan Dormitory on
the predominantly white campus. For the first time, she was confronted
with the notion of her racial, gender, and sexual identity in the white
environment of OSU. She experienced extreme culture shock from the
new experiences of living with a white female roommate, meeting an
African American man in the elevator, and being tutored by a bisexual
Cuban American woman. Later, she found strength in her circle of friends
that included the wives of graduate students. Her struggles as a college
student from a working-class background—a lack of knowledge about
how to navigate the college system and the lack of financial resources for
college—required her to find a way to supplement her income. Developing a sense of agency, she bought a typewriter at Goodwill to make extra
money by charging twenty-five cents per page for typewritten papers
and reports in spite of her limited English proficiency. She sacrificed

her grades because her business was so successful. Her experiences as a working-class college student show that she had to pay for the privilege of an education. And, it was her working-class consciousness that helped her to develop a Chicana feminist consciousness.

After completing the language program, she enrolled at the UO and graduated in 1974, but because she was missing one course, she did not receive her diploma until 1976. She struggled academically, even though she recorded her class lectures due to her limited English proficiency. As the first to go to college, María represented hope to her family. Her siblings, Eduardo and Yolanda, followed her to UO. Initially, María resented that they chose UO, which she felt restricted her autonomy. Undeterred, she went on to receive a master of science in Education Administration and Policy Foundations at PSU in 1998. Paradoxically, in order to transform the university in support of community activist initiatives, María had to ascend the institutional hierarchy to utilize its privileges and resources. She went on to work as an admissions counselor and minority student recruiter at PSU, where she helped provide higher education access to formerly excluded ethnic minority students, particularly Chicanas/os. Her struggles to attain full citizenship have paved the way for others to follow.

Working in the Fields and Factory—*"No sabia de surcos"*

As she matured, Maria's own female body became the site of a new subjectivity that rejected subjugation. The accumulated experiences of work—the backbreaking field labor, the grinding factory work, and the objectification of the body as mere instrument—was what led her to consciousness. Her first job outside of the home was at age sixteen at a Chinese restaurant in Matamoros, Tamaulipas, which involved the policing of her female sexuality. Horrified to find her working at the restaurant's bar, her father ordered her to resign immediately. *Un viejo mañoso* (a dirty old man) was watching her and tried to persuade her dad not to take her. To help her family, María found work as a salesperson at Las Tres Hermanas, at a shoe store La Moda, and at Marco Polo selling fabric, cashmere, and electronics in Brownsville.

Having migrated from an urban environment, María recalls, *"no sabia de surcos"* ("I didn't know about rows"). She had no experience in the fields, picking, thinning, or hoeing. She described the labor conditions at the Jensen Farms migrant camp near Salem as oppressive and exploitative, with squalid cabins made for chickens, a picnic table, gas stove, refrigerator, and public showers—incomparably deplorable: "not even in México." Eventually they moved to Eola Village, the largest migrant labor camp in Oregon with 5,000 people. The pay was five dollars per day or by the crop, which was eight cents per pound for green beans, a dollar fifty per crate for strawberries, and seventy cents per hour for hops. After the hop harvest in mid-September, the family worked in other fields. María worked for two years as a farm worker, an occupation marked by the disciplining of bodies through organizational hierarchies and productivity demands.

In 1969, María found work at a local factory, Diane's Foods (now called Mission Foods, which is owned by the Gruma Corporation), in McMinnville, manufacturing hard-shell tacos. She sometimes worked double shifts for ninety cents per hour. For eleven months, she endured working the night shift, the nature of shop-floor work, the heat from the folding presses, and worst of all, the *mal olor* (bad odor). Before long, María became aware that the routinization of labor was exploitative and that it marginalized workers, particularly female employees. The difficult and dangerous job, with high stress levels, low wages, few benefits, and little job security, gave her the impetus she needed for self-improvement. She was involved in the union struggle for fair wages—demanding increases from $1.10 to $1.60 per hour and fair labor practices. With a few of the Mexican women dissenting, the effort was defeated. She recalls one of her dissenting co-workers, Ms. Salinas, who thought María's aspirations of learning English and going to college was possible "*solo en sueños*" ("only in her dreams").

While María worked hard and was loyal to her employer, she refused to internalize any patriarchal restrictions on her mobility as dictated by her family, co-workers, and society. She credits Berna Wingert, a Chicana from New Mexico working at the VML with providing the affirmation and encouragement she needed to confront the oppression. Her farm worker experience later prompted her activism on behalf of the United Farm Worker (UFW) boycotts. During a weekly picket on Friday in front of a Safeway store, a hostile white male onlooker threw a piece of lettuce that struck María in the face. Agitated, María rolled up her UFW flag and went in pursuit of the man with her picket sign to physically confront him. José Romero, a MEChA (Movimiento Estudiantil Chicano de Aztlán) member, beseeched María on the philosophy of nonviolence and diffused the racial incident. Shifting her spiritual understanding, María's capacity for tolerance deepened; however the racial confrontation allowed María to see her lack of power as a female and to find other forms of resistance. She would continue participating in the picket lines, first with the grape boycott, then lettuce, Gallo wine, and the Coors company in the 1970s.

CHICANISMA AND ACTIVISM—*"ME SALIO EL ACTIVISMO"*

Even before entering college, María demonstrated such political consciousness that her parents and siblings teased her that she was "born in the wrong family." Her oppositional consciousness surged, María claims, at age fifteen, when "*me salio el activismo*" ("my activism was born"). President John F. Kennedy's assassination in 1963 was imprinted in María's memory by the attendant emotional turmoil and the closure of the U.S/Mexico International Bridge. Her fierce self-determination and radicalization primed her for the training and leadership experience that followed next.

Although the Chicano movement did not reach Oregon until the early 1970s, it was at the University of Oregon at the Chicano Student Union where the ideology of the Chicano movement took hold. María embraced the Chicana/o label. She had developed a sense of racial identity, a cultural awareness, and an activist zeal in college, and she benefitted from the collective transformation that challenged white supremacy.

María Alanís Ruiz at a demonstration in the 1970s. *Photo courtesy of María Alanís Ruiz.*

María's activism began in the farm worker struggle and incorporated the urban struggle for education as she navigated college. The historical and social circumstances, such as the farm worker movement and the anti-war movement, elevated her consciousness and provided training for the roles she would later play. With financial aid and recruitment programs, there was also a large concentration of first-generation Chicana/o college students, particularly Chicana students, entering the university under the Three Percent Program, or the Experimental Modification of Admission Requirements (EMAR), which was implemented in the Oregon University System (OUS) in the fall of 1968. In addition, SESAMEX and Project Life, under the auspices of Educational Opportunities Services (EOS), provided opportunities and educational access for Chicana/o students. Graduate students and an activist couple with an affinity for farm workers, José Romero and Kathy Romero, were among a group of Chicanos/as María met who recruited her into MEChA, which they started in 1972. Graduate students such as José Romero, brothers José "Simon" Villa and Roberto Villa, Roberto Loredo, and Senon Valadez, who had farm worker experience, were instrumental in organizing students around campus and the community for *la causa*. The alienation Chicanos/as felt was assuaged by their numbers even as class tensions between the Chicano Student Union and the Latin American Student Union were growing. A pan-Latino unity between the two student organizations may also have been hindered by different group identities based on their social locations and personal histories.

While at UO, María became the director of the Migrant Labor Project (MLP), a student-based organization that provided teacher aides, child care, and food for migrant workers. She recalls calling the state health department to conduct an investigation that led to the closure of the labor camp. For her work with the MLP, María was honored with the Whitman Award given by Senator Wayne Morse in 1973. The group held fundraisers, which included selling *mole* plates and *capirotada* (bread pudding). She also helped organize a symposium that included Chicano activists Rodolfo "Corky" Gonzales and José Angel Gutiérrez. She participated in a sit-in at the Board of Higher Education and marched in protest of the 1978 Supreme Court's Bakke case, which limited affirmative action in higher education. In 1970, she attended the statewide Poor People's

Conference in Salem organized by and for the poor, and she attended the Chicana Conference at Lewis and Clark College in Portland. María acknowledges that this was the first time the issue of lesbianism emerged for her, even though gender and sexuality issues were raised in the movement in Oregon.

Selected to participate in the *Centro Intercultural de Documentación* (CIDOC), María spent a summer in Cuernavaca, México, in 1972 where she was disparaged as a *pocha* (assimilated) and a *traidora* (traitor) to her Mexican culture. As a Chicana student activist, her encounter with Mexican nationals' racialized notions of her identity was confusing; however she resisted. They also deflected her gendered identity as a woman, and imposed the dominant nationalistic constructions of identity. She was also stereotyped as a tourist, which further diluted her ethnic identity. Issues of race, ethnicity, gender, class, and sexuality surfaced during the trip that made María question any transnational political solidarity movement that could have been empowering.

María was also active with the Young Women's Christian Association (YWCA), serving as the Western Region Chicana Caucus Representative for three years and attending annual conferences in San Diego, New York, Chicago, and Oklahoma. During that time, resolutions to support the UFW were passed. Even though María did not attend the 1971 *Conferencia de Mujeres por la Raza* at Houston's YWCA that ended with a walkout, the regional factions helped her to explain some of the breakdowns in the conference. Among other complaints was that the YWCA was an Anglo institution that was dominated by white, elite, Christian women at the conference. María negotiated the ideological fissures and formed a gendered solidarity with women across age, race, and class. At one of the conferences, where César Chávez spoke, the YWCA adopted the imperative "[t]o trust our collective power towards the elimination of racism, wherever it exists, by any means necessary." María met Chávez again aboard an airplane when he requested they not serve lettuce on the flight. She also met other male leaders of *el movimiento* including Reies López Tijerina at Mi Tierra Restaurant in San Antonio in 1976 after his release from prison following the Tierra Amarilla courthouse raid, and José Angel Gutiérrez in Oregon.

María credits José and Kathy Romero with fomenting her critical consciousness. Recruited by José, who was then director of Chicano studies and later became the director of academic affairs, María started working at Colegio César Chávez at Mount Angel in September 1974 as a recruiter. With her independence and a $10,000 salary, María moved to Portland with her sister. Her relationship with the Romeros was also personal; she would babysit their daughter, Shelli. She was gaining independence as she learned to drive, and bought her first car, a 1973 green Chevy Vega, for $99 a month. However, the staff was growing frustrated by the mounting legal and financial problems plaguing Colegio following the resignation of Sonny Montes and eventually José Romero. Interestingly, it was mostly women, including Irma Gonzales, Gloria Sandoval, Hortencia Antillón, and Elizabeth Gorman-Prunty, who remained to stave off closure. For a time, the Colegio staff did not get paid and would divide honoraria among the staff. Despite its ten-year run and national attention, El Colegio never recovered and ceased to exist a short time later.

El Colegio was a part of a consortium of Chicano-oriented colleges in the U.S. Unique in its bilingual/bicultural approach, the Colegio administered the College Without Walls program, which granted credit for life experiences and a documented learning portfolio, and was facilitated by a *comité* (committee). El Colegio attracted prominent speakers to campus, such as its namesake César Chávez, the poet Alurista, Teatro Campesino, and Daniel Valdez. At Colegio, María coordinated *Los Norteñitos*, a youth dance program. She says of the beauty of Colegio, "*Sembramos la semilla... Brotó, pero sigue 30 años despues*" (The seed was planted, it grew, and it continues thirty years later). In spite of its closure, the fruit of leadership had transformed the community.

In 1975, María was recruited to work at Washington State University in Pullman, Washington, in the Chicano Studies Program in the Bilingual Bicultural Training Institute to prepare teacher-aides in the Yakima Valley to graduate from college. She lasted a year because she felt isolated being away from her family and friends and she returned to work for Colegio César Chávez.

In 1980 she took up her next challenge in the admissions office at Portland State University. Roberto, her husband, noticed the job announcement in the newspaper and encouraged her to apply. The arduous interview process that started with the committee and concluded with the dean would characterize her experience in that position. María's resilience is evident in the face of institutional and interpersonal violence. In one instance, she was told, "You need to go back where you came from." María submitted her resignation letter when she was offered a better suited position as the director of Latino Student and Community Relations at PSU.

THE FIGHT FOR CHICANO STUDIES PROGRAMS

As part of the active Chicano movement, there was a push to develop and institutionalize Chicano-Latino studies at Portland State. In 1992, the Hispanic Studies Committee was tasked with developing a proposal for faculty enhancement and curriculum development "in existing courses, development of a team-taught course...and development planning for an expanded program on Hispanic and Latin American studies." The committee was composed mostly of white faculty members and a few token Chicana/o faculty and staff. The white members of the committee wanted to enhance their own departments through a faculty seminar with invited faculty speakers and local Hispanic groups. Despite the lofty, long-term goals of "interdisciplinary faculty research projects on Hispanic issues in Oregon that would involve undergraduate student research and fieldwork; increased Hispanic enrollment at PSU; enhanced faculty involvement with Hispanic students through mentoring programs, informal advising, orientation programs, or freshman/new student seminars; and support for the hiring of Hispanic faculty in tenure-track positions," the struggle was hard-fought.

The timing of the committee coincided with the 1992 annual MEChA National Conference at Eastern Washington University (EWU). Politicized MEChA students from PSU attended the conference with a renewed sense of identity and heightened consciousness. Students were formalizing their ethnic and political identities distinct from the Hispanic Student Union and the International Latino Student Union. The students returned to campus, organized, and demanded that PSU adopt EWU's Chicano studies program model with curricula and services, not the committee's proposed piecemeal program. EWU's Chicano Education Program (CEP) included recruitment, student support services, and the Chicano studies program. Carlos Maldonado, who was the CEP director, was also the first executive director of the National Association for Chicano Studies (NACS) at Washington. The EWU Chicano studies program, which was established in 1977, received advice and support from Washington State University (WSU). The University of Washington also had a Chicano studies program, which was established in 1970. Washington proved to be the state for the germination of Chicano studies programs across the Pacific Northwest. One of the administrators at PSU, vice provost and dean of students Juan Mestas, supported the students, who mobilized to rally support for the bachelor's in Chicano-Latino studies on campus. As the MEChA founding advisor in the 1990s, María witnessed the students' call to action, mobilizing, and gathering signatures on petitions. Several challenges, from budgetary to bureaucratic, impeded the progress of the program. As an urban public university, the push came from community organizations off-campus. Faculty from the international studies and Latin American studies programs were not supportive.

In 1995, a Chicano-Latino studies certificate program was established at PSU with core courses in the College of Liberal Arts and Sciences. Following a national search, Rubén Sierra was hired as the founding director of the Chicano/a studies program with a joint position in the theater department. Originally from San Antonio, Sierra was as an actor, director, and playwright who founded the Seattle Group Theatre. María was recruited by Rubén as founding faculty to develop the program, and she stepped in as interim director at the time of Sierra's untimely death in October of 1998. Later, as associate director of Chicano-Latino studies, she continued to create new curricula (courses such as Southwestern Borderlands, Mexican American Folklore), teach classes (four every term), and serve as advisor to student organizations including MEChA. She established partnerships with off-campus entities such as PSU's Salem Center, Continuing Education, and Portland Community College in Beaverton, and outreach programming such as the Oregon Leadership Institute (OLI), Sí Se Puede Leadership Project, and the Scholarship Gala. She hired adjunct faculty such as Narce Rodríguez, who graduated and worked at Oregon State University. She also invited noteworthy speakers to PSU including Lalo Alcaraz, Chicano cartoon artist; Victor Villaseñor, Chicano author; and Peter Bratt, film director. For the first three years, she also hosted the César Chávez Leadership Conference for Oregon high school students on the PSU campus. She remains involved with the conference by offering workshops.

The year 2004 marked a turning point in her career when she faced a devastating political battle of macho or "chingón" politics, ironically after the institutionalization of Chicano-Latino studies. In her role as associate director, she confronted male supremacy, hierarchical and individualized leadership when she was called into a meeting by two male faculty members who authoritatively told her she was being "promoted and transferred" to another department. Up until then, there was a racialized and gendered division of labor: however it was becoming classed. María felt that PSU had institutionalized a male-centered Chicano-Latino studies program. As the only Chicana, María faced subjection, alienation, and censure by exclusion and marginalization from the conversation and decision-making process. The divide along gender and class lines mirrors the inherent contradiction between the discourse of liberation and practice of oppression. The two male faculty members used their male privilege to demote María because of her degree (or lack thereof), erase her feminist vision and critical role in the formation of the Chicano-Latino studies program, and reinscribe the hierarchies of privilege.

As one of the administrators of the program, María had solidly helped to build the Chicano-Latino studies program through Chicana feminist collaboration, participation, and humility. Her Chicana feminist consciousness and activism were influenced by her own lived experience in the fields, on the picket lines, and in the community, which translated into a daily commitment to awareness of the site of her own privilege in higher education. Nevertheless, the gap between her position and her colleagues' devalued perception of her labor made her dispensable. She described the incident as devastating and demoralizing—"as if she had lost part of her soul." Despite the hidden injuries from heteropatriarchal institutional violence, María demonstrated tolerance, political clarity, and ethical integrity with her decisiveness. During María's tenure at PSU, she saw professors including Elizabeth Flores and Carlos Blanton—two Chicano/a studies faculty members—leave the program either because they were denied tenure or because of race and gender inequalities. Systematic exclusion and isolation has contributed to the underrepresentation of Chicana/o faculty, resulting in negative implications for the institution, program, faculty, and students.

María claims she was naïve about gender issues when she entered college and yet she challenged the traditional ideologies of womanhood, which is to maintain a home and family, and instead made her own independent trajectory as well as a collective one. For María, feminism was intersected by race, class, gender, and sexuality, and drew from multiple traditions and lived experiences. María acknowledges the agency of her mother, who was unused to rural life, but united the family and wielded authority with resourcefulness to protect them from poverty. It was in the daily rhythm of migrant life that her mother disrupted patriarchal authority and redefined motherhood. As a stay-at-home mother, she made the labor camp a home for the family, taking care of the everyday routines, particularly the meals, from meager resources. For most of the time, her mother raised the children as a single parent. In addition to peanut butter and jelly sandwiches, her mother prepared dishes of *barbacoa*, *lengua*, and *menudo*, delicacies that sustained the family.

One of María's earliest feminist role models was Berna Wingert, who she met at the migrant camp at Eola Village, and who invited her to visit the University of Oregon. Education was the site where María subverted hegemonic female roles. Her father had offered her only two options: marry (his *compadre's* son) or go to school. During college, she met Gloria González, a radical Chicana feminist from Tijuana, Baja California. Gloria taught her how to drive a car in a state vehicle while visiting the labor camps. They formed a mostly female *ballet folklórico* group at the UO that provided a sense of female solidarity and was an outlet for cultural expression. The Chicana students also formed *Las Mujeres de la Raza*, an organization for Chicanas to develop gender and sexuality consciousness; however it folded because of internal problems caused by *chisme* (gossip) based on female competition and alienation. Chicanas struggled to find their own voice while simultaneously balancing the competing demands of the family and the university.

The gender and sexual politics of Chicano nationalism in the Chicano movement in Oregon were subtle, and the emergence of Chicana feminism occurred from within. Chicana activists questioned the concerns of the Chicano movement and deconstructed the machismo. The balance between the collective identity of Chicano nationalism and a Chicana's individual consciousness was tensely held. One example of this tension was during a concert at a nightclub where the band members objectified Chicanas with overt sexist and misogynistic jokes. The Chicanos enacted their male supremacy in defense of Chicanas' sexuality based on idealized notions of Chicanas in traditional gender roles as wives and mothers. Moreover, Chicanas rejected the Chicanos' nationalist ideologies of race, gender, and sexuality dictating who they could and could not date. María's personal experiences of being sexualized or sexually harassed include an overtly macho Chicano graduate student who felt entitled to ask if she was a virgin. María felt Chicanos were "trying to get in bed" with Chicanas and demanding that "they prove it," using heterosexuality as a weapon to restrict and control their sexual freedom; yet, Chicanos claimed the sexual freedom to date white women. María had a saying for the sexual double standard: "*Chicano de día, gabacho de noche*" (Chicano by day, white male by night). Chicanos saving Chicanas from other men was not gender and sexual equality.

As a young woman, María eschewed the feminist label as she did not explicitly identify with white feminism. While noting the complications within the feminist tradition, María reveals her ambivalence toward Chicana feminism saying, "I was feminist in a way," which demonstrates the negotiations for Chicanas. Recognizing feminism as too narrow, she redefined feminism broadly in relation to her gendered life experiences through race and class. When asked about her feminist consciousness, María critiqued the racial politics in the women's movement and the subordination of Chicanas because white feminists "used us." The complexities and contradictions which suffused the women's movement, María felt, were restricted to white women's experiences. She felt excluded by the women's movement because she did not share the same feminist identity nor claim the same interests. She explains that her mother and father were egalitarian and that respect toward the family took priority.

Biculturally adept, María learned how to negotiate boundaries that included racist, gendered, and class-based language standards reflecting the whiteness of academia. Speaking with an accent that reflects her immigrant/migrant narrative, María has had to invent her own bilingual-bicultural language, challenging notions of citizenship based on national origin. While at PSU, her Mexican-accented English became the target of discrimination by her white female supervisor. Evoking nativist politics, she insisted to María, "People like you need to start at the bottom," indicating a racialized class hierarchy that requires policing to keep people in their place. Denied the relevance of her cultural experience, María was "othered." She had her credentials questioned, her accent pathologized, and was told to conform to linguistic norms and acquiesce to psychological behavior modification. Because of her linguistic difference, she was ostracized and subjected to hostile treatment, including intense language repression, negative evaluations, and punitive sanctions such as demanding travel obligations no one else wanted, which ironically required bilingualism. Her supervisor's arrogance allowed her to transfer the burden of sexism to María, who faced a workplace culture that was oppressive and reproduced a racialized gendered hierarchy. Consequently, María was reassigned to the College of Liberal Arts as the director of Latino and Community Relations under the direction of Dean Marvin Kaiser. Kaiser, an advocate of multiculturalism, retired in 2011. In her and her family's best interest, and as an act of resistance, María decided to retire from PSU after thirty-one years of service. After all, she had witnessed the impact of the cycle of abuse on her women of color colleagues as their intellectual labor and emotional and physical health were compromised at the predominantly white institution. Rather than be silent, María claimed her agency and consciousness to voice her protest against intolerable working conditions rather than be objectified. By claiming a personal subjectivity, she confronted the harmful effects within the collective.

With greater awareness of issues of gender and sexuality, María was also involved in coalition-style politics. One such organization was *Las Mujeres de Oregon* (Women of Oregon), a statewide grassroots community-building organization, which formed in 1980 and met twice monthly before it disbanded. The ethnic diversity of the group was its strength; however, its internal contradictions such as class heterogeneity and forms of political action were not resolved. María was involved in organizing *El*

Poder de la Mujer Latina (The Power of the Latina Woman) conference in 2005 at PSU to celebrate and honor the legacy of Chicana activism in Oregon. This event also helped to temper Chicana's individual self-serving agendas and perpetuate cooperation.

For María, motherhood was a choice to practice the "personal is political" dictum. As a Chicana adoptive mother, she used motherhood as a model of engagement for lifting the next generation. Her construction of motherhood included a redefinition of familism, which has allowed her to work outside the home without guilt. She acknowledges that PSU's administration was accommodating to the facts of her life as a mother raising two children.

Underscoring her Chicana feminist consciousness, she used her insight and understanding of Chicana/Latina girlhood practices to develop the curriculum for the Sí Se Puede program at PSU, which was integrated with the Chicano-Latino studies (ChLa) capstone course. She also developed the Adelante Academy, which aims to empower fourteen- to eighteen-year-old Latinas by using embodied knowledge and a feminist activist pedagogy. The leadership program was developed to inspire and counter the myths of and about Chicana/Latina girls from a health issues approach. Funds from the Legacy Hospital paid for stipends to the twenty to sixty girls to participate in monthly sessions and hear from invited Latina speakers. The program was short-lived, as María describes it, as "*la avaricia*" (avarice) took over. As she prepared the women leaders of tomorrow, she passed on her ethos of love, which has served to protect María from falling into the trappings of materialism and instead focus on spiritual rewards.

Spiritual Activism—"*Una espiritista*"

From María's neck hangs a necklace with a pendant of *la Virgen de Guadalupe*, which attests to her embodiment of Chicana resistance and transformative spiritual agency. Bold-spirited, María has reconciled the contradictions of her Catholic identity by recreating her spirituality, which has been a source of female strength and healing. María's survival has depended on her ability to interpret signs and her gift in combatting oppression. As a card reader, María utilizes her *facultad* (ability)—which includes faith, humility, and intuition—for healing alienation, illness, and despair, and for offering redemptive remembrance. She constructs her knowledge and identity as *un espiritista* (spiritualist). Her multiple perceptions have allowed others to change who they are and their behavior for personal healing and collective liberation from intergenerational trauma. Her spirituality has facilitated a self-reflexive heightened consciousness and a critical awareness for others.

María's spiritual work is deeply personal and political, bringing together mind, body, and spirit, and providing her a vision for emphatic action. María's stories themselves are spirits that show her love of self and compassion for others and passion for social justice. As a mode of cultural expression, she uses her spiritual activism as a guide toward personal integrity and political empowerment. As a witness to the trappings of materialism and individualism, María's commitment to social justice is undergirded by her humility and way of being.

COMMUNITY-BRIDGE WORK—*"YOU DO IT BY HEART...DO IT BY PASSION"*

María's transformative work has been guided by an ethic of love and purpose carried out with feelings, dreams, and passion that transgress boundaries. Determined to eliminate the exclusionary patterns, María's activism has evolved into a transnational focus in which she has improved the social and cultural lives of Chicanos/as in Oregon as well as the transborder lives of Mexicans in Guadalajara. She broadened the civil rights approach to include human rights to make connections with transnational activist groups for social justice. Her involvement with organizations focused on Chicanas/os-Latinas/os has had a gendered focus. *Una "rielera moderna"* (modern trailblazer), María draws on the genealogy of Chicana female activists with transnational and multiracial perspectives to promote economic, social, and cultural rights. A well-respected community leader, María has served on countless committees, councils, and boards.

Having been actively engaged in social struggles for more than thirty years, María remains involved in making and sustaining community. For over thirteen years, beginning in 1997, she organized the Scholarship Gala to raise over one hundred $1,000 scholarships for students at PSU, challenging the exclusivity of access to higher education. With the help of Bel Hernandez Castillo, she has appealed to philanthropists and celebrities such as Yareli Arizmendi, Ricardo Chavaria, Esai Morales, Edward James Olmos, Lupe Ontiveros, and Tony Plana to serve as keynote speakers.

In addition to the gala, she has also organized the *Cinco de Mayo* festivities, which is a way to create space, forge memory, and reinforce a transnational ethnic Latina/o identity and culture. For Latinas/os in Oregon, the cultural isolation can be quite unsettling. As founder and President of the Portland-Guadalajara Sister City Association (PGSCA), she transcends national borders and builds a sense of collectivity. Started in 1985, the *Cinco de Mayo* celebration at Portland's Waterfront Park is symbolic of Chicano/a-Latina/o civic and political life, cultural suste-nance, and inclusion. When she first made the suggestion, a conflict arose between a male Mexican nationalist leader and María along generational, racial, class, and gender divides. This is documented in the PGSCA board meeting minutes of February 5, 1985. The first festival included a Cantinflas film series and high school art contest with a $75 budget. The long-established festival now attracts more than 300,000 people and a million-dollar budget, proving it to be an important cultural link to the community. Given the geographic isolation of the Pacific Northwest, María recognized that the communal and performative aspects of the Mexican diaspora exist beyond the *fronteras* of the Southwest.

As part of the PGSCA, María receives funding from foundations, but the work is broad-based and reaches organizers and constituents. She established Jardin Portland at El Bosque Las Colomos in Guadalajara, México, which is a replica of Multnomah Falls, Crown Point, and Pioneer Courthouse Square in Portland. Other projects include Villas Mira Valle, which serves as an orphanage; El Colegio Unico, a culinary program; and the *Bombero* (firefighter exchange) program. In recreating the foods from her youth, María has developed an ethnic transborder identity. (Three of her favorite recipes, Aztec pie, *capirotada* pudding, and a *nopalitos* and egg dish, were featured in *The Oregonian* for the third annual *Cinco de Mayo* celebration in 1988.)

Among her many accolades, she was knighted an Honorary Dame under the Banner of the Rose by the Royal Rosarians in 2006 for her many contributions to Portland. Financially independent, she started her own consulting company in 2011, *Sin Fronteras*, which has partnerships with school districts offering parent education workshops in Portland and at *La Universidad Autónoma de Guadalajara.*

María has been married to Roberto Ruiz since 1985. He has encouraged her to tell and write her story and has been her biggest supporter. True partners in life and work, they share interests and a commitment to the community. They met in 1976 at a *tamalada* (tamale-making party) hosted by their mutual friend Irma Flores Gonzales, then board member of Colegio César Chávez. Originally from Victoria, Texas, Roberto lost both his parents when he was a young child. He joined the army and was stationed in Portland, where he has lived since his discharge. With a business degree from Portland State University, he has worked as a licensed realtor. He and María have been married for thirty-one years and have raised two adopted children—Antonio Roberto, who is twenty-four, and Alejandra María, who is twenty. Her decision to adopt is part of her motherwork to share her maternal love and transform assumptions about family. The way she speaks about her children—finding them and supporting them—demonstrates her unrelenting commitment to social justice. Adoption doesn't define her family. As a loving and devoted mother, she has helped her children on their journeys of self-discovery and self-identity through critical reflection. She is conscious of the hegemonic construction of motherhood, but she holds fast to her feminist convictions of maternity.

Lessons

María's complex life is a panorama of migrant crossings to and within the United States, from the fields to the academy, accented by language that weaves both Mexican and Chicana identities. Empowered by the Chicana/o movement, she created her own identity in both public and private spheres and consistently challenged boundaries of inclusion and exclusion. Her sustaining power to keep her family together and her survival in racist environments are her rewards individually and collectively for her organizing. Documentation of María's feminist activism during the Chicano movement in Oregon powerfully exposes the racism, classism, and sexism railed against her in her courageous struggle for access to higher education and for Chicana/o studies.

Conducting oral history interviews is a rich and powerful site for knowledge production about race, class, gender, sexuality, and belonging. As a privileged witness, I have received from María intellectual lessons, emotional lessons, and most importantly spiritual lessons about courage, survival, and hope. During our first interview at the Woodburn Public Library, I showed deference by referring to María as "*usted.*" She insisted on being addressed as "*tú,*" and it took several more interviews before I crossed the cultural border where I felt we had established a sense of solidarity and I had become an intimate witness. Through the telling of her individual truths and collective experiences, she has imparted her memories as *testimonio* and has bridged the transcendental divide of thinking and acting.

Feeling overwhelmed at the start soon gave way to exhilaration, as I felt that this project had a longer life and expanded in ways I had not imagined. Pedagogically, I have incorporated students into the oral history project who have directly interviewed María to draw knowledge from her lived experiences and from within Chicana/o communities. By engaging in praxis that applies both theory and method in service of social change, students will sow the seeds of self-empowerment to reclaim their history and become activists in their own right as María's dreams live on. Another goal of the project is the creation of a Chicana oral history archive that resists the epistemic violence of historical erasure. Finally, the project contributes to a feminist testimonial discourse that pays homage to, and is a testament of, María's social justice activism and voice that inspires solidarity.

References

Alaniz, Yolanda and Megan Cornish. *Viva la Raza: A History of Chicano Identity and Resistance.* Seattle: Red Letter Press, 2008.

Blackwell, Maylei. *!Chicana Power!: Contested Histories of Feminisms in the Chicano Movement.* Austin: University of Texas Press, 2012.

Castañeda, Antonia I. "'Que se pudieran defender (So you could defend yourselves)': Chicanas, Regional History, and National Discourses." *Frontiers: A Journal of Women Studies* 22, no. 3 (2001): 116–42.

Chabram-Dernersesian, Angie. "I Throw Punches for My Race, but I Don't Want to Be a Man: Writing Us—Chica-Nos (Girl, Us)/Chicanas—into the Movement

Script." In *The Chicana/o Cultural Studies Reader*, edited by Angie Chabram-Dernersesian, 165–82. New York: Routledge, 2006.

Gamboa, Erasmo. "El Movimiento: Oregon's Mexican-American Civil Rights Movement." In *Nosotros: The Hispanic People of Oregon*, edited by Erasmo and Buan, Carolyn M. Gamboa, 46–60. Portland: Oregon Council for the Humanities, 1995.

García, Jerry. "A Chicana in Northern Aztlán: An Oral History of Dora Sánchez Treviño." *Frontiers: A Journal of Women Studies* 19, no. 2 (1998): 16–52.

Gonzales-Berry, Erlinda and Marcela Mendoza. *Mexicanos in Oregon: Their Stories, Their Lives*. Corvallis: Oregon State University Press, 2010.

Hernández, Ellie. *Postnationalism in Chicana/o Literature and Culture*. Austin: University of Texas Press, 2009.

May, Glenn Anthony. *Sonny Montes and Mexican American Activism in Oregon*. Corvallis: Oregon State University, 2011.

Mulcahy, Joanne B. "'Know Who You Are': Regional Identity in the Teachings of Eva Castellanoz." *Oregon Historical Quarterly*, 2007: 444–57.

Nusz, Nancy and Gabriella Ricciardi. "Our Ways: History and Culture of Mexicans in Oregon." *Oregon Historical Quarterly*, 2003: 110–23.

PGSCA. "Board Meeting Minutes." February 5, 1985.

Ruiz, María Alanís, interviews by Norma Cárdenas, March 3, 2012; April 27, 2012; July 9, 2012; July 17, 2012; July 30, 2012; August 22, 2012; August 29, 2012; September 5, 2012; September 17, 2012.

Ruiz, Vicki. *Memories and Migrations: Mapping Boricua and Chicana Histories*. Champaign: University of Illinois Press, 2008.

Salas, Elizabeth. "Latinas in the Pacific Northwest." In *Latinas in the United States: A Historical Encyclopedia Volume 1*, edited by Vicki L. Ruiz and Virginia Sánchez Korrol, 24-28. Bloomington: Indiana University Press, 2006.

Salas, Elizabeth. "Mexican-American Women Politicians in Seattle." In *More Voices, New Stories: King County, Washington's First 150 Years*, edited by Mary C. Wright, 215–31. Seattle: Landmarks & Heritage Commission, 2002.

Stephen, Lynn. "Latino Roots in Lane County, Oregon." 2007. //cllas.uoregon.edu/wp-content/uploads/2010/06/Latino_Roots_booklet.pdf (accessed July 3, 2013).

The Sunday Oregonian. "Migrant Makes Big Jump from Fields to Social Work." September 10, 1978: 125.

Valle, Isabel. *Fields of Toil: A Migrant Family's Journey*. Pullman, WA: Washington State University Press, 1994.

Xing, Jun, Erlinda Gonzales-Berry, Patti Sakurai, Robert D. Thompson, and Kurt Peters. *Seeing Color: Indigenous Peoples and Racialized Ethnic Minorities in Oregon*. New York: University Press of America, 2007.

PART THREE

COMMUNITY, LABOR, AND IMMIGRATION

CHAPTER 7

The Mexicanization of a Northwest Community: The Case of Woodburn, Oregon

Carlos Saldivar Maldonado and *Rachel Maldonado*

INTRODUCTION

As of 2014, the U.S. Census reported that the U.S. Latino population reached 55.5 million or 17.4 percent of the total U.S. population. Since 1990, the Latino population has averaged 3.7 percent annual growth (Pew Research Center, 2015). The bulk of the U.S. Latino population is of Mexican descent, representing nearly 65 percent of all Latinos in the U.S. (Pew Research Center, 2015). This significant growth has captured the attention of scholars interested in becoming more informed about and documenting the Mexicana/o community's presence in various regions of the country. This expanding regional attention is an important development as research on the U.S. Mexicana/o community has historically focused on a southwest regional context. The 2010 U.S. census figures clearly reinforce the fact that the Mexicana/o community is indeed a national community. It is therefore important to examine the Mexicana/o experience and presence in various regions, including the Pacific Northwest. This paper is an ethnographic community study that highlights the Mexicanization of Woodburn, Oregon, a small rural community located in Oregon's agriculturally rich Willamette Valley. This chapter illuminates how Mexicana/os are impacting the social-cultural milieu of this local community. A regional historical sketch of the Mexicana/o presence in the Northwest sets the context for the discussion and is followed by a historical sketch of Woodburn, Oregon. This chapter then discusses four dimensions of community that demonstrate the Mexicanization of Woodburn's local community: demographics, business development, the church, and the school setting. We close the chapter by presenting sentiments from some non-Mexicana/os regarding the Mexicanization of Woodburn that illuminate some interesting views.

The research methods utilized in this study include interviews with community members; participant-observation at community cultural events and meetings; review of historical newspaper articles, city directories, and census data; collection of historical photographs; and photographing and being part of community life of Woodburn, Oregon. This study offers a developmental pattern of Mexicanization that may provide explanations or insights into what may be occurring in other rural Northwest communities as Mexicana/os become a larger percentage of the population.

HISTORICAL SKETCH OF MEXICANA/OS IN THE NORTHWEST

Mexicana/os have deep roots in the Pacific Northwest. These roots extend to the eighteenth century when Spanish ships supported by Mexicana/o crews departed from Mexican ports for the northwest coastal waters (Cutter 1981; Engstrand 1991). These Spanish ships journeyed to the northwest coast to establish and extend the Spanish colonial presence already entrenched in Mexico. The Spanish failed to establish any enduring territorial presence in the region and formal Spanish territorial claims ended with the signing of the Transcontinental Treaty in 1819. Nevertheless, contact and exchange between colonial northern Mexico and the Northwest territories continued. Mining, cattle ranching, and mule transportation activities brought Mexicana/os to the Northwest. Such efforts were well in place by the 1860s (French 1965; Watt 1978).

After the turn of the century, the Mexican Revolution of 1910 and the economic development of the West coupled to pull Mexican labor to various regions of the U.S. including the Pacific Northwest (Gamboa 1990; Maldonado 1995). By the 1940s and the advent of World War II, the need for Mexican labor sharply increased to help offset the drain on U.S. labor. This drain was due to a growing U.S. military and the heightened economic production needed to support the war effort. Mexican labor was actively recruited through the Bracero Program, a 1942 labor agreement between the U.S. and Mexico. Mexican braceros helped harvest the agricultural crops and maintained the railroads of the Northwest (Gamboa 1990). Additionally, Mexicana/o migrant farm workers from south Texas (Tejana/os) heeded the labor call and the 1940s and 1950s became watershed years for the recruitment of Mexican nationals and Tejana/os to the Northwest. It was during these years that Mexicana/os began to establish roots in numerous rural communities supported by agriculture.

During the 1960s and 1970s, Mexicana/o farm workers continued to come to the region. Some returned to their places of origin between harvest seasons, while others made the decision to settle out of the migrant farm worker stream. During the 1980s and subsequent decades, Mexican immigrants deepened their roots in the Northwest. Continued immigration and a high birthrate among Mexicana/os contributed to setting the stage that would later socially transform some small rural communities in the Northwest. The Mexicanization of these communities is evident in Mexicana/o community-wide cultural celebrations, mainstream and specialty Mexicana/o owned businesses, school enrollments, church attendance, and arts and culture in the public domain. The remainder of this study focuses on the gradual Mexicanization that transformed the northwest rural community of Woodburn, Oregon.

Brief History of Woodburn, Oregon

Founded in 1889, Woodburn is located in the heart of the agriculturally rich Willamette Valley in western Oregon (Woodburn Centennial Commission 1989). Woodburn is located on Interstate 5 and is nestled seventeen miles north of Salem (Oregon's capital), and thirty miles south of the metropolitan city of Portland. Woodburn is centrally located, with quick access to Oregon's coast to the west and the Cascade Mountains to the east, including Mt. Hood. The U.S. 2010 Census estimated Woodburn's population at 25,000 (U.S. Census Bureau 2010). The community consists of four diverse population sectors. First are the long-term Anglo residents who founded and contributed to the city's early development. Second are the Mexicana/os, including Tejana/os, who began arriving in Woodburn during the 1940s, 1950s, and early 1960s as a result of active agriculture labor recruitment. Third are the Orthodox Russians who began a hopscotch journey out of Russia in the 1940s and continued into China and South America during the 1950s and finally ended in Woodburn in the early 1960s. And fourth are senior citizens who make up the sizeable senior retirement community of Woodburn's Senior Estates, which was developed during the early 1960s (Woodburn Centennial Commission 1989).

Over the years, Woodburn's primary business sectors have focused on retail and services, agriculture, food processing, and manufactured home construction (Woodburn Chamber of Commerce 1994). Its three distinct business districts include the historical downtown, a business corridor along Highway 99E located east of downtown, and a second business corridor along Interstate 5, west of downtown. Residential areas separate these two business corridors from the community's downtown.

Woodburn's historical downtown encompasses twelve city blocks, two blocks wide by six blocks long. (See Figure 1 below.)

During the 1980s, Woodburn began to experience an exodus of Anglo businesses from its downtown business district. The development of Woodburn's business districts situated beyond the historical downtown played an important role in this exodus. Beginning in the 1980s, these business corridors began to experience significant growth. This increased business development encouraged some downtown merchants to relocate

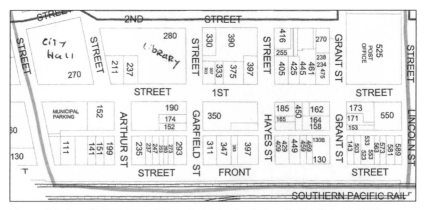

Figure 1: Map of Downtown Historical District (City of Woodburn, 2005)

to these emerging business corridors. As a result, their vacant storefronts became part of the business rental market in the historical downtown.

The businesses established in the I-5 and 99E corridors brought competition to small downtown local businesses. National stores such as the Walmart Supercenter, Payless Shoes, Safeway, Bi-Mart, and others created stiff competition to downtown merchants. Some of the downtown establishments soon became casualties of the local vs. national business scenario. Other downtown merchants retired and closed their doors. Their vacant storefronts, too, became part of the downtown rental market. Additionally, most of the historical downtown buildings were old and small, and many were damaged by an earthquake during the mid-1980s. The increase in the vacancy rate translated into low rents for these old, small, earthquake-damaged downtown buildings.

The preceding historical sketch highlights the local community's population change and economic development impacting the nature of its local business districts. The remainder of the chapter focuses on the community changes brought about by this population shift as the community became Mexicanized.

THE MEXICANIZATION OF WOODBURN, OREGON

Since its founding in 1889, Woodburn has historically been a community dominated by Anglo demographics and control of the social-political local structure. In the past forty plus years, the local community has gradually undergone some social shifts that resulted in changing the character of the local community. One of these social shifts has been a gradual Mexicanization of the town. This segment highlights four dimensions of community that reflect this Mexicanization. These four community dimensions include demographics, business development, the church, and the school setting.

Demographics

One of the important community dimensions in Woodburn that reflects the Mexicanization is a shift in demographics. This shift mirrors statewide demographic changes. Latinos comprise 12 percent or 466,000 of Oregon's population (Pew Research Center: Demographic Profile of Hispanics in Oregon, 2011). Latinos reside in every county in Oregon. In five communities Latinos represent 50 percent or more of the total local population (U.S. Census Bureau 2010a). Oregon's Latino population increased from 112,707 in 1990 (U.S. Census Bureau 1990) to 275,314 in 2000, and to 466,000 in 2011—a 413 percent increase since 1990. Most of Oregon's Latinos are of Mexican descent and account for 85 percent of the state's 466,000 Latino population (U.S. Census Bureau 2010). These statistics are reflective of national and regional demographic trends that identify Latinos as the largest and one of the fastest growing populations, with persons of Mexican descent representing the bulk of the growing Latino community.

Since 1980, Latino population trends in Woodburn, Oregon, clearly echo the increase in national and state Latino population. According to the 1980 U.S. Census, Woodburn's total population numbered 11,196 (U.S. Census Bureau 1980a). Persons of Spanish origin numbered 2,035 (U.S. Census Bureau 1980b) or 18 percent of Woodburn's total population (see Table 1 below). In 1990, the U.S. Census recorded Woodburn's total population at 13,404 (U.S. Census Bureau 1990). The Hispanic-origin population comprised 4,211 or 31 percent. Of Woodburn's Hispanic origin population, 3,932—or 93 percent—were of Mexican descent.

In 2000, the U.S. Census recorded 20,100 for Woodburn's total population (U.S. Census Bureau 2000c). The Hispanic population comprised 10,064 or 50.1 percent of Woodburn's total population, 88.9 percent of whom were of Mexican origin. By 2011, Woodburn's Latino population had reached 14,750 or 59 percent of the city's population. Based on the 2010 Census, people of Mexican origin represented 93.6 percent or 13,275 of Woodburn's Latino population.

The figures in Table 1 show that Woodburn has experienced continued growth through recent decades. The census data shows a 20 percent increase in population from 1980 to 1990 and another 50 percent increase from 1990 to 2000. While these figures are dramatic, Table 1 indicates that this population growth is being driven by the rapid growth in Woodburn's Latino community. For example, Woodburn's Latino population increased 107 percent between 1980 and 1990, by 139 percent between 1990 and 2000, and again by 40 percent by 2011. The resulting Mexicanization is reflected in the increasing Latino percentage of Woodburn's total population. Latinos went from representing

Table 1
Woodburn Census Information
(Source: U.S. Census Bureau: 1980, 1990, 2000, 2011)

	Total Population		Latino Population		
		% Change		% Change	% Latino
1980	11,196		2,035		18%
1990	13,404	+20%	4,211	+107%	31%
2000	20,100	+50%	10,064	+139%	50.1%
2011	25,000	+12%	14,750	+40.3%	59.0%

18 percent of the population in 1980 to comprising 50.1 percent by 2000 to nearly 60 percent by 2010. This upsurge in the Mexicana/o/ Latina/o population in Woodburn since 1980 is attributed to a growth in the birthrate, immigration, and internal migration.

The dynamic demographics described above show a rapidly expanding Mexicana/o population that impacts various sectors of the local community. However, Mexicana/os have been noticeably absent or sparsely represented in the elected governing body of Woodburn. The city's 2016 web page (www.ci.woodburn.or.us) shows that, of the seven elected city officials (mayor and six council members), only one is of Latina/o descent, and yet, Mexicana/os represent over 60 percent of the population. It is unclear whether this is due to a lack of Mexicana/o candidates, lower voter registration among Mexicana/os, or a political scene dominated by the predominantly Anglo Senior Estate population.

Business Development

A second major shift reflecting the Mexicanization of Woodburn is the emerging dominance of Mexicana/o businesses in the downtown business district. This growth is the result of two simultaneous trends. First, there is a natural link between growing Mexicana/o demographics and an expanding Mexicana/o business sector. This pattern has been repeated numerous times in Texas, California, and other southwestern states. In the past few decades, this pattern has emerged in other regions and local communities beyond the southwest. The Mexicanization of Woodburn's downtown business district is another example of this relationship between demographic growth and business development. As Woodburn's Mexicana/o population grew, there was a corresponding demand for products and services unique and familiar to Mexicana/o consumers. The fact that existing businesses were not providing these products or services created the opportunity for Mexicana/o entrepreneurship. Second, there was an exodus of Anglo businesses from downtown Woodburn leaving many vacancies in the area. These vacancies and the deterioration of many historic buildings translated into low rents. Mexicana/o entrepreneurs viewed the low rent vacancies as an opportunity to establish their businesses. The demographic shift resulting in an increased demand for products and services unique and familiar to Mexicana/o consumers and the low rents created by the exodus of Anglo businesses provided an inevitable impetus for the explosion of Mexicana/o business development in the historical downtown.

In 1957, Armandina Garcia and her family and half-dozen other Mexicana/o families came to Woodburn from South Texas. Her family traveled in a canvas-covered truck. They had immigrated to South Texas from Mexico and lived in Mission, Texas, for a short period before extending their trek to Oregon, where they worked on Woodburn area farms. Armandina also worked at Birdseye, a local processing plant. In 1964, she met and married Rogelio Medina. In 1966, the Medinas decided to open El Mexico Lindo, a small store in Woodburn's historical business district. El Mexico Lindo was the first, and for many years the only, Mexicana/o owned business in Woodburn. The Medinas sold Mexican records, curios, jewelry, and a limited selection of Mexican groceries (Medina 2005).

It was not until the 1980s that other Mexicana/o owned businesses became established in Woodburn's historical downtown. Two Mexican restaurants opened in the early 1980s. The first was Regina's Mexican Restaurant; the second was La Linda, opened in 1981 by the Carbajal family. The Carbajals had come to Woodburn to work the crops from south Texas during the 1950s. The elder Carbajal soon became a labor contractor and began to supply workers to Woodburn area farms. The family also established Carbajal Farms labor contracting business in downtown Woodburn (Merriman 1988). In the late 1980s, a third Mexican restaurant, La Michoacana, opened for business, as well as Jose

Parra's Panaderia Casas Blacas, Woodburn's first Mexican bakery (Parra 2005). Parra's bakery was short lived, and another Mexicano entrepreneur from Fresno, California, opened Salvador's Bakery in 1987 (Te 2005) and filled the void left by Parra's Mexican bakery. While most of these Mexicana/o businesses focused on cultural foods, Jose Castro and his family opened SOLO, a T-shirt and print shop, in 1987. The Castro family had begun their business venture in their garage a couple of years earlier (Merriman 1988). These businesses represented the first significant efforts by Mexicana/o entrepreneurs in downtown Woodburn and led to the Mexicanization of the historical downtown district. The 1980s were challenging economic times. The historically low success rate of small businesses, limited resources, and the economic slump during the Reagan administration collectively undermined some of the upstart Mexicana/o businesses established during this period. The majority of the businesses established during these years were closed as the decade of the 1990s began.

Mexico Lindo, Salvador's Bakery, and SOLO T-Shirts and Design were three of the four Mexicana/o businesses that weathered the economic challenges of the 1980s. Fortunately, the continued influx of Mexicana/o immigrants combined with the growth of the Mexicana/o population in Woodburn during the 1980s brought renewed interest from Mexicana/o entrepreneurs in the downtown business district during the 1990s. The 1990s can be characterized as the decade when Woodburn's Mexicana/o businesses continued to solidify as well as expand their business base and diversity.

During the 1990s, Mexico Lindo ventured into production of tortillas and tamales and secured additional downtown business space as a restaurant. The owner of Salvador's Bakery went on to open a second site beyond the downtown business district that focused on wholesale bakery production for distribution to area stores. He moved his original bakery to another downtown site and expanded the Mexican products he offered to the community. These expansions included meat and vegetable market sections, groceries, tortilla production, and a restaurant. These diverse selections as well as the bakery section made Salvador's a significant Mexicana/o anchor store in downtown Woodburn. A review of city business license listings and reverse telephone directories indicate that

Carniceria (butcher shop) in Woodburn, Oregon, 2005. *Maldonado collection*

thirty-four new Mexicana/o owned businesses were opened in the 1990s in the Woodburn downtown district. The expanding base contributed to the diversity of Mexicana/o businesses, and included clothing, shoe retail and repair stores, a meat market and other food-related stores, auto repair, telephone and money wiring services, hair salons, an attorney, social and health services, home furnishings, video rentals, music stores, novelty imports, a substantial tortilleria, and several eating establishments including taquerias (taco restaurants).

While the 1990s witnessed the significant expansion and diversity of Mexican owned businesses in downtown Woodburn, a natural attrition reflecting traditional small business failure was evident. Many of the business categories mentioned above saw significant business turnover as businesses came and went. Likewise, a few businesses relocated to other Woodburn business districts. By 2000, approximately 20 Mexicana/o businesses remained in downtown Woodburn (see Table 2 below). However, at least 37 new Mexicana/o businesses were established between 2000 and 2005. This significantly increased the level of direct competition in the area. By 2005, in the 12-block radius, there were 35 businesses

Table 2
Downtown Mexicana/o Business Growth
(*First half decade 2000-2005)

Decade	Number of New Mexicana/o Business Entrants	Number of Businesses Remaining at end of Decade			Number of Mexicana/o Business Categories
		Total	Non-Mexicana/o	Mexicana/o	
1980s	7	30	26 (87%)	4 (13%)	5
1990s	34	41	21 (51%)	20 (49%)	16
2000s*	37	52	17 (33%)	35 (67%)	16

including 3 bakeries, 2 carnicerias, 2 auto repair and towing, 3 money wiring services, 3 hair salons, 2 music stores, 6 clothing and or shoe stores, 5 novelty or import stores, and 7 eating establishments. These figures indicate multiple, direct competitors within the same business category.

While businesses come and go, a few comparisons can be made to show the transformation of the Woodburn downtown business district (see Table 2). For example, in the 1980s there were only 7 new Mexicana/o businesses that came into the business district. These represented five business categories and only 4 of the businesses remained at the end of the decade. During this decade, 87 percent of the businesses in the district were non-Latino owned. The decade of the 1990s was a turning point in business ownership. By 1999, only 51 percent of the businesses were owned by non-Mexicana/os. The number of non-Mexicana/o businesses declined from 26 to 21 while the number of Mexicana/o businesses increased from 4 to 20.

The explosion of Mexicana/o businesses in the 1990s can be seen in the 34 new entrants, the increase in types of products or services offered (see Number of Business Categories in Table 2) from 5 to 16, and in the number of businesses remaining at the end of the decade (approximately 20 in 1999 versus 4 in 1989). Table 2 indicates that the rate of new business entrants continued to grow in the 2000s. While around 34 businesses were started in the 1990s, approximately 37 new businesses were started in the first half of the next decade alone, between 2000 and 2005. The table also shows a substantial increase in the number of concurrent businesses remaining open. At the end of 1999 there were 20 storefronts occupied by Mexicana/o businesses. By 2005, the number had increased to 35. The number of business categories, however, remained fairly stable and competition within categories became much stronger. For example, at the end of 1999, the 20 remaining businesses represented 16 different business categories. By 2005, there were 35 Mexicana/o businesses in 16 categories.

It is also important to note that the number of non-Mexicana/o businesses continued to decline from 21 in 1999 to 17 in 2005 and only represented 33 percent of the total businesses in downtown Woodburn. Just as Woodburn's demographic growth had been driven by growth in the Latino community (see Table 1), the growth in the downtown business district was due to growth in Mexicana/o businesses. The increase in the number of Mexicana/o businesses was enough to offset the loss of non-Mexicana/o businesses and still show a significant increase (27 percent from 2000 to 2005) in the number of occupied storefronts in the downtown business district.

The Mexicana/o businesses also include an independent and mobile entrepreneur sector that do not occupy storefronts. This sector includes strolling musicians who petition restaurant patrons and downtown visitors to pay for a song, strolling flower vendors, paleteros (ice cream vendors) on bicycle carts, and street-side temporary food vendors selling tamales and Mexican-style corn on the cob.

Paletero (ice cream vendor) in Woodburn, Oregon, 2005. *Maldonado collection*

Several interviewees commented on the active trade in forged documents such as social security and immigration identification cards. While visiting downtown businesses, an individual peddling forged document approached one of the authors of this study. As the peddler closely walked by the author he whispered from the corner of his mouth, "¿Necesitas una mica?" (Do you need a green card?) The author engaged the peddler in further conversation, but the peddler soon realized that the author was not a likely client and continued walking down the street.

In visiting and interviewing downtown Mexicana/o business merchants, a number of conclusions can be made. First, an overwhelming number of the merchants are immigrants from Mexico. The Tejana/os who came to Woodburn in the 1950s and early 1960s were farmworkers by trade and were visibly absent in the downtown business ownership. Second, many of the Mexicana/o merchants or their extended family members have had previous business ownership experience before moving to the Woodburn area. Therefore, the notion of businesses ownership was not a novel idea. For example, Armandina Medina's father operated a small grocery store in Mexico as well as an orange grove farm. Her husband's family operated a hamburger drive-in in South Texas before moving to Woodburn (Medina 2005). Martin Ochoa, owner of Lupita's Restaurant, was part of a family run restaurant in Hillsboro before opening his restaurant in Woodburn (Ochoa 2005). Lara Jasmin Banvelos opened music stores in Independence and Gresham, Oregon, before opening Koritas Musical Imports, Inc. in Woodburn in 2001 and Mi Lindo Nayarit in 2005 (Banvelos 2005).

Third, many of the Mexicana/o businesses are family operated. This is an important point in minimizing labor costs of start-up businesses. Fourth, an overwhelming number of the Mexican businesses rent rather than own their buildings or storefronts. This precludes the businesses from building capital investment equity. It can also contribute to the deterioration of the buildings as many absentee building owners refuse to update and refurbish their buildings. The lack of ownership also reinforces the transitory nature of the small businesses. Fifth, the customer base that supports the Mexican downtown business is predominately Mexicana/o. The Mexicana/o businesses have not reached out to non-Mexicana/o consumers, thus ignoring a significant potential consumer base.

Sixth, the businesses predominantly occupy small storefronts, which may impact their potential for future growth. Seventh, most Mexicana/o downtown merchants do not participate in civic or business associations including the Woodburn Downtown Business Association. This prevents

their input into significant legislation and activities impacting their business and inhibits business networking. Eighth, most Mexican downtown
merchants do not use traditional advertising media such as the Yellow
Pages, the local newspaper, or mainstream radio or television. The most
consistent avenues of advertising are the local Spanish radio station and
word of mouth. This undermines their outreach to patrons outside of the
local Mexicana/o community. Ninth, many of the business owners have
limited or no English speaking abilities. This impedes their interactions
with city officials regarding business regulations, and presents a communication challenge to non-Spanish speaking customers.

As indicated in the preceding discussion, the Mexicanization of
Woodburn's historical business district is firmly established. This strong
Mexican presence was reinforced in August 2005 when the City of
Woodburn completed construction of a downtown city park fashioned
after the traditional Mexican plaza. In September, the city sponsored
the annual Mexican Independence Celebration at the new plaza. City
officials hope that the new plaza will contribute to increasing business
activity in the downtown by bringing more visitors and patrons to the
area (Perfecto 2005).

La Placita, the downtown city park modeled after a traditional Mexican plaza,
Woodburn, Oregon, 2005. *Maldonado collection*

Religious Life

The above sections show Woodburn's Mexicanization through the shift of demographics and the firm establishment of a Mexicana/o downtown business district. The third demonstration of this Mexicanization is the growing presence of Latinos in the religious life of the local community. This is illustrated by the level of participation by Mexicana/os in the local Catholic parish, the establishment and growth of independent Spanish Protestant churches, and active outreach efforts by mainstream Protestant churches to the Mexicana/o community.

Woodburn's St. Luke's Catholic Parish

St. Luke's Catholic Parish has a long history of serving the spiritual needs of the local Mexicana/o community (Zegar 2005), dating back to the 1950s and early 1960s. when Mexicana/os from South Texas first started coming to Woodburn as part of the migrant farmworker stream. As more Mexicana/os from South Texas came to harvest the crops in Woodburn and surrounding communities, St. Luke's implemented an outreach effort to these families. Parish representatives visited labor camps and brought Mexicana/o children to the church by bus during the summer months to attend catechism classes. These classes culminated in Mexicana/o children being confirmed as members of the church and making their first communions. The parish also conducted religious education retreats for parents. These retreats were focused on spiritual development but they also contributed to solidifying relationships and building community among the few Mexicana/o families attending St. Luke's. During the harvest season, visiting priests from Mexico came periodically to serve the growing Mexicana/o farm workers being integrated into St. Luke's. Likewise, Spanish-speaking individuals studying at the Catholic Seminary in Mt. Angel also contributed to meeting the spiritual needs of St. Luke's Mexicana/o families. Early on, Spanish mass was held once a month in the parish's basement. In 1972 and 1973, St. Luke's had its first full-time Latino priest. Several non-Latino priests over the years who spoke Spanish likewise served the Mexicana/o parishioners (Zegar 2005).

Much has changed at St. Luke's since the 1950s and early 1960s. In 2005, St. Luke's priest reported serving about 1,500 families. Sixty percent of the

Spanish mass at St. Luke's Catholic Parish, Woodburn, Oregon, 2005. *Maldonado collection*

parishioners were reported to be Mexicana/o/Latino while 40 percent were non-Latino. The overwhelming majority of Mexicana/o parishioners were Mexican immigrants who came to Woodburn in the 1980s. Many of these Mexicana/o immigrants came from the Mexican state of Oaxaca (Zegar 2005). Father Dave Zegar, St. Luke's pastor for the past eleven years, speaks Spanish and has worked with other Spanish speaking Catholic communities in Oregon and has traveled and lived in Mexico. Father Jamie Rojas, a Mexican priest from Oaxaca has been with St. Luke's since about 2000. The church celebrates Spanish mass twice on Sunday and once during the week. On the authors' recent visit to a Sunday mass, the main sanctuary, the balcony, as well as the pews in the entrance foyer were overflowing with Mexicana/o parishioners. Father Zegar established a parish office in downtown Woodburn for several years in an effort to connect with immigrant Mexicana/os visiting or living in the downtown area. He spent part of his workday at this downtown office for three years. During this time, Father Zegar was able to listen to many personal stories of immigrant men highlighting their difficult economic, immigration, family, and settlement struggles.

Fifty percent of the St. Luke's Parish Council is Mexicana/o and Mexicana/os are also well represented in the parish staff. St. Luke's operates a school as part of its mission. In 2005, the enrollment at the school was 170, of which 35 percent were Mexicana/o students. The church leadership has been actively raising scholarship funds to support Mexicana/o student enrollment (Zegar 2005). St. Luke's stages a number of Mexicana/o religious events including Las Posadas, La Fiesta de La Virgin de Guadalupe, Mesa de Gallo, and Miercoles de Ceniza (Ash Wednesday), among others. An altar dedicated to La Virgin de Guadalupe is prominently situated within the sanctuary. A Spanish-language choir resonates throughout the church during Sunday Spanish mass. St. Luke's periodically stages a bilingual mass as an effort to further integrate the Mexicana/o parishioners. Father Zegar points out that St. Luke's has strived to establish new parish ministries and ways of doing things to respond to the challenge of better serving a parish community where Mexicana/os represent the majority.

Father Zegar acknowledges that the Mexicanization of St. Luke's is clearly connected to the social-demographic shifts taking place in the wider community. He warmly shares an experience he recently had when he took a bicycle ride in Woodburn early one morning. "As I rode my bike to the edge of town, I saw the horses grazing in their fenced up area, the rooster was crowing, people were going about the daily chores, Mexican music escaped the homes, and I could smell the cooking of tortillas. The sight, sounds and smells pleasantly took me back to the days when I lived in a small Mexican town some time ago." Father Zegar shared this experience with a friend, and the friend asked him, "How long have you lived in Woodburn?" Father Zegar answered, "Eleven years." His friend replied, "And you are just realizing where you live?"

Protestant Spanish-Speaking Churches

St. Luke's represents just one dimension of the Mexicanization of religious life in Woodburn. This Mexicanization is also reflected in the founding of Protestant Spanish-speaking churches run by Mexicana/os. Within blocks from St. Luke's and close to downtown Woodburn are three such churches. Iglesia Pentcostes is the pioneering non-Catholic Spanish-speaking church in Woodburn. It is associated with the Pacific Conference of the Mennonite Church and was established in the early 1960s. When the pastor and a member of Iglesia Pentcostes were interviewed by a news source (Wozniacka 2005), the church member stated, "There are places in Mexico where Pentecostals are not welcomed. The church here is like a family. It's very peaceful in Woodburn. It's a little Mexico." Victor Vargas, the church's pastor stated, "The church offers the kind of social interaction that reminds them of home." Another early church in this classification is El Centro Cristiano associated with the Assemblies of God. This church is actively reaching out to Mexicana/os in downtown Woodburn. On one of the authors' Saturday evening visits to downtown Woodburn, some members of El Centro Cristiano handed them a religious tract that included a religious message and the church's contact information. By the mid-2000s, there were about six other denominational Spanish-speaking churches with Mexicana/o pastors active in outreach efforts towards Mexicana/os in Woodburn.

Beyond St. Luke's and Mexican-run Protestant denominational churches are the mainstream Protestant churches that have mounted an active effort at attracting the Spanish speaking community to their church. Often, these churches have established Spanish-language ministries for their members, while still working with the mainstream community. These churches are likewise active over the local radio waves with Spanish-language Christian programs. These shifts taking place within religious life are another demonstration of the Mexicanization of Woodburn, Oregon.

The Woodburn School District

Finally, the fourth community dimension that illuminates the Mexicanization of Woodburn, Oregon, is the rise of Mexican student enrollment in Woodburn schools. According to David Bautista, bilingual services director for the Woodburn School District, the district's 2005 total student enrollment was 4,800 (see Table 3 below). Latino students accounted for 3,600 or 75 percent of the district's total student enrollment. Overall, 70 percent of all Latinos were English language learners. At the high school level, 60 percent of the Latinos were English language learners (Bautista 2005). Enrollment figures for 2015-2016 show that Mexicanas/os con-

Table 3
2012 Woodburn School District Enrollment by Ethnicity

Ethnicity	Number of Students	% of Total Students
Latino	4,323	77.8%
White	1,105	19.9%
Black	44	0.8%
Asian	17	0.3%
American Indian	17	0.3%
Total	5,557	

tinue to be the largest ethnicity in the Woodburn School District with 79.8 percent of the 5,648 students Latinos (Puente 2016).

The Woodburn School District is striving to meet the challenges that these student demographics bring to the school setting. Mexicana/o students from immigrant families make up the major student population that the district works with in its bilingual programs. The district has implemented an English Transition Program (ETP) incorporating five different models or approaches that address the English language development and content learning needs of kindergarten through grade 12 English Language Learners (ELL) (Woodburn School District 2005).

Depending on the student's English language ability, an ELL student may: (1) Receive as much as a half day instruction in their native language with gradual transition into English instruction (Transitional Bilingual Model, Grades 6-12); (2) Receive instruction in English but supported with some native language instruction (Structured Immersion Model, K-12); (3) Receive instruction at a literacy center where instruction is given in English and/or a student's native language. ELL students placed in the literacy center have special language and/or academic needs that the literacy center can focus on (Literacy Center, 4-12); (4) Receive instruction in mainstream, English language classrooms. ELL students enrolled in this instructional model have a reasonable command of verbal English skills and exhibit academic abilities in English (Mainstream Instruction Model, K-12); (5) Receive instruction in a two-way bilingual approach. ELL students involved in this approach receive instruction in English and second-target class (Russian or Spanish) in kindergarten and gradually increase English language instruction in the upper grades (Two-Way Bilingual Model, K-12). Both ELL and fluent English speakers participate in these bilingual classrooms (Woodburn School District 2005).

The district's goal is to secure academic success and bilingual literacy for English speakers and targeted language speakers (Russian or Spanish). Woodburn School District has an articulated priority to train certified and classified staff in bilingual education to effectively implement the English Transition Program. An important aspect of the program is that parents are informed and given the choice to have their child enrolled in a particular ETP program after an assessment has been completed. A significant point, however, is the noticeable absence of integrating or recognizing culture as an important element in the district English Transitional Program efforts.

In order to address the need to integrate culture into school programs, the district has instituted a mariachi band initiative as part of the high school's music curriculum (Te 2005). Woodburn High School's mariachi band is the only such initiative in Oregon. One of Woodburn's middle schools named and dedicated its library in honor of César Chávez. Additionally, the district has been co-sponsor of the Annual César Chávez Commemoration, and the 2005 commemoration was staged at the high school. This is an important link to Mexicana/o immigrant students who come from families whose livelihood is often connected to the agricultural sector. Additionally, the district has placed a bilingual assistant principal at each of the district's schools.

During fall 2005, the author participated in a professional educational conference sponsored by the district that focused on language and culture. Sessions such as "Family, Language and Culture in the Classroom," "Voices from the Gap: A Qualitative Look at Hispanic Achievement Gap," and "Bridging the Family and School Culture," were of particular relevance to issues generated by the Mexicanization of the Woodburn School District.

Mentioned above are specific strategies the district has implemented to respond to issues related to the Mexicanization of school enrollments in Woodburn. There are additional issues the district will need to examine in its efforts to further respond to the continued Mexicanization of the district. These issues include Latino bilingual staffing, integration of language and culture in the academic development of students, high school completion rates of Mexicana/o students, progression of Mexicana/o graduates into higher education, Mexicana/o representation in the district's leadership, and other related and critical issues.

SOME COMMUNITY SENTIMENTS REGARDING WOODBURN'S MEXICANIZATION

The above sections document the Mexicanization of Woodburn reflected in the school setting, community demographics, the historical down business district, and local churches. This transformation has not gone unnoticed by non-Mexicana/o community members. We interviewed several non-Mexicana/o community members who shared some positive and negative perceptions concerning the Mexicanization. The following are examples of some of the sentiments shared by these informants. Most of these informants requested that they remain anonymous.

Positive Sentiments

"Hey, they (Mexicana/os) are basically coming here for the same reasons that some of us came here many years ago. We came to find jobs and make a life."

"My parents came here from Idaho in 1923. Our wheat crop was destroyed by a severe storm so my father came here and found work at a dairy."

"The Hispanics are keeping the downtown alive. If it was not for them, the downtown would have died."

"The Mexicans are hard working. What is happening is a natural progression."

"I have not had any problems with Mexicans. In fact, I came to know this Mexican guy who lived near the downtown. He would come over to my gas station and we would have coffee at the Club Café. He was a prince of guy."

"I have never been bothered by any of them (Mexicans) and I work downtown.

"There is a great deal of intermixing and acceptance on the younger level."

Negative Sentiments

"They get government money and that is how they start their businesses."

"You read the paper, and the majority of those arrested are Mexicans. Drunk driving and selling drugs."

"The ladies don't like to go downtown because they feel uncomfortable with the Mexican men just loitering around. They just stand around and watch people go by and that gives people the creeps."

"The city should not favor just one group. The Plaza does just that. The city should make a park for everyone not just one group."

"Some people feel like they are losing control. When there were a few Mexicans it wasn't a concern, but now (that) the Mexican community has grown, some people feel threatened."

"Some old retired men in the community that no longer have to deal on a regular basis with the public are very racist, very racist and don't have a good thing to say about anyone of Mexican origin."

"There have been cars broken into, houses, and our motor home was broken into too. A woman was assaulted in our neighborhood. And all of it, all of it was Hispanics. The newspaper constantly is, you know, all the police reports are Hispanic. You have a mistrust, that is kind of basic and it is growing because the problem is growing."

"Some young guys hit my mail box and took off. The police got them. They had no driver's license, no insurance, and it was difficult to know who really owned the car. If they are in a car accident, they get out of the car and run. That doesn't make for good relations, race relations. It does not make for trust. It does not make for easy acceptance."

"The Anglos don't go downtown. Why should they? What is down there for them?"

These comments from some non-Mexicana/o community members in Woodburn demonstrate both positive and negative sentiments. Comments that Mexicana/os are closely linked to crime activity surfaced as a reoccurring sentiment. Such perceptions certainly reinforce old stereotypical images of Mexicana/os. While these perceptions may be based on some actual illegal activities downtown, the perceptions have been generalized to the entire Mexicana/o community and undermine positive inter-ethnic relationships. Additionally, some perceptions are based on false assumptions. For example, the notion that Mexicana/o businesses are started with government money is not accurate. Most business owners interviewed in this study started their businesses on a shoestring without loans. This limited investment capital is one of the reasons for the high attrition rate among Mexicana/o businesses. Another foundation for the negative perceptions is the result of cultural differences. For example, Mexicana/os are accustomed to using the downtown streets, sidewalks, and parks as social gathering places. Anglos view this social gathering practice as loitering, and feel uncomfortable because they feel that they are being watched.

Perhaps a more serious foundation for the negative comments was the expressed sense of losing control. It is conceivable that many of the negative perceptions could have been overlooked until the majority demographic standing of the Anglo population became threatened and many began to feel a loss of social control. This sense of losing control very likely magnified the perceived issues undermining ethnic relations. This sense of losing control was also reflected in comments that the downtown was now only for Mexicans, that there was no longer anything for Anglos downtown, and that the plaza was constructed for Mexicans only. One informant stated that the city should not make a park for just one group. This sense of losing control of the downtown was expressed as an attitude of loss rather than an attitude of gaining an expanded diverse community brought about by Mexicana/os and Mexicana/o culture. It is also interesting to note that the sense of loss or exclusion expressed a notion of ethnic parallel existence that was not to be bridged. It is as if informants were saying, "If the downtown is now for them, it is no longer for us." There is no indication of sharing or mutual appreciation in these comments. In fact, very few Anglos attended the Mexicana/o celebrations observed by the authors in this study.

Even though the preceding discussion highlights some negative ethnic relations issues, the positive comments offered by some Non-Mexicana/os indicate that some have an appreciation of Mexicana/o presence. One informant even recognized that the Mexicana/o businesses are what kept the Woodburn historical business district alive.

Conclusion

The Mexicanization of Woodburn, Oregon, is firmly in place. This is demonstrated in community demographics, the presence of Mexicana/o businesses in the historical downtown, the local churches, and student enrollments in the Woodburn School District. Demographics have been the driving force in the changing character of Woodburn. This local social change will continue as the Mexicana/o presence becomes reflected in other dimensions of community in the future. Specifically, Mexicana/o representation in local politics will be one such area. This representation will include positions on the local city council, city boards and committees, as well as the local school board. Mexicana/os hold or have held posts in the local political structure but their presence has been minimal. The natural progression of the Mexicanization wave in Woodburn, Oregon provides an opportunity to study Mexican questions of immigration, Mexicana/o entrepreneurship development, ethnic relations, the social dynamics of changing communities due to demographics, and a host of other contemporary social issues.

References

Banvelos, Lara Jasmin. 2005. Interview, October 8. Woodburn, OR.

Bautista, David. 2005. Interview, October 14. Woodburn, OR.

City of Woodburn. 2005. GSI Map of Woodburn, Oregon. City of Woodburn Planning Department.

Cutter, Donald C. 1981. *Malaspina and Galiano: Spanish Voyages to the Northwest Coast, 1971–1792*. Seattle: University of Washington Press.

Engstrand, Iris H.W. 1991. "Jose Mariano Moziño: Pioneer Mexican Naturalist." *Columbia: The Magazine of Northwest History* (Spring): 19–22.

French, Giles. 1965. *Cattle Country of Peter French*. Portland, OR: Binford and Mort Publishers.

Gamboa, Erasmo. 1990. *Mexican Labor and World War II: Braceros in the Pacific Northwest, 1942–1947*. Austin: University of Texas Press.

Maldonado, Carlos S. 1995. "An Overview of the Mexicano/Chicano Presence in the Pacific Northwest." In *The Chicano Experience in the Northwest*, edited by Carlos S. Maldonado and Gilberto García. Dubuque, IA: Kendall/Hunt Publishing Company.

Medina, Armandina. 2005. Interview, July 28. Woodburn, Oregon.

Merriman, Ed. 1988. "Hispanics Build on Heritage." *Statesman-Journal* (Salem, OR) May 13, 1988, pg. 1F.

Ochoa, Martin. 2005. Interview, July 15. Woodburn, Oregon.

Parra, Jose. 2005. Interview, October 8. Woodburn, Oregon.

Perfecto, Javier. 2005. Interview, October 10. Woodburn, Oregon.

Puente, Benito Jr., 2016. Interview October 13, 2016. Woodburn, Oregon.

Te, Michelle. 2005. "Just a Little Mariachi Music Magic." *Woodburn (OR) Independent*, August 3, 2005, pg. 8.

U.S. Census Bureau. 2000a. "GCT-P6. Race and Hispanic or Latino: 2000," in Oregon—Place. American FactFinder. Washington, DC: U.S. Census Bureau.

_____. 2005. "Hispanic Population Passes 40 Million, Census Bureau Reports," in U.S. Census Press Releases, edited by Robert Bernstein. Vol. 2005, June 9. Washington, DC: U.S. Census Bureau News.

_____. 2004. "Population Finder Woodburn City, Oregon," Vol. 2005. American FactFinder. Washington, DC: U.S. Census Bureau.

_____. 2000b. "QT-P9. Hispanic or Latino by Type: 2000," Oregon, Vol. 2005. American FactFinder. Washington, DC: U.S. Census Bureau.

_____. 1990. "Table 6: Race and Hispanic Origin," Geographic Area: Woodburn Oregon. Washington, DC: U.S. Census Bureau.

_____. 1980a. "Table 56: Summary of Social Characteristics," Geographic Area: Oregon. Washington, DC: U.S. Census Bureau.

_____. 1980b. "Table 59: Persons of Spanish Origin, Race and Sex," Geographic Area: Oregon (Ed.). Washington, DC: U.S. Census Bureau.

_____. 2000c. "Table DP-1: Profile of General Demographic Characteristics: 2000," Geographic Area: Oregon. Washington, DC: U.S. Census Bureau.

_____. 2004. "U.S. Interim Projections by Age, Sex, Race, and Hispanic Origin," Vol. 2005, March 18. Washington, DC: U.S. Census Bureau.

Watt, James W. 1978. *Journal of Mule Train Packing in Eastern Washington in the 1860s*. Fairfield: Ye Galleon Press.

Woodburn Centennial Commission. 1989. Woodburn Centennial Program." City of Woodburn, Oregon.

Woodburn Chamber of Commerce. 1994. "Woodburn Area Growth and Diversity." In *1994-95 Business Directory and Community Guide*, edited by Jane Kanz, Executive Director. Woodburn: Woodburn Chamber of Commerce.

Woodburn School District. 2005. "Educational Approach and Setting Goals," Vol. 2005. Woodburn, OR: Woodburn School District.

Wozniacka, Gosia. 2005. "Thriving Latino Community Builds a Better Life in Woodburn." News story. KATU (ABC-TV affiliate).

Zegar, Father Dave. 2005. Interview, October 7. Woodburn, Oregon.

CHAPTER 8

Norteada/Northed: My Tears Created the Great Lakes

Theresa Meléndez

In Tomás Rivera's *Tierra*, when a migrant worker is asked why she won't be going to Utah, she replies: "se nos hace que no hay ese estado" (We don't believe there is such a state). The other migrant tells her that in fact, Utah is close to Japan (Rivera 1995, 21). Here Rivera's migrants, in an ethnicized Orientalism perhaps, extrapolate "el Norte" to any unknown territory—the point being, that wherever this place is, it does not belong within the known realm of the Chicano. It might as well be in Asia. To contemporary southwestern Chicanas/os, the Midwest often presents them with a similar situation: The Midwest is an unknown site, an unknown direction, and an unknown quantity when thinking about Mexicans.[1] The existence of midwestern Mexicans complicates a Chicana/o cultural identity, already contested, contradictory, multi-formed, and historically inscribed as pertaining to a particular geographical and cultural landscape.

In the history of Mexicans in the United States, place, of course, has been decidedly significant when defining and constructing cultural identity, especially in the aftermath of the Mexican American War, when the entire Mexican population of northern Mexico had to readjust the boundaries of nation, self, and identity; to name *place* was to define homeland. During the Chicano movement of the late 1960s, especially with "El Plan Espiritual de Aztlán,"[2] the Southwest became reified as that homeland in the appropriation of the myth of Aztlán—although according to colonial documents, the Aztec themselves considered the valley of

Mexico their promised land, led there conclusively by their gods; in fact, they took the name "Mexica" to affirm their new identity (Duran 1964). To Luis Leal, the theme of Aztlán in both Chicano and Mexican novels appears to be the "peregrination" itself, the departure from or the search for the promised land (Leal 1989, 22-23). Aztlán was the place we left, and so it appears to be for midwestern Mexicans.

But as a transplanted Tejana in Michigan, I have found that Midwest Chicanas/os don't necessarily feel they have "left" anything, and certainly not their "culture." My use of the vernacular *norteada* (disoriented) is, of course, ironic, because Mexicans have migrated *al norte* since the beginning of the century, if not earlier, hailed by agriculture as well as the auto and steel industries. Two colleagues and I have interviewed senior "immigrants" to Michigan, who, in their *testimonios* clearly emphasize both their attachment to the Midwest and the continuation of culturally-based behaviors, including establishing community associations, maintaining food culture, re-creating various types of Mexicano music, participating in Mexican community celebrations, continuing traditions, and expressing (less easily defined) Mexicano social values.[3] They are not disoriented in the least. Although many midwestern Mexicans proudly claim to be Tejano, they equally proudly stake their claim to Michigan. In this state, the Southwest and Midwest often meet in imagined landscapes of cultural appropriation in a dynamic that gives diaspora a new meaning, as in the line quoted in the title, from a ninety-two-year-old woman from Kalamazoo who begins her interview by stating: "I suffered so much I think my tears created the Great Lakes." A similarly expressive articulation is the transformation of the state capital Lansing to "Aztlansing" by the local chapter of Brown Berets, also picked up by a high school Chicana theater group who called themselves Aztlanzing Productions. Chicano students at Michigan State University often describe themselves as Michicanos (or MiXicanos) and bilingual community publications keep us informed of events, issues, and people, in a mode that would indicate the region is primarily Latino. Even so, the sense of a perpetual migrant-hood continues to obtain, when in fact, demographic research tells us that the majority of Michigan Latinos are native born. The presumed community boundaries of geography, ethnicity, and culture at times appear to be questioned, at other times fiercely affirmed.

Some theorists on the relationship between diaspora and cultural identity have framed the migratory experience as fundamental to identity. For example, the brothers Boyarin writing on Jewish identity, describe diaspora as the "ground," a basic logical condition or a basis for thought and action (Boyarin 2002). For Chicano history and culture in the Midwest, this identity is marked by at least three interrelated foci that are constructed through the lens of place or homeland:

1) the original loss of the homeland to the U.S.;

2) a secondary loss at being "displaced" in the mythification or symbolization of the Southwest as the homeland; and

3) the individual experience or subjectivity of each Chicana/o's concept of homeland.

In the dynamic of our identity politics—not only in the 1960s when expertise in barriology (knowledge of the barrio) was sometimes seen as a requisite for participation in the movement, but also going back to the nineteenth-century Spanish-language newspaper critics who decried the loss of the language, the values, and the culture of the newly emerging Mexican American—the search for authenticity is still an underlying tension. Often, among Chicanas/os, "Where are you from" translates to "how Chicano are you." In other words, are you the real thing? Did you originate in the "authentic" barrio, state, or region?

My work in the oral tradition has taught me the futility of looking for "origins," that ineffable beginning, as if it held the key to the authentic and could explain the present, while dismissing the versions as pale copies or corrupted images of the true. The mark of the authentic in oral tradition in fact is the existence of versions, a concept that displaces the authentic from the text to the process, that is, culturally speaking, from the originary native culture to the historical and social processes that make the culture. About the question of authenticity, Rey Chow in *Writing Diaspora* says: "…whenever the oppressed, the native, the subaltern…are used to represent the point of 'authenticity' for our critical discourse, they become at the same time the place of myth-making and an escape from the impure nature of political realities" (Chow 1993, 44). It is this process of myth-making and escape that is at play in the question of identity for Chicanos in a location not conventionally or symbolically their own.

What makes the Midwest Mexican "authentic" is the same process that created the Southwest Mexican: exploitation and resistance; racialization and oppression; and the consequences of the continual influx of Mexican culture due to our proximity to the homeland, the transnational experience. This historical process joins with the symbolic construction of community, and "assertion of community," to create a Mexicano/ Chicano identity. Yet, the Chicanos/as of the Midwest do have a sense of displacement, and often decry their distance from "their land," while at the same time, remain firm in their loyalty to the Midwest. For me, the question becomes: what is at stake in this identity, and what is the relation between individual identity and community identity? And, when/ how does the construction of a Mexicano identity serve as a vehicle for progressive political movement?

The two examples I draw from our interviews of pre-World War II migrants to Michigan come from two distinctive conceptualizations of Mexican/Chicano identity as well as political positioning; while all three informants would describe themselves as Mexicanos, it is their relationship to the homeland, in whatever guise, that creates these differences. I chose narrative selections, which describe most strongly their relation to Mexican culture, or what Raymond Williams would call, a "structure of feeling." The first interviewees were the Garcías, a couple in their late seventies; they had five children, both worked in the auto industry, both have visited their relatives in Mexico, and are well-known in the Chicano community of Lansing. They were among the ten or so couples who in 1947 began *El Comité Patriotico*, one of the many mutual-aid organizations that were formed in other Mexicano communities throughout the United States. The second, Edelmira López, in her late sixties, is now a single woman, also politically active and among those who began *El Comité*, less affluent than the Garcías, who married and left Texas, vowing never to return, in order to get away from her relatives.

In the first example, Mr. Luciano García begins his narrative by explaining that he was born in Mexico but "has been here for the rest of my life." His first anecdote, in English, explains how at the age of two and a half, he rejected his mother's attempt to cross the border into the U.S. "Evidently, I realized I was leaving my country. I got away from my mother and ran back to Mexico, my home. I just didn't want to have anything to do with the U.S." He tells us he still plans to return to live in the beautiful village of his birth, describing it in some detail. He explains how the town has its own history, which he traced through the cemetery and church records, that it survived "revolutions of different governments," and that its fiesta in August is "wonderful…I didn't see anything like that up here." He has visited it on a few occasions and will return to live at his birthplace, he says, because "they got everything there," again describing in detail its marketplace, the many fresh fruits, vegetables, meats, and *pulques* (traditional alcoholic beverages) available there. His father left Mexico, he says, only because of the dangers of the Revolution and because he heard of the "big opportunities" in the U.S., but "he always thought we'd go back." They all traveled "up North" by Pullman train, in a manner very distinctive from that of his wife's family.

Mrs. Rafaela García, whose grandparents were from Mexico, begins her interview with their story, one she has been told many times by her family because "they suffered so much on the way." This arduous journey was indeed a pilgrimage, in Leal's sense of peregrination—a journey of great sacrifice and much hope. Her grandparents walked from Ciudad Juarez, Chihuahua, to Rockford, Illinois, with their eleven children; although they began as a family of eighteen, seven died from typhoid at the border. Following the railroad tracks all the way, they traveled for over a year until they reached their destination. As she tells us this, she weeps quietly and says: "from then on they suffered. They told me all these stories when I was growing up. How they suffered!"

When describing her early marriage, she says she lived with her in-laws, "al estílo mexicano," but had to return home, to Rockford, often because of homesickness. "That old disease for which there is no medi-cine," interjects Mr. García. They finally move into their own apartment in a house owned by "unos arabes" (again Mr. García interjects, "amigos míos"), who treated her "like I was one of their own." Mrs. García's experience in Rockford was multi-ethnic, with Italians as her best friends, but her Mexican identity and culture were never at question when she talked about herself. For example, she remembers an aunt, educated in Mexico, who would have the children participate in community dramas, such as a *pastorela*. In 1947, both Garcías, helped create *El Comité Patriotico* with ten other couples: "Siempre nos reuniamos, los poquitos que eramos aquí, nos juntabamos." (We always came together, the few that were here, we got together). About the eventual loss of *El Comité*, she said, "Era poquito doloroso, siendo mexicano, pierde uno algo." (It was a little painful, since it was Mexican, one loses something). Even discussing interracial marriages among her children did not break the frame of their Mexican identity. Mr. García says to her at one point: "Begin telling them about your gringos," in mock sternness, "gringos con Mexican faces." They proudly speak of two grandsons, both interracial, who work very hard at speaking Spanish. "My father says I'm a wannabe," he reports his grandson saying, "aren't I Mexican?" His grandfather answers, "You're already half, a wannabe makes up a fourth, so you're all Mexican."

To both of the Garcías, the departures from the homeland are significant and are valued memories. Obviously, neither has had a direct memory of this experience, but their identity as Mexicanos has been fixed by a painful or wistful departure. Their origins in Mexico are very important to them, as signified by the relative length of the description of their "villages." The Garcías have been active in social and political organizations in the community and are proud of how they instilled the love of Mexican culture in their home, "where it should be learned," says Mr. García, "not in schools." Mrs. García, a third-generation Mexicana, says about her parents' family: "Nos criaron con el mismo tema y cultura que se criaron ellos, que trajieron de Mexico," (We were brought up with the same subject matter and culture that they were raised in and which they brought from Mexico), and relates how they continued this tradition with their own children.

It is clear that the Garcías' Mexican identity originates in a very consciously constructed past, around a perceived set of cultural values, and one fraught with the dangers of nostalgia, albeit a self-created nostalgia, since neither of the Garcías have lived in Mexico. It is this framework that serves as a vehicle for self-definition. They have constructed their identities—of community, families, and themselves—in an imagined homeland of plenitude and beauty. This construction of identity serves to create a sense of solidarity and allegiance to the culture and recognition of shared and valued characteristics (Hall 1996).

The second interview was with Mrs. Edelmira López, who moved to Michigan, she tells us, to get away from her relatives, and she vowed never to return to Texas. Her young life was marked by the death of her mother and her subsequent care by a relative, with whom, she says tartly, she learned about "inequality." A short time after they arrived in Michigan, she and her husband rented a "flat" in an apartment building where they were the managers:

> *Metimos mucha gente mexicana con nosotros y así se hiso como un barrisito, para juntarnos, porque no había mucha gente mexicana...La majoría de la gente era mexico-americano, entonces no había muchos hispanos de otras partes, o latinos, o comoquieren llamarse.* (We brought in many Mexican people with us and that was how it became like a little barrio, so that we could meet together because there were not many Mexican people...the majority of the people were Mexican-American. At that time, there were not many Hispanics from other parts, or Latinos, or whatever they want to call themselves.)

She tells us how their friends would gather in one or two homes, simply to be together:

> *Se juntaba la gente...los poquitos que había...Se fue viniendo gente— braceros de mexico y otros migrantes de California, Texas, Arizona, etc...y así nosotros fuimos haciendo raíces...Entre más raíces, empezamos a creser, hacimos un grupito politico.* (The people would gather together...the few there were...people were coming—braceros from Mexico and other migrants from California, Texas, Arizona, etc...and in that way we began to make roots...With more roots, we began to grow, we created a small political group.)

She also explains their many activities, celebrations of Mexican national holidays, fiestas, and dances:

> *Y así empezo la gente a juntarse y seguir la culture mexicana.... Porque nosotros fuimos los que traimos aqui los tamales, el pan dulce, los riñones de res, las cabezas, el menudo. Todas esas cosas no se conocian aquí y ahora todos los anglos y morenos y todos comen la misma cosa.* (And that is how the people began to gather together and to continue the Mexican culture...because we were the ones that brought the tamales here, the pastries, beef kidneys, beef heads, and menudo. All those

things were not even known here and today all the Anglos and Blacks and everyone all eat the same thing.)

She explains how the people would go to slaughterhouses to pick up the leavings—all part of Mexican cuisine, she laughs. In describing her political activities—working to improve the living conditions in the migrant community, creating a credit union and the mutual aid organization, and instigating marches and demonstrations—she states, "We all did what was needed." When working with the migrants, she would take her children, she says, so that they could see "el campo...para que supieran las raíces de la gente mexicana" (the fields...so they could know the roots of the Mexican people). All these activities, she describes as "abriendoles el camino a los nuevos, los demás" (opening the pathway for the newly arrived, for the rest of us).

In this narrative, we learn that Mrs. López literally constructs community by gathering Mexican immigrants to form "a little barrio." She delineates the ethnic boundaries, not exclusively but descriptively, including both Mexican nationals and Chicanos from other states, in the formation of community. Reproducing traditions, celebrations, and foods, allows them to "continue the culture," but what is interesting to note is that she describes the creation of community, as a process that she calls making "roots." Her own roots, her origin in Texas, do not appear to be a factor in determining the identity of community and personhood because her objective is a specific political one: to gather the sufficient numerical strength that will lead to the empowerment of her community. This political agency is what she describes as "roots." And here, paradoxically we might say, she clearly defines Mexicano identity as one of migrant-hood since she identifies *el campo*, the working fields of the migrants, as the symbolic "roots of the people." The journey of migrant-hood itself is her metaphor for this rootedness, this stability in instability that allows for the journey to continue: "the opening of the pathway."

In *Borderlands*, Gloria Anzaldúa writes of this instability, this disorientation also: "Estoy norteada por todas las voces que me hablan/ simultáneamente" (I'm lost because of all the voices that speak to me simultaneously). She argues that this state arises from the clash of cultures and subsequently we undergo "a struggle of borders, an inner war" that can leave us floundering (*norteada*). Or the struggle can move us towards "a tolerance for ambiguity" if we embrace a "new consciousness—a mestiza consciousness." As mestizos, she says, we have no country, no race, and no culture except that which we participate in creating and shaping into new myths and new perspectives (Anzaldúa 1987, 79–82). I believe that Senora López has succeeded in creating just such a mestiza consciousness.

Stuart Hall describes migrant-hood in this way: "Identity is formed at the unstable point where the 'unspeakable' stories of subjectivity meet the narratives of history, of a culture. And since he/she is positioned in relation to cultured narratives which have been profoundly expropriated, the colonized subject is always 'somewhere else': doubly marginalized, displaced always other than where he or she is, or is able to speak from" (Hall 1996, 135).

These two narratives—from Luciano and Rafaela García, whose identity is caught up in the mythification of the past, and from Edelmira López, who rejects her origins for a re-creation of Mexican community in the present—inform us, as Anthony Cohen says, "that people assert community, whether in the form of ethnicity or of locality, when they recognized in it the most adequate medium for the expression of their whole selves" (Cohen 2002, 107). Although neither the Garcías nor Mrs. López focus directly on the experience of racism and exploitation in their narratives, this marker of their ethnicity is definitely an underlying theme that colors their sense of themselves and their people—and how they arrived in this locale. The expression of self for the Garcías places community in the past, a community with a history and a culture that are important to preserve and to celebrate. For Edelmira López, however, her assertion of community is placed in the present and the future, a people with a destiny to forge. Both exemplify how the loss of the geographical bases of community boundaries has led to a renewed assertion of identity in symbolic terms, however different.

With these brief examples, I do not wish to make any totalizing statements about Chicano identity in the Midwest, except to suggest how formation of self and community emerge from the "drive for a homeland" (Padilla 1994, 114) in these testimonies. The material conditions obtained by Chicanos throughout the Midwest are framed by a sense of displacement felt from being out of Aztlán, that is, twice over landless, historically and intraculturally. And yet, as another migrant, Arturo Rocha Alvarado, has written about the Midwest in *Cronica de Aztlán: A Migrant's Tale* (1977), while recognizing that "the poor Chicanos did not own a single inch of that fertile land" they worked, "[he] had traveled the Migrant routes for such a long time that he felt all the country was his home" (Alvarado 1977, 29, 109). In migrant-hood, one understands the ideology of possession and rejects it. One is free from the strictures of identity that others have imposed. And one acquires the necessary conditions for the war of position: self-reflexivity and agency. Or as a MiXicana poet has written: "Aztlán is everywhere I've ever walked."

Notes

1. Of course, Dennis Valdés and Zaragosa Vargas, among others, have given us excellent studies on immigration, labor, and living conditions on Midwest Chicanas/os.
2. "El Plan Espiritual de Aztlán" was the manifesto adopted by the first National Chicano Liberation Youth Conference in Denver, Colorado on March 1969.
3. Javier Pescador and Diana Rivera and I received a small grant to interview Michigan seniors from 2000–2002; all interviews are in the MSU Library CLS collection.

Works Cited

Alvarado, Arturo Rocha. 1977. *Cronica de Aztlán: A Migrants Tale*. Berkeley, CA: Tqs Publishers.

Anzaldúa, Gloria. 1987. *Borderlands/La Frontera: The New Mestiza*. San Francisco: Spinsters/Aunt Lute Book Company.

Boyarin, Jonathan and Daniel Boyarin. 2002. *Power of Diaspora: Two Essays on the Relevance of Jewish Culture*. Minneapolis: University of Minnesota Press.

Chow, Rey. 1993. *Writing Diasporas: Tactics of Intervention in Contemporary Cultural Studies*. Bloomington: Indiana University.

Cohen, Anthony. 2002. *Self-Consciousness: An Alternative Anthropology of Identity*. New York, NY: Routledge Press.

Duran, Fray Diego. 1964. *The Aztecs: The History of the Indies of New Spain*. New York, NY: Orion Press.

Hall, Stuart. 1996. *Modernity: An Introduction to Modern Societies*. Cambridge, MA: Blackwell Press.

Leal, Luis. 1989. "In Search of Aztlán." In *Aztlán: Essays on the Chicano Homeland*, edited by Rudolfo A. Anaya and Francisco A. Lomeli. Albuquerque, NM: Academia/El Norte Publications.

Padilla, Genaro M. 1994. *My History Not Yours: The Formation of a Mexican American Autobiography*. Madison, WI: University of Wisconsin Press.

Rivera, Tomás. 1995. *...y no se lo tragó la tierra*. Houston, TX: Arte Publico Press.

CHAPTER 9

Becoming Aztlán in the Northern Borderlands

Jerry García

"♪ *Salieron de San Ysidro, procedentes de Tijuana /Traían las llantas del carro repletas de hierba mala /Eran Emilio Varela y Camelia la Tejana ♪*." (They left San Ysidro from Tijuana/they had the tires of their car filled with "the bad weed"/They were Emilio Varela and Camelia the Texan woman.) This is the first line from a famous song, "Contrabando y Traición," sung by Los Tigres del Norte, one of the most beloved bands for people of Mexican origin in the United States. Composed in the early 1970s, "Contrabando y Traición" explored the taboo topic of illicit drug trafficking and became one of the first narcocorridos, a subgenre of *corrido* music.[1]

As teenagers this was my cousin Mundo's anthem and mine as we set out on the weekends to raise whatever hell we could in a community of three thousand people located in North Central Washington. I remember cruising in Mundo's Black Trans AM 6.6L with Los Tigres blaring from the Blaupunkt speakers and doing our best to emulate our fathers' *gritos* (shouts). Our gritos were often followed by the lines: "♪livin' easy, lovin' free season ticket on a one-way ride/askin' nothin' leave me be…/I'm on the highway to hell ♪. "Highway to Hell" by heavy metal rock gods AC/DC was our secondary (mainstream) anthem as we tried to stay cool and current with our white peers in Quincy, Washington.

Mundo and I felt a strong connection to "Contrabando y Traición" not because we were involved in drug trafficking, but rather for how the corrido spoke to us regarding the ideas of freedom, rebellion, and identity.

The corrido was also very popular within the Mexican community because it spoke of betrayal, something the Mexican community experienced on numerous occasions from mainstream society. More important, Los Tigres del Norte, like many of their fans, were immigrants/migrants "who crossed the border and made it to America, but never shed their most precious commodity, their Mexicanidad or their Mexicanness."[2] On another level I believe the popularity of "Contrabando y Traición" can be explained by the fact that it reminds many ethnic Mexicans that they, too, regardless of status, are treated as contraband as they move from state-to-state or from Mexico to the United States. When this song emerged in the early 1970s the movement of marijuana to the United States was commonplace. This smuggling speaks to the idea of borders and the dangers of navigating such terrain with a cargo of contraband. The same comparison can be made with the smuggling of human beings along the same pipelines as illicit drugs. The confrontation between *La Migra* (immigration authorities) or law enforcement with both smugglers and immigrants/migrants/Chicanx resonates with the lived experience of many Mexicans. Danger lurked on multiple fronts for Mexicans entering the United States, and simply being Mexican was layered with peril. As a result, "Contrabando y Traición" is imbued with many elements of the Mexican lived experience, both real and metaphorical. Ultimately, the images of freedom, borders, treachery, betrayal, and rebellion are why Mundo and I gravitated so strongly to this groundbreaking song.

My adolescent experiences allowed me to explore the various borders, cultures, and contradictions I had to navigate in an attempt to maintain my *mexicanidad* or Mexican identity, in a location with few Mexicans. At the same time, I struggled against assimilation forces that often subsumed part of my identity.[3] This chapter provides a personal insight, an auto-ethnographic examination, of a Chicano existence in the Pacific Northwest, a borderland experience different from that of Mexicans in the Southwest. I submit that living and growing up in the Pacific Northwest provided unique experiences that varied from those along or within the traditional U.S.-Mexico borderlands. Gloria Anzaldúa wrote: "Borders are set up to define the places that are safe and unsafe, to distinguish *us* from *them*."[4] Anzaldúa spoke from her experience as a queer Chicana from the U.S.-Mexico borderlands, yet her experiences resonate with all borderlands people.

We, as Chicanxs in the Pacific Northwest slipped in and out of various cultural identities as a coping mechanism for survival. This experience also illustrates the multi-dimensional spaces occupied by Chicanxs in the northern borderlands and the various corridors of our lived experience. The northern borderlands of the Pacific Northwest also provided many contrasts. For example, the dichotomies of modernity/traditionalism, Mexican culture/U.S. culture, U.S.-Canadian border/U.S.-Mexican border came to represent my lived experience. We lived in multiple worlds, sliding in and out of what seemed parallel universes, never forgetting our origins and the culture of our family, but also embracing mainstream ethos as teenagers. This is the world we created for ourselves, the one I remember—and when out of the Northwest—the one I long for.

THE FUTURE MEETS THE PAST—BORDERLANDS IN THE TWENTY-FIRST CENTURY

I was raised in the small, segregated, rural farming community of Quincy, Washington, where, in the 1970s, Mexican-origin residents represented approximately 12 percent of the overall population of 3,237. During that time Quincy epitomized many of the concerns that were raised by Chicanx activists in the Northwest: a population with few opportunities beyond agriculture; a high push-out rate of Chicanx high school students; objectionable attitudes towards people of Mexican ancestry; and a social-economic-political structure that offered little concern for the Mexican population. As a young boy I recall a summer gathering of Chicanx college students at the local park when a Brown Beret from the University Washington suddenly jumped to his feet and shouted, "Let's not fight amongst ourselves; let's unite and fight the white man!" At that age I was not able to fully understand the meaning of that proclamation, but this memory resonates with me today because it was my first, albeit limited, introduction to community mobilization and how a small group of Chicanxs dared to confront a system that viewed them in a negative light. Demographically, Quincy has changed dramatically since the 1970s and 1980s and yet it remains embedded in my memory as the beginning of my cultural and political awakening.

Besides the remarkable growth of the Mexican population in Quincy in the past twenty-years, another transformation has changed the landscape of the region: the migration of technology giants to the fertile, irrigated Columbia Basin. My hometown is located in the northern region of the Columbia Plateau, approximately 170 miles south of the Canadian border. The Columbia River, which begins in Canada, flows within a ten-minute drive of Quincy. Modern technology, through a series of dams and canals, carries the Columbia's water right into the community. Until recently Quincy was primarily known for its agriculture production. However, since 2006 Internet titans Microsoft, Dell, Intuit, Sabey, Vantage, and Yahoo have built huge data centers in Quincy, drawn by the inexpensive and reliable hydropower furnished by the Columbia River. The cheap energy is used to cool the hundreds of massive tower servers in the data centers that provide a variety of tasks for companies and internet clients. In the midst of green cornfields, apple orchards, and potato and wheat fields stand massive cold, colorless, glass-and-concrete structures that in their own way bring a form of sustenance to the world that consumes data via the internet. Although appearing lifeless, within these large and bulky structures is the hum and cadence of a digital existence transmitting billions, perhaps trillions of bytes of data. This data is the new food source that sustains life on a global scale. Yet, these structures stand in stark contrast to an environment forged decades earlier from a landscape dotted with jackrabbits, tumbleweeds, and sagebrush. When water arrived

Data centers like this one are changing the landscape of the Columbia Basin. *J. García collection*

from the Columbia River in the 1950s, a green, yellow, and orange bio-network of fields teeming with life appeared to provide nourishment to the consumer on a global scale. Similar to the data centers, the reach of agricultural production, still the heart and soul of the Columbia Basin, is global and transformative.

Over the span of human history, billions of people have negotiated natural borders—mountains, rivers, deserts, oceans. It has only been relatively recently that artificial borders have been created to disrupt the unfettered flow of human migration. My family became part of what is considered one of the longest sustained movements of labor anywhere in the world, the movement of Mexican labor to the United States. This movement has ebbed and flowed over the past century, forcing immigrants and migrants to cross natural barriers such as the Sonoran Desert, Rio Grande River, or the Cascade Mountains. Equally important are the unnatural borders that are negotiated once in the United States. These man-made borders include Immigration, Control, and Enforcement (ICE or *La Migra*) checkpoints, walls and fences, the unscrupulous *enganche* (labor contractor), violence, and in general, a society that simultaneously despises yet embraces immigrants for doing the work "hard-working" Americans will not do. These conditions have allowed U.S. consumers to buy meat and vegetables at bargain prices, but have deprived its workers of a living wage. This is the world my parents entered and negotiated, a world in which I was forced to maneuver through a precarious landscape created to subordinate and suppress my identity and opportunities.

THE NORTHERN BORDERLANDS EXPERIENCE

The contemporary high-tech industry of Quincy, my hometown, is not part of my historical past, yet Mexican immigrants continue to be pulled to the region for the same reasons my father and mother were. Economic opportunities in Quincy, grounded initially and primarily in agriculture, but now in technology for a limited number of individuals, are dependent on the same natural resource. The data centers are operated with minimal human interaction, but provide the community with a substantial tax revenue stream. And, as the CEO of Vantage Data Centers acknowledged, "Our location in Quincy benefits from access to abundant, low-cost hydropower as well as significant tax incentives."[5]

Imagine these same incentives provided to migrant laborers, the backbone of the agricultural industry.

The water that flows out of the Columbia River and into the various canals that irrigate the crops defines North Central Washington and the Canadian-U.S. border region. Without this resource the region would be a very different place and certainly not one of the largest producers of potatoes in the world or known as the "apple capital of the world."[6] North Central Washington provides a clear example of human settlement gathering around an essential resource, whether we are talking about Native Americans, farmers, migrants, or Internet companies. Over fifty years ago the transformative power of water pulled my family to the area. Had the Columbia River not been harnessed, my parents would have remained in Arizona or Mexico. As a second-generation son of Mexican immigrants, I straddled numerous borders that were disparate from the experiences of other Mexicans and Chicanxs such as my cousins and relatives who continue to live along the U.S.-Mexican border, in particular the Rio Grande Valley in Texas. Perhaps listening to Los Tigres del Norte, Ramon Ayala y Los Bravos del Norte, or AC/DC, Van Halen and Black Sabbath is not much different from other Chicanxs with similar backgrounds, but I submit what adds a layer of contrast and distinction is residing in *El Norte*—not the *Norte* that many Mexicans imagine, which is the U.S.-Mexican border, but *El Extremo Norte* (the Far North), the Pacific Northwest, far removed from the familiar and the recognizable. And, yet, this is the region that defined my experience and made me who I am today.

Borders, whether created by our own imagination, community, society, or institutions, are erected out of a sense of fear of the unknown, to protect, and are an attempt to control and contain, especially the movement of labor and people. We can no longer simply conceptualize the term "border" as reflective of a Chicanx experience from the Southwest, especially with nearly eight million people of Mexican origin residing in the two regions discussed in this volume (Pacific Northwest and Midwest). People of Mexican origin have struggled with borders ever since United States invaded and conquered what was once Northern Mexico and shifted the U.S. border westward while forcing Mexico's south. My parents negotiated a multitude of borders as they made their way to

Washington. My mother, Gloria, at the age of five, and her six-year-old brother, Cruz, were placed on a train to Washington to live with relatives after their parents were tragically killed. She and her brother traversed various states as they left Arizona in 1945, becoming Washingtonians at a very young age and like me, the northern borderlands became their experience as they lived most of their lives in the Northwest. My mother was raised on the Yakama Indian Reservation (Wapato and Toppenish), an area that in the 1940s and 1950s had a significant Mexican population. However, *la frontera* (border) that defined her identity is not the U.S.-Mexican border, but the northwestern region of the U.S., specifically, the state of Washington, which borders the Canadian province of British Columbia. Ironically and perhaps not surprisingly, these two international borders (Canada and Mexico) or regions share the same violent history of invasion and conquest where indigenous peoples were removed and killed for their land and white settlers quickly invaded and developed the

Cruz Torres and Gloria Torres (author's uncle and mother), Phoenix, Arizona, ca. 1945. *J. García collection*

areas that were, as Gloria Anzaldua states "either eternally Indigenous or temporarily Mexican."[7]

The two regions also display dissimilarities. Until the mid-twentieth century Washington, Oregon, and Idaho had relatively small populations of Mexican origin people or Latinxs in general. As Mexicans began to migrate in greater numbers into the Pacific Northwest, unlike on the southern border, the racial status quo in many rural farming communities was disrupted. On the one hand, migrant labor was welcomed to the Northwest to harvest highly perishable crops, but on the other hand, the dominant culture preferred transient labor and were reluctant to accept Mexican migrants as permanent members of their communities.

If farm laborers became permanent residents, they remained marginalized within the community. These dualities are what my parents encountered, and I too, as I became aware of the disparities and inequalities that existed within a bifurcated community. Farm labor became my first exposure to the economic stratification of the community and the many lessons I learned regarding class, race, and race relations were a direct result of my family's working-class status.

From an early age I realized my parents were farm laborers or worked in positions related to agriculture production, and whenever possible, I accompanied my parents to the fields to provide what little help I could or simply enjoy the adventure of the outdoors. At this age (eight to ten years old), the economic necessity and viability of my parent's labor did not resonate; however, I recall admiring my parents' hard work as well as that of my paternal grandfather, who remained active as a farm laborer into his seventies. I also recollect, with fondness, how during our lunch breaks, while we ate our tacos of *frijoles* and *huevos*, my grandfather Don Juan would take each of our hoes and with his stone sharpener hone our instruments so they would effortlessly slice through the weeds as we cleaned sugar beets for ten to twelve hours per day. I can also still see my father, Ruben, bundled from head to toe to protect him from the cold wintery wind of late fall in Eastern Washington as it swept across the dry fields as he loaded, transported, and unloaded sugar beets at a designated depot. There he would drop the beets onto a pile that appeared to my ten-year-old eyes as a towering black mountain speckled with early snow. I also remember my mother coming home late in the evening during the spring with a layer of dust over her face, body, and clothing after spending twelve hours sitting behind a monstrous tractor planting potatoes with a constant stream of dirt hitting her face. Those are the days I saw my parents in a different light, not just as man and woman or father and mother, but protectors, givers, and providers. At this age I did not contemplate whether or not I would follow in their footsteps, but rather, if I had the strength and courage that my parents displayed.

As I resurrect these long-held memories, I realize that although my family was performing difficult manual labor, in many cases damaging stoop labor, it was also a time of family bonding. Often my extended family worked side-by-side and my tías (aunts) Lola, Felicitas (Fela),

Rebecca, Alicia, and Isabel (Chavela) would suddenly break out in song with renditions of Mexican favorites such as *Cielito Lindo,* or one of my cousins would begin to tell jokes, or I would hear the latest *chisme* (gossip) of the community. This camaraderie sustained us, especially the adults, who for brief moments throughout the day could forget about the back-breaking labor and enjoy a laugh, a smile, or gaze at the foothills of the Cascade Mountains to dream of what could be or simply know that perhaps tomorrow would bring a better day.

The hardships, marginalization, discrimination, and our working-class status did not prevent my family from trying to make the best of a tough situation. From my parent's perspective, Washington offered better economic opportunities and relief from their life along the U.S.-Mexican border, especially the overt racism my father experienced. Despite oppression and discrimination, my parents never succumbed to their victimization.

Our family's history in the state of Washington also included an urban chapter. Although I was very young (age four to seven) when our parents moved us to Seattle, this experience remains vivid in my recollection. The distinction between an urban area such as Seattle and the rural community of Quincy is powerful and perhaps is why over forty years later the memories remain lucid.

MEMORIES OF THE EMERALD CITY

Among my first memories are the wet, lush fields by my elementary school and the green forest behind our house in Seattle (or what seemed like a forest to someone about to begin preschool). I attended Head Start, kindergarten, and first grade in Seattle-area school districts. I went to first grade at Mirror Lake Elementary in the suburb of Federal Way. My father and mother, who were both twenty-something during the late 1960s, were attempting to navigate away from farm labor and into blue-collar positions. Neither had graduated from high school. My father entered the United States at the age of thirteen with a third-grade education and my mother had completed the eleventh grade. Although my father attempted school while in the Yakima Valley in the 1950s, he felt awkward as a fifteen-year-old placed into the fifth-grade class. In the

Mrs. Fenstad's Roosevelt School fifth grade class, 1953-54 school year, Granger, Washington. The author's father, Ruben D. García, is sixth from the right, top row. *J. García collection*

end my father felt more at peace with adults in the fields than with ten-year-olds in elementary school.

Once in Seattle, my father was able to find an entry-level position with Jorgensen Forge, which supplied the region with steel and titanium alloys, including Boeing. As a young child I had no perception of race, racism, and the prejudice and discrimination my parents faced during our brief time in Seattle, which they would later share with me. After several years we returned to Eastern Washington as a result of discrimination my father encountered while at Jorgensen Forge, and my mother's sense of isolation in a city where she had no friends or relatives.

My mother's lived experience was primarily in small communities such as Toppenish, Wapato, and Quincy, Washington, all with small but significant Mexican populations and among relatives. Although she was willing to uproot to Seattle, she simply was not prepared to deal with loneliness and the treatment she received. One recollection my mother shared was an encounter with a white woman who was a neighbor and encouraged her children to beat up and harass my siblings and me because of our race. She confronted this woman and it turned into a shouting match, an event that left my mother deeply concerned about the strong racial animosity declared by this white woman. My mother also indicated that as a young Chicana in Seattle she felt very isolated with almost no friends. When a Mexican family did move into the neighborhood, the wife refused to forge a friendship with my mother because she viewed our working-class background as beneath her family's middle-class status. When I spoke to my mother about this situation she put it into a late 1960s and 1970s context by stating the Mexican family were "*Tío Tacos*" or sellouts (literal translation "Uncle Tacos").[8]

Around 1970, and without my father's knowledge, my mother surrendered to the isolation, packed our bags and returned us to Eastern Washington. A few days later my father quit his job and also returned to our hometown of Quincy. Although our Seattle experience was brief—approximately three years—it is deep-rooted within our family's historical memory. Over the years we returned often to Seattle for weekend getaways and to enjoy the outdoor activities our parents introduced to us while living there.

As an adult with an advanced degree I have been given the tools to analyze my family's experience, yet I remain bewildered by the courage my parents exhibited to venture into the unknown; a city such as Seattle must have seemed enormous and complicated to navigate after spending most of their lives in a rural setting. And my parents did this at a very young age, with four small children. There is no doubt that my father and mother have always had an adventurous streak and are willing to traverse mainstream culture whenever possible and necessary. Indeed, my father introduced our family to recreational culture that was completely foreign and unfamiliar to us: water skiing. This is a man who in his twenties had barely mastered the basic elements of the English language and remained very traditional regarding Mexican culture, yet here we were, perhaps the only Mexican family on Lake Washington and Lake Sammamish in Seattle, water skiing. (My mother, who was terrified of water and never learned to swim, navigated the boat). My mother later explained to me that my father had received a medical settlement for a work-related injury and with part of the proceeds purchased the boat. Not only did my father use this boat for water skiing, but also used it to take his sons to Westport, Washington, for deep-sea fishing (even though it was not built to handle the waves of the Pacific nor navigate in deep fog). My father would surprise us with these sudden outbursts of mainstream activities, then revert back to his traditional, comfortable, and recognizable Mexican culture consisting of cockfighting, Mexican music, and speaking Spanish in the home.

I was raised in this traditional family structure. My father, although dominant, was not domineering; nonetheless, the notion of machismo was strong in my family and it shaped my own masculinity during my adolescent years. My family's patriarchal structure was reinforced by displays of machismo and masculinity, whether within the household, where my father insisted that his sons were not to do housework, or in the arena of cockfighting, where I witnessed my father and uncle carrying pistols with bravado. Furthermore, machismo played a significant role in the rural farming community. There were clearly defined roles for boys and girls in the K-12 educational system. The overt displays of masculinity, as many scholars have indicated, are oppressive towards women regardless of the definition or rationalization.

As my formal education commenced I was fortunate that the Mexican culture remained vibrant and constant in my life, providing a bilingual and bicultural experience that has given me many opportunities since I left high school. Regardless of my criticisms and critiques of the primary and secondary education I received in the northern borderlands, I am proud to say that all of my formal education, from Head Start to PhD, took place in my home state of Washington. My Northwest experience became even more apparent to me when visiting relatives along the U.S.-Mexico border or when I was with relatives who made the journeying to the Pacific Northwest. It was during these moments I began to see the differences between borderlands.

MIGRATING TO THE NORTHERN BORDERLANDS

As my cousins in south Texas crossed into Reynosa, Matamoros, or Nuevo Laredo, Mexico, our family crossed into Osoyoos, Penticton, Kelowna, and Vancouver, British Columbia, or journeyed over the Cascade Mountains to Seattle to enjoy a weekend or summer vacation. During my adolescent years our family traveled to both the northern and southern borders for extended trips. I have fond memories of both locations. Each offered their own unique experience and as children we easily adapted to the changing environment as we navigated the borderlands of U.S.-Mexico and U.S.-Canada. Yet, unlike my father and other relatives, I do not have extended memories of Mexico nor do I long for it. I have no attachment to the U.S.-Mexican border region in the manner that I am connected to the northern borderlands.

When I voluntarily exiled myself to the Midwest for a decade to pursue my academic career, I yearned for the wide open expanses of the Wenatchee or Quincy Valleys, or for the clear blue sky that was so elusive in humid places like Iowa and Michigan. I learned to snow ski as a child at Mission Ridge near Wenatchee, Washington, and on Snoqualmie Pass in the Cascades. A good friend of mine, Juan Gabriel Ibarra, who grew up in the border town of Eagle Pass, Texas, became fascinated with snow skiing when I introduced it to him while we were in graduate school at Washington State University. This relatively common recreational activity in the Northwest is completely foreign to my relatives along the U.S.-Mexico border. Yes, my father spent time in south Texas as a teenager after crossing in from Mexico and I am aware of the historical significance of the region, but my roots and lived experience are in Washington, the Northwest, and the northern border. Nonetheless, part of my identity stems from my father's background in Mexico.

My father was born in a place called *El Rancho de Agua Fresca* on the outskirts of Monterrey, Mexico. You will not find this community on any map; in fact, when I interviewed my father he was uncertain whether it still existed. Growing up, I always enjoyed knowing that it was also my place of origin. There is a certain mystical quality to the name and I want to believe that it's an actual place. Most likely, *El Rancho de Agua Fresca* was simply a few dwellings located in a rural site with a fresh-water well, as my family put it, and has long since disappeared. Nonetheless, it was my father's place of origin in Mexico before his family immigrated to Texas in the late 1940s. After listening all my life to family oral history and interrogating my father and his siblings I have deduced that my father's side of the family were perhaps one generation removed from the peasant class in Mexico. I also learned that a branch of my father's family originated from the ranching class of northern Mexico. I witnessed

Mexican culture alive and well in the form of Mexican Catholicism, the musical genres *corridos, norteno,* and *ranchera,* and the types of food we ate—*menudo,* flour tortillas (rather than corn)—and a tendency to raise, butcher, and eat cattle, pigs, and goats. And my father and uncle brought with them the Mexican sport of cockfighting.

Prior to coming to the Northwest my father's family survived by moving frequently within Texas in search of farm work. According to my family the average wage in Texas during the early 1950s was approximately $2.50 per day. By the mid- to late-1950s my father and his family began their migration north, following long-established routes that took them through Montana, where they worked sugar beets, then to Idaho to pick potatoes, and finally to the Yakima Valley in Washington, where they worked sugar beets, hops, and potato crops. Their motivation for this arduous journey was both economic and social. Texas growers tended to pay wages by the day; while Northwest growers paid laborers by the hour. In the early 1950s, when my father arrived in the Northwest, the prevailing wage for a farm laborer was $1.00 per hour, a significant income for a family of migrant workers.

Racial discrimination was another aspect of the marginalization experienced by my family in their relations with the dominant white culture in Texas. In an interview with my father and uncle, I was told about one experience in west Texas during the 1950s:

> There were many Mexicans, but it was mostly Anglo people living in this region. I will never forget that we once went to the movies and after getting my popcorn and soda I went to sit in the center of the theater. Shortly after, a young white girl poked me on the shoulder and said, "You are not supposed to sit here. You are supposed to sit up there in the balcony." In those days we did not know our rights and we did as we were told.[9]

As my family traveled the migratory routes from Texas into the Rocky Mountain region up to Montana and finally the Northwest they recall a significant change in treatment once they arrived in Washington in the mid-1950s. My father indicates they did not experience the overt forms of racism and discrimination they were subjected to in Texas. Other Mexican American migrants who came to the Northwest during the same period have made similar statements. The only explanation I have to offer for this variation in treatment between regions is the small number of Mexicans in the Northwest at the time. Without a critical mass of Mexicans, Mexican culture posed no threat to the dominant culture. It might also be argued that still fresh in the minds of many Anglo families and growers were the Mexican braceros that came to the Northwest during World War II to harvest their crops. Many communities throughout the Northwest praised the braceros for saving their crops during a critical period. Prejudice certainly existed in the Pacific Northwest and my parents experienced it, it just was not as prevalent as in Texas. As my father's family settled into the Northwest as permanent residents they still had to navigate and negotiate the terrain of assimilation in order to survive and maintain economic viability. My father and mother have had a unique experience regarding their adjustment to the United States that reveals a distinctive Northwest form of acculturation.

My father, as an immigrant and undereducated, was a farm laborer for most of his life. He eventually went from unskilled to semi-skilled work and finally to skilled blue-collar positions, and was generally well respected in the community. My father and mother along with my grandparents and my father's siblings eventually settled in the Columbia Basin located in North Central Washington. When the Columbia Basin became the beneficiary of a massive reclamation project that turned the semi-arid desert into a cornucopia of agricultural production that needed significant farm labor, my parents were one of the pioneering families of Mexican origin to arrive in the late 1950s.

My father provides contradictions on multiple levels regarding his transition into U.S. society. He's has often been an enigma to me because of his uncanny ability to adapt, negotiate, and infiltrate cultures with an ease, something I have never been able to duplicate. In many ways his integration resembles what much of the literature indicates on assimilation; he learned English and moved up the social economic ladder through "hard work." On the other hand, after living in the U.S. for sixty-plus years he has on many occasions returned to Mexico as if he never left. Indeed, after retiring from the workforce in the early 2000s my father returned to Mexico to live permanently, but returns to Washington for about five months out of the year. My father has been able to maintain much of

The author's father, Ruben García (left) and uncle, Roberto García, with trophies won at at a cockfighting derby, Quincy, Washington, ca. 1976. *J. García collection*

his culture of origin due to selectivity on his part. The underground and illegal sport of Mexican cockfighting played a large role in my father's life and kept him grounded and attached to Mexican culture.[10] From his adolescent years to his late thirties my father worked long hard hours performing stoop labor: picking potatoes by hand, thinning beets, and as a general farm laborer. However, he never received the admiration or respect on the job that he achieved as a cockfighter. Thus, the cockfight became a world of acceptance and success for my father, a place where he became a clear winner, and where he could display his self-worth, have a sense of accomplishment, and practice a non-white, Mexican form of masculinity.

What makes my family's continued practice of Mexican culture noteworthy is that we are thousands of miles away from the U.S.-Mexican border and within a small community of Mexican origin people. The co-existence of the Mexican and Mexican American communities within these various border constructs has obscured many of their cultural differences. Offsetting this are the counter-pressures for Mexican acculturation and assimilation to the dominant society. Overall, my father is imbued with an extraordinary ability to traverse through dominant mainstream culture and Mexican culture, almost seamlessly. For example, in order to survive in the United States, my father has had to assimilate as a laborer in the workplace, yet he chooses to relate primarily with his own ethnic group and has only secondary interaction with individuals and institutions of the dominant culture. Some sociologists have called this process "selective acculturation."[11] This selective acculturation partially explains why Mexican culture remains intact for such individuals as my father. First-generation immigrants find a cultural cocoon to protect them from alienation, domination, and isolation within American society and culture. My father's participation in cockfighting was a means of maintaining his cultural identity as a Mexican, part of which includes the notion of machismo and masculinity. The notion of machismo remained strong in my family, and it shaped my own masculinity during my adolescent years. My father played a major role until my fourteenth year, when my parents divorced. Thereafter, my mother became the primary role model and I gained much of my identity from her. Raised in a traditional Mexican household allowed me to appreciate and understand Mexican culture, but like most Chicanxs I lived a bifurcated existence negotiating the world of my parents and home, while simultaneously being pulled and tugged by assimilation forces, especially in the education environment.

A Pacific Northwest Education

In my youth and adolescence, surrounded by agriculture, growers, and farm workers, an unexpected event or discussion could lead to a life-changing moment. For example, one day when I was eleven or twelve my father's employer, *el patrón*, a kind Anglo man who farmed several hundred acres of various crops, stopped by and carried on a conversation with my father. He suddenly turned to me and asked this timeless question, "Jerry, what do you want to be when you grow up?" My response, "Like my father, I want to work on a farm." Not wanting to perhaps offend my father, my response was met with silence from the "boss." My father simply smiled at me and rubbed the top of my head. My father never spoke to me about my response, but I knew he expected more of me. Perhaps, my response was my unconscious appreciation I felt towards the community bonds I felt as a migrant child and was a reflection of what I had been exposed to regarding labor and occupations. I also argue that it is a manifestation of my educational experience. Very few teachers during my education in Quincy ever motivated, inspired, or spoke with me about opportunities, occupational goals, or higher education. Perhaps it was not a deliberate attempt to see me fail, or a conscious withholding of opportunities afforded to my white peers, but rather, incompetence and neglect on the part of school administrators and faculty when it came to non-white students. Yet I am conscious now as I was then that Mexicans, like my mother and father, were racialized within the labor market by mainstream white culture and that racialization was superimposed on Mexican children within the educational system. As Edward Telles and Vilma Ortiz point out, "Practices leading to racialization include direct discrimination by educators, structural or institutional discrimination in education, and issues of self-perception—all which derive from ideas about race."[12]

Through my adolescent years I remained very proud of what my father and mother did for a living because I witnessed their strong work ethic. Exposure to another life than farm work, or aspirations to attend college came slowly for two reasons. One, my parents had little experience with secondary or higher education. They understood the importance of education and the pinnacle of that achievement, from their perspective, was to complete high school. Second, my kindergarten through twelfth-grade education reflected the treatment of Mexican students during this period (1970s and 1980s), with few teachers or counselors encouraging us to move beyond farm labor. There was a clear disconnect between the all-white faculty and staff and the Mexican students, and those teachers and administrators were a reflection of the community. Educators' view of the Mexican population was seen through the lens of their labor. The only occupations Mexicans held within the school district were as janitorial personnel or city or county laborers, otherwise they toiled in the fields or packing sheds. Many educators projected this image upon their students, creating yet another obstacle for students to overcome. Even as the Mexican student population increased, the school district did little to hire teachers of Mexican ancestry as role models.

In fact, I have no memory of any member of the all-white faculty and staff ever asking me if I wished to attend the university, not once! At the very least what I experienced was institutional discrimination designed to keep Chicanx students subordinated. There was a significant divide between school administrators/teachers and the Chicano community. School outreach or contact with parents simply did not exist. Educational historian Rubén Donato, in his observations of early twentieth century educational practices, indicates that many social scientist and educators held strong beliefs that Mexican culture was not supportive of education: "The belief that Mexicans were indifferent about education was used as a pretext for educators to absolve themselves from responsibility for the Mexican child. Educators blamed school failure on poor school attendance, high transience, bilingualism, and a culture that was unresponsive to school."[13]

By the late twentieth century directives and policies had been created to alleviate this neglect, but with slow progress. By 1972, for example, the lack of community outreach and communication with Mexican parents was in fact a direct violation of a mandated policy for all school districts with more than five percent minority students. The policy disseminated by the Office for Civil Rights, stated, "School districts have the responsibility to adequately notify national origin-minority group parents of school activities, which are called to the attention of other parents. Such notice in order to be adequate may have to be provided in a language other than English."[14]

This neglect and indifference was one of the main catalysts for the national Chicano student movement of the 1960s and 1970s. In fact, similar to high school students in California and Texas, Chicano high school students in Quincy walked out of their classrooms in the early 1970s because of mistreatment directed towards them by school officials. When I graduated high school in the early 1980s I was tracked into the military and served three years. In the end, it was people in the military, not at my high school, who recognized my college potential and encouraged me to exit the military and apply to the university. My high school experience was not much different than most Chicanxs, with few exceptions. Those of us who found a way to graduate, despite the obstacles, did so through a variety of mechanisms, including acculturation.

Participating in athletics provided on one level a sense of assimilation and belonging, and on another level, a means for survival. My brother Juan and I participated in all the ritualistic sports that we were supposed to as male high school students such as football, baseball, and wrestling. We both chose wrestling over basketball because it was as close to boxing as we could get in high school. Like cockfighting, boxing was a family sport. My father, while in Seattle, was a professional boxer and fought a handful of fights until my mother forced him to stop. Wrestling allowed us to participate in a semi-blood sport and was considered more macho from the perspective of the Mexican and Chicanx community.

Juan had better skills than me in most of those sports and throughout high school we maintained a sibling rivalry, sometimes too competitive. Part of the male high school experience, especially in a small rural community, is the constant evaluation of your Americanness and masculinity, and what better way than through the "all-American" sports of football and baseball, and the ancient sport of wrestling. Both Juan and I were admired because we excelled in sports, which is one of the reasons we were able to pass in and out of dominant mainstream culture, and may have mitigated the discrimination that our non-athletic Chicanx brothers and sisters felt. We were accepted because we maintained an acceptable level of acculturation, a survival mechanism against the dominant culture. It also became clear to both Juan and me that the extra-curricular activities, become part of our identity as students and provided a level of protection, and also acceptance from our white peers.

Ethnic relations in the Quincy School District revolved around a Mexican–white binary model reflective of the demographics of the community. While I went to school with one or two individuals of Japanese-American background, I have no recollection of any Native Americans or African Americans in the district. (My first encounter with someone of African American ancestry occurred when I entered the military after high school). Quincy was stratified based on class and labor, with growers (virtually all white with the exception of a few Japanese-American farmers) at the highest echelons, followed by district and county employees, then farm laborers. Farm labor had its own hierarchy based on whether you were a permanent resident of the community or a transient undocumented worker. Transient workers often supplied the field work, while permanent Mexican Americans residents worked either in the packing sheds or as foremen of the various ranches and orchards. Chicanas primarily worked as sorters within the numerous facilities that required steady eye and hand coordination. In fact, one can argue that this specialization has become gendered and is seen as female work, with very few men willing to engage in this type of labor.

On occasion a Chicanx might move outside of agriculture and find employment as a teacher's aide, a janitor with the school district, or as a general laborer for the county utility district, but these were the exceptions. One exception I recall is Doña Rita Puente, who had a traditional migrant background and moved to the Columbia Basin for agricultural labor, but eventually became a *contratista*, a labor contractor, which was primarily the domain of men. The *contratista* has not been viewed kindly within Chicanx history because this individual often took advantage of migrant laborers through unscrupulous payment methods and broken promises of employment. Doña Rita's position within the Mexican community was one of respect, but also one of caution due to a history of exploitation by *contrastistas*, regardless of gender.

Relations in school were a microcosm of the greater community, with evident race, class, and ethnic distinctions and divisions. Most of the curriculum revolved around the European-American experience and "captains of industry." Based on my experience in the Quincy School District, I have to agree with sociologist Alfredo Mirandé who wrote, "…the role of the school was to maintain Chicanxs in a subordinate and dependent position."[15] A hostile environment certainly existed in the form of neglect and indifference from teachers, counselors, and administrators. How else am I to explain the lack of mentorship, grooming for college, and tracking into the military? During my senior year in high school, as my classmates, primarily white students, were taking the SAT to enter higher education, I was removed from my classroom to take the military entrance exam without warning. No one consulted me on whether I wanted to take the SAT rather than the military exam. This neglect and failure is why I waited for nearly three years to commence my university studies as I served in the armed forces. I graduated despite the lack of support, but many of my Chicanx classmates did not. My cousin Mundo did not, and three of my siblings did not. This neglect stemmed from several factors: a curriculum that ignored the background, heritage, and contributions of Chicanxs; the lack of training and preparation of the educators about the Chicano experience and the educational needs of Chicano students;[16] and a consistent lack of access to and guidance from school officials.

AZTLÁN IN THE NORTHERN BORDERLANDS

By the time I graduated high school, nearly two decades had passed since the beginning of the national Chicano civil rights movement or *El Movimiento*, which is generally considered to have started in 1962 with the establishment of the United Farm Workers Organizing Committee lead by Cesar Chavez and Dolores Huerta. In the state of Washington *El Movimiento* had multiple origins beginning in 1965 with the establishment of the Yakima Valley Council for Community Action. In 1966 Tomas Villanueva and Guadalupe Gamboa trained with César Chávez and the United Farm Workers in California, and in 1967, they returned to Washington to create the United Farm Worker Cooperative. A chapter of United Mexican American Students (UMAS) and the Brown Berets were founded at the University of Washington in 1968 and UMAS became El Movimiento Estudiantil Chicano de Aztlán (MEChA) in 1969. El Centro de la Raza, a grass roots civil rights organization, was created in 1972; and Sea Mar Community Health Clinic was established by students in 1978. This short list illustrates Washington State activism seeking economic, social, and political justice for the Chicanx community long before I entered high school. While there was limited discussion on the African American civil rights movement and Martin Luther King Jr., my high school curriculum contained no mention of César Chávez , the United Farm Workers, or any Chicano movement activities in Washington State. Though the Chicano community in Quincy was actively involved with progressive politics seeking social and economic justice, for a long time it remained invisible to me.

I learned about the Chicano movement through individuals connected to Quincy, such as Alfred "Freddy" Mata, was one of the first Chicanxs to attend the University of Washington and became a Brown Beret. When I was twelve or thirteen, I heard Freddy give an impassioned speech to unite the Chicanx community in Quincy. He was also in a local band

An early 1970s flyer for a United Farm Workers Union fundraiser, featuring the Quincy, Washington, band Zapata. *J. García collection*

called "Zapata." This band traveled in an old school bus with the word Z-A-P-A-T-A and an image of a man in a charro suit with a rifle in his hands painted on the side. I later learned this was the great Mexican Revolutionary hero Emiliano Zapata, the namesake of the band. This was the birth of Aztlán for me, a slow awakening to a history and past hidden by school officials, teachers, and counselors. Whether this was intentional is unclear. However, I have very little doubt there was a severe lack of cultural awareness, which raises the question of how this could be with such a significant population of Mexican Americans in the community and in the schools. Based on the history I later uncovered regarding the origins of the Mexican community in Quincy there appeared to be neglect and simply indifference to Mexican Americans at all levels, not just in the educational system.

As a master's degree student I did my thesis on the development of the Mexican community in Quincy and discovered that in the early 1970s Chicano high school students walked out of their classrooms to protest unfair treatment. My investigation lead me to Andy Martinez, a longtime community activist from Quincy who was the Washington State delegate to the 1972 La Raza Unida Party National Convention held in El Paso, Texas. Not only did the Pacific Northwest have a vibrant and ongoing movement, Washington State appeared to be leading, and more important to me, individuals from the small community of Quincy played vital roles during the 1960s and 1970s. It was only in the pursuit of my own education that I made these discoveries of Aztlán in the northern borderlands. In the end, it would take three years in Japan (military service) and my return at the age of twenty to begin to uncover what had been erased and neglected by the high school curriculum in Quincy and other places regarding Chicanx history and culture at the local, regional, and national levels. The attempts by the high school curriculum to indoctrinate the grand U.S. narrative and colonize my mind was nearly complete and would have been fulfilled had it not been for my family's daily dose of *Mexicanidad*. The attempts to silence this history ultimately served to invigorate my desire to find the truth and decolonize my mind as a student in higher education.

When I began my first semester as an undergraduate my intent was to pursue a degree in technology, specifically, the burgeoning field of computer science. These plans were quickly interrupted when I took my first course in Chicanx studies. This particular class was on the ancient Mesoamerican cultures of Mexico and it literally changed the direction of my life. I began to learn of my own past, not one disconnected from my Mexican heritage, but one fully articulating the important influences the cultures of Mexico had on the Western Hemisphere and the world. This was the very first time I learned of the contributions Chicanxs had made to the development of the Pacific Northwest, and to the United States in general. I was also fortunate to take a class with the internationally recognized artist Rubén Trejo, who had a long and distinguished career at Eastern Washington University. Professor Trejo introduced me to the ancient art of Mesoamerican cultures. I went to college with an understanding of my Mexican culture, but not its history, and my self-identity through a process of politicization did not emerge until after my introduction to Chicanx studies. In many ways I was a classic example of how self-awareness and the development of a positive identity provides stability and in the end scholastic achievement. I now realize that I did not have to travel to some far off distant land to understand Aztlán. Embedded in the concept of Aztlán is the idea of liberation and self-determination. That vision is here in Washington, the Pacific Northwest, and Great Lakes region and not restricted by borders, boundaries, or archaic ideas of regionalism.

CONCLUSION

In some measure Los Tigres del Norte and other bands like them helped me maintain equilibrium between my Mexicanness and mainstream culture. Like most teenagers anywhere, we saw music as central to our lives. Mexican, Norteño, and Tejano music was our counter-weight to mainstream music, but it was also a constant reminder of who we were and it represented our attempt to emulate our fathers, who each maintained a strong sense of their culture and identity through music and other elements of Mexican ethos. I think Mundo would agree when I say we admired our fathers for their strong sense of manhood, courage, and for not succumbing to their victimization and remaining strong. It was our fathers who introduced us to Mexican music and we learned how to appreciate it for the role it played in our family and culture. Further, Mundo and I were the only siblings on either side of the family allowed to accompany our fathers to cockfights, a sign that as teenagers we had garnered the respect and trust of our fathers. It was on these trips we witnessed them being brothers and not fathers, and were immersed into another layer of our culture very few are allowed to witness. Mundo and I remained tight friends throughout high school. Mundo adapted better to the rural environment and had the personality to maneuver easily through the various worlds, especially the dominant culture. Although Mundo was pushed out of high school during our sophomore year, he nevertheless was a constant presence because of our family relations. Put simply, Mundo was the guy you wanted to hang with because of his charisma and popularity with all groups. Together, on these trips with our fathers we learned that cockfighting was alive and well in the Pacific Northwest and witnessed Mexicans, whites, and Filipinos in a competition in which race and class were subsumed by the code of cockfighting. After completing high school, I went into the military, eventually got my BA, MA, and PhD, lived in the Midwest for ten years, and am currently living in the Southwest, which means I have not lived in Quincy as a year round resident since I was seventeen years old. Nonetheless, I remain drawn to the northern borderlands because of the memories I shared in this article and all of my immediate family remains in the Pacific Northwest.

Decades later, with the migration of hundreds of thousands of Mexicans to the state, the population of Quincy has more than doubled to over 7,000 people. Today 75 percent of my hometown is of Mexican origin![17] Similar demographic shifts have occurred throughout the Pacific Northwest. Aztlán is not off in some distant mythical place far-removed from our lived experience. Aztlán exists in places like Quincy, Seattle, and Yakima, Washington; Woodburn, Portland, and Mt. Angel, Oregon; Lansing and Detroit, Michigan, and other regions of the northern borderlands. My family's ability to hold on to its culture and my exposure to greater Aztlán revealed the beauty of the Chicanx experience. And a whole new world opened up when I decided at the end of my first course in Chicano Studies 101 to be an educator to introduce others to this culture and history, especially to the unique northern borderlands experience. I continue to do so.

Notes

I wish to thank Angelina Castagno, Esperanca Camara, and Theresa Meléndez for reading an early draft of this article and providing important insight and suggestions. 1.   Los Tigres del Norte, "Contrabando y Traición," written and composed by Ángel González, 1971, recorded by Discos Fama (now Fonovisa), LP, 1974. "The corrido, like the romance, relates a story or event of local or national interest—a hero's deeds, a bandit's exploits, a barroom shootout, or a natural disaster…" Américo Paredes, *With His Pistol in His Hand: A Border Ballad and Its Hero* (Austin: University of Texas Press, 1958).

2.   Ramiro Burr, *The Billboard Guide to Tejano and Regional Mexican Music* (Austin: University of Texas Press, 1999).

3.   In Quincy during the 1970s and 1980s the Mexican origin population was never above 15 percent of the community. Since the 1990s Quincy is now a predominately Latinxs community with the majority of Mexican origin. In general, Quincy and the state of Washington are excellent examples of the demographic shift that occurred in the late twentieth and early twenty-first centuries.

4. Gloria Anzaldúa, "The Homeland, Aztlán/El Otro México," in *Aztlán: Essays on the Chicano Homeland,* eds. Rudolfo A. Anaya and Francisco A. Lomelí (Albuquerque: El Norte Publication/Academia, 1989), 194.

5. "Vantage Completes 4.5MW Data Center Expansion in Quincy." www.datacenterknowledge.com. Accessed April 23, 2016.

6. Wenatchee, Washington, located approximately thirty miles northwest from Quincy makes this claim. North Central Washington, which includes both Quincy and Wenatchee, produces the largest amount of apples in the U.S. The United States is the second largest producer of apples. China is the number one producer of apples in the world. Accessed April 18, 2016. www.wa.gov/esd/farmworkers/ag_info.htm.

7. Anzaldúa, 193.

8. This phrase has been used since at least the 1960s within the Chicano community. It is the equivalent to "Uncle Tom" or someone who is considered a "sellout" to the white establishment. This image is largely based on Harriet Beecher Stowe's novel *Uncle Tom's Cabin* and refers to an individual who is excessively subservient to white people.

9. Interview with father and uncle, January 3, 2003, Quincy, Washington.

10. For a more complete discussion on Mexican cockfighting see Jerry García, "The Measure of a Cock: Mexican Cockfighting, Culture, and Masculinity," in *I AM AZTLÁN: The Personal Essay in Chicano Studies,* eds. Chon A. Noriega and Wendy Belcher (Los Angeles: UCLA Chicano Studies Research Center Press, Regents of the University of California, 2004), 109–38.

11. Alejandro Portes and Ruben G. Rumbaut, *Immigrant America: A Portrait.* (Berkeley: University of California Press, 1996), 250–51.

12. Edward E. Telles and Vilma Ortiz, *Generations of Exclusion: Mexican Americans, Assimilation, and Race* (New York: Russell Sage Foundation, 2008), 131–33.

13. Rubén Donato, *The Other Struggle for Equal School: Mexican Americans during the Civil Rights Era* (Albany: State University of New York Press, 1997), 18–19.

14. The Excluded Student: The Educational Practices Affecting Mexicans Americans in the Southwest, Report III. A Report of the United States Commission on Civil Rights, 1972.

15. Alfredo Mirandé, *The Chicano Experience—An Alternative Perspective.* (Notre Dame, Indiana: University of Notre Dame Press, 1985), 91.

16. Ibid., 93.

17. Quincy, Washington, 2013 population: 7,242, of whom 75 percent are Hispanic.

Contributors

Oscar Rosales Castañeda is originally from Guadalajara, Mexico, and came to Washington State as part of the Mexican diaspora of the 1980s. He grew up in Yakima and moved to Seattle in 2002 to attend the University of Washington. As an undergraduate, he was involved in student government and was a member of the coordinating board for the UW chapter of Movimiento Estudiantil Chicana/o de Aztlan (MEChA), a student group that traces its roots to the Chicana/o movement of the 1960s. He was a founding member of the Student Labor Action Project at UW and was involved with the anti-war movement. He graduated with a BA in American ethnic studies and history, and contributed writing to the Seattle Civil Rights & Labor History Project as an undergraduate researcher. He has also written for HistoryLink.org, the Online Encyclopedia of Washington State History, and contributed to the anthology *Writing History in the Digital Age*. He has been a board member for El Comité since 2010.

Norma L. Cárdenas teaches in the Chicano Education and the Race and Culture Studies Programs at Eastern Washington University. She has published in edited collections such as *Rethinking Chicana/o Literature through Food: Postnational Appetites* (2013) and *Latin@s Presence in the Food Industry: Changing How We Think About Food* (2016). Her current book project is a cultural history of Tex-Mex food in San Antonio. She has a BA from Amherst College in political science and an MA in bicultural-bilingual studies and PhD from the University of Texas San Antonio. Her PhD examined literacy, culture, and language. Professor Cárdenas has held academic appointments with the Ethnic Studies Department at Oregon State University.

Josué Q. Estrada is a doctoral student in history at the University of Washington. He is also an instructor for the department and collaborator on the UW digital history project, "Mapping American Social Movements." His research interests include migration, voting rights, labor, and the social/political movements of Mexican people in the Pacific Northwest. He previously was director of the College Assistance Migrant Program at Washington State University (WSU).

Jerry García was born and raised in the Pacific Northwest. He received his PhD from the department of history at Washington State University and has held academic appointments with Iowa State University, Michigan State University, and is the former director of the Chicano Education Program and the College Assistance Migrant Program at Eastern Washington University. Dr. García's research focus is on Chicano history, Latin American history, history of Mexico, Asians in the Americas, immigration, empire, masculinity, and race. He has published numerous articles and books on the Mexican experience in the Pacific Northwest. His most recent book is *Looking Like the Enemy: Japanese Mexicans, the Mexican State, and U.S. Hegemony, 1897-1945* (2014).

Carlos Saldivar Maldonado was an associate professor at Eastern Washington University and director of EWU's Chicano Education Program from 1987 to 2008. Maldonado also served as director of the College Assistance Migrant Program, a program designed to enroll students from the migrant and seasonal farm worker background in post-secondary education. His publications include *Chicanos in the Northwest* (1995) and *Colegio Cesar Chavez, 1973-1983: A Chicano Struggle for Educational Self-Determination* (2000, 2016).

Rachel Maldonado retired from Eastern Washington University where she was an assistant professor of marketing in the university's College of Business. Prior to entering academics full time, Rachel owned and operated a Mexican food store and restaurant in Spokane, Washington. In addition to their involvement at Eastern Washington University, Rachel and Carlos served together on many Mexicana/o community-based boards and organizations focused on developing a sense of community among the growing Latino population in the Spokane region.

Theresa Meléndez is associate professor of English emeritus, Michigan State University, where she founded and directed the Chicano/Latino Studies program for ten years, bringing in Chicano professors, graduate students, and undergraduates, and creating a CLS PhD program. Her fields of study include Chicano literature, Mexican folklore, and medieval literature.

Dylan Miner is a Wiisaakodewinini (Métis) artist, activist, and scholar. He is director of the American Indian Studies Program and associate professor (RCAH) at Michigan State University, as well as member of the Justseeds artist collective. Miner has been featured in more than twenty solo exhibitions and was granted an Artist Leadership Fellowship from the National Museum of the American Indian in 2010. He is author of *Creating Aztlán: Chicano Art, Indigenous Sovereignty, and Lowriding Across Turtle Island* (University of Arizona Press, 2014). He is presently working on two books—one on contemporary Indigenous aesthetics and a book of poetry, *Ikidowinan Ninandagikendaanan (words I seek to learn)*.

Ernesto Todd Mireles holds a PhD from Michigan State University's Department of American Studies. His emphasis is in Chicano studies where he is working to develop his ideas of Xicano resistance literature, national theories around low intensity organizing models, while studying and focusing on anti-colonialist theory, indigenous liberation and the methodologies and rhetoric of mobilization and organization for radical movements within the Americas; with an emphasis on the Chicano movement from 1848 until the present. He currently teaches at Prescott College in the Masters in Social Justice and Human Rights Program. His main commitment is working with undergraduate students in the classroom to help them develop a disciplined principled approach of non-hierarchical anti-authoritarian pedagogy to achieve their desired goals both in and out of the classroom.

Dionicio Nodin Valdés is professor of history at Michigan State University. He has written extensively on labor and social history, including the books *Organized Agriculture and the Labor Before the UFW* (University

Texas Press, 2011); *Barrios Norteños: St. Paul and Midwestern Mexican Communities in the Twentieth Century* (University of Texas Press, 2000); *Voices of a New Chicana/o History* (Michigan State University Press, 2000); and *Al Norte: Agricultural Workers in the Great Lakes Region, 1917–1990* (University of Texas Press, 1991).

Index